OLE MAN ON THE PORCH

OLE MAN ON THE PORCH
THE TROOPER

Bryan Gregory

BRYAN GREGORY

ENHANCED SOME BY:
LEVI POWELL

iUniverse, Inc.
New York Lincoln Shanghai

Ole Man on the Porch
The Trooper

Copyright © 2006 by Bryan Gregory

All rights reserved. No part of this book may be used or reproduced by any means, graphic, electronic, or mechanical, including photocopying, recording, taping or by any information storage retrieval system without the written permission of the publisher except in the case of brief quotations embodied in critical articles and reviews.

iUniverse books may be ordered through booksellers or by contacting:

iUniverse
2021 Pine Lake Road, Suite 100
Lincoln, NE 68512
www.iuniverse.com
1-800-Authors (1-800-288-4677)

ISBN-13: 978-0-595-39276-6 (pbk)
ISBN-13: 978-0-595-67685-9 (cloth)
ISBN-13: 978-0-595-83671-0 (ebk)
ISBN-10: 0-595-39276-8 (pbk)
ISBN-10: 0-595-67685-5 (cloth)
ISBN-10: 0-595-83671-2 (ebk)

Printed in the United States of America

What Others Say

A few statements, listed in order received

"I already knew Bryan and expected comical episodes, but the serious ones were somewhat of a surprise and reminded me of how stressful law enforcement really is, and how little we talk about it. For those who don't know him it's a shame, because I can hear his voice as I read his stories. Unlike many others would do, he exposes himself emotionally and in doing so, reminds us that we're all human."
…Lisa Stokes, Parole/Probation Officer

"As they have stood witness to the terrible things that human beings do to one another, only in the past few years has grief counseling or psychological help been made available to members of the law enforcement community. It was considered a sign of weakness to show any emotion. Sadly, many turned inward to the bottle, divorce, extra marital affairs and suicide. Thankfully there was humor. This was the escape that the large majority used to deal with the stress of the job. Thus this book deals with the humor of law enforcement, especially within the North Carolina State Highway Patrol. The ability to laugh at each other and ourselves provided the outlet needed to go out and do the job year after year. I commend the author for his hard work on a project that must truly be fulfilling, and this book to your perusal that will bring laughter and a tear to the eye."
…Fred Patton, "An Old Field Soldier"

"After reading only two stories, I was hooked by Ice Cream & Cake and then reeled in by Heather's story. I laughed and then cried…I cried for Heather and the uphill battle she faces. My co-workers were affected the same way…They were speechless. The author tells it EXACTLY as it is! He says out loud what everyone has thought, who has worked in the Criminal Justice System."
…Jeri Hinson, Department of Corrections

Dedication

When I look at pictures of my Ancestors or Troopers who have gone on before me, it saddens me that I have so little knowledge of their lives. These efforts will insure that those coming after me will know me better.

With that, I dedicate this book to my children, Trip and David Gregory, and to The North Carolina State Highway Patrol.

Acknowledgements

I've lied and I've cheated. Contrary to what the cover indicates, this book is not "by" me at all, but is by me and a crowd of others. Since there's no way that this would all fit onto the cover, let me make it plain right now…I did not accomplish all of this by myself! Now that I've explained my lie, let me clarify my cheating.

I've used an endless number of proofreaders and editors, and I've solicited help from everyone I could find. Anyone who would go over what I'd done and would offer an opinion, I've paid attention to them. From *"I like that"* to *"You can't put that in there!"*, I've listened to all of them, and I treasured every criticism they gave me…But then I turned around and did it just like I wanted to.

I've paid them. I've begged them. I've threatened them. Even total strangers, I've pestered to death. Just as soon as I would write a story, I'd shove it in somebody's face. Some helped me more than others but they all helped me some…But it's those who made discouraging remarks, questioned my capabilities or wouldn't even look at my work that I thank the most. Thank you, thank you…You just drove me harder! I didn't trust your judgment anyway. Then comes my brother…

Of all, my younger brother, Bill Gregory, was of the most value to me. As he has done throughout his life, he has constantly encouraged me and whenever I've asked him, he'd have something to say. Without him, his ear to listen and his calmer nature than mine, this would've been an absolute disaster and I would've made a complete ass of myself. As always, he has been right there with me every step of the way. Thank you, Bro…For always being there with me. Then comes Levi…

When I first started this project, I knew I wanted Levi's work to enhance it. Levi Powell retired from the North Carolina State Highway Patrol in 1985 and about ten years before I did. I'd never met him until I started this mission and that's when I looked him up. But I remember back when we were working, every once in awhile, one of his cartoons would appear. His work has been such a colorful part of our organization that I knew I could settle for nothing less. I just knew it…It would be either his cartoons, or nothing! I don't think Levi ever accepted payment for any of his work until I suckered him into this. Thank you, Levi. I know your health hasn't been the greatest and you didn't complete as much as you wanted to, but you did the best that you could and I appreciate all that you did…As will everyone else who reads much further than this.

If you're a member of the North Carolina State Highway Patrol or ever have been, you're in for a disappointment…Don't expect to find your name here. The rest of this book is about you and for you anyway. And the rest of you…

Well, you may be disappointed too. I'm just not very good at remembering names anyway. And for those that I could remember, there's just no way that I could do it without hurting somebody's feelings. In what order would I put them and who could I say had helped me the most…But I had to come up with something to fill up this space and to not recognize anyone would be a total disgrace. So included below are just some of the voices that I've listened to. These are just some of those who when I sought their help…Have prodded me, prompted me, prepped me and pumped me up. And they're not listed according to importance…They're just thrown in here in a random way.

> Mark Frederickson *(For opening a door for me)*
> Nicole Kaylor *(My first decent proofreader and editor…Not bad-looking either)*
> John Cashier *(One of my best critics. I didn't listen to him much, but he kept trying anyway)*
> Eddie Cathy *(For making a priceless connection for me)*
> Kelly & Denise Borrell *(For not slapping my face)*
> Paul Avenick *(For picking me up when I fell)*
> Tyler Schock *(For taking up where I left off)*
> Ernie Oppenheimer *(For having enough sense to beat me in a fighting hairs contest)*
> Kate Fine-Harth *(For just being there)*
> Coyt Atkinson *(I loved to listen to his words of wisdom, but never believed a word that he said)*
> Vinnie Romanille *(Another redneck like Coyt)*
> Big Jim Benedetto *(Always read my stories and never tried to get away)*
> Rifka Keilson *(For being the first true professional I would deal with)*
> Don Hurst *(For believing in me even more so than I did)*
> Noemi Lazares *(For putting a song in my heart and zest to my step)*

Victor Cozzone *(For keeping me busy and throwing peanut hulls on the floor)*
Quilt Patch Fabrics *(They're going to sell a ton of books for me)*
Walt Venator *(Took a big chance by first publishing my work)*
Joe Yakonowski *(For laughing at all of my jokes)*
Myah Russian *(For cleaning up after me)*
Heather Thompson *(For living a story that will now be told)*
Terrell Blackbat *(I'm sure he did something, I just can't remember what)*
Andrea Fleming *(For providing me with a place to contact so many proofreaders and editors)*
Fred Coffey and Tommy Price, Jr *(For remaining right where they are)*
Bill Funderud *(Oops, I didn't mean to put his name here! Where's that damn delete button?)*
Donald Honeycutt *(He didn't do anything either. I just thought his name would look good here)*

I give up. I'm getting tired and I'm not even going to try anymore…It's just too much! There's just no way that I've covered all the bases. But know that although your name doesn't appear here, if I could remember it, I would certainly appreciate all the work that you did. And last of all…

I will acknowledge myself. I think you've done an okay job, ole boy. I think you've lived a pretty good life and I think you've now expressed yourself fairly well. I'll bet you've proofread this damn book more than a hundred times and for a year and a half now, you've allowed it to consume your whole life. Because of it, you've put everything else on the back burner and you've allowed your relationships to suffer. But there comes a time and that time has now come…You've done the best that you can do, ole boy. Put it down now. It's time to move on.

Table of Contents

Warnings!	xv
Introduction	xvii
Preface	xxi
Terminology	xxv
The Waiting	1
Labor	2
The Spectrum	4
The Boxing Match	5
End of the Beginning	7
The Hard Ass	9
Other Mother	12
Sneaky Snake	14
Autoway Floyd	18
Bribe to Survive	22
Old Man on the Porch	25
Arrest of a Trooper	27
Preacher's Kid	31
The Fickle Female	33
The Air Conditioner	35
Blowing the Boss	37
All Rise!	39
King of Beers	41
Loud Mufflers	43
Advantage or Disadvantage?	45
English Bobbies	47
A Better Door Lock	48
Donkey Basketball	50
Deep Cover	53
Drunk at Church	55
Bubba & the Drag Race	57
Flying Shit	59
Gully Washer	62
The Cattle Prod	64
Scratch My Back	66
Smoke & Mirrors	69
Better than Most	72
Mud	74
The Silo	76
Unanswered Prayer	79
My God	82
Friend of an Angel	83
Bottomless Pit	86
The Trash Collectors	88
The Fox Drive-In	91
Railroad Tracks	93
Hot Foot	97
Man with the Plan	99
Obscene Gestures	101
A Normal Speeder	105
The Biltmore House	106
Little Black Book	108
The Head	110
The Young Marine	112
The Secret Supervisor	114
The Door Knob	117
Ice Cream & Cake	120
Pop Quiz for Police Officers	122
How to Stop Smoking	124

Special Ingredient	126	Two of a Kind	199
Never There	128	Blood Pressure Problem	203
Weak Bladder	132	Early Retirement	205
The Best Shot	135	Guardrail	208
Lying Eyes	138	Hello Henry	210
Wired	141	The Paper Trail	212
Mistaken Identity	143	Proper Authority	216
Snoot Full	147	The Rookies & the Flat Tire	218
Insignificant Job	151	The Deacon's Submarine	221
The Trooper Bowl	152	The Heels of Death	224
Free Firewood	156	Breaking a Bad Habit	227
Bullethead	158	The Hidden Word	229
The Kidnapped Wife	163	Nightmare on Wheels	233
The Wildcat	165	Soft & Tough	236
Chitlins	170	How to Correct a Supervisor	238
Upset Stomach	173	Decent Tomatoes	242
Bad News for the Doctor	176	One of the Best	248
Dial a Page	178	Bullet on the Wall	251
Stolen	181	Long Lost Rookie	255
Payback	183	It's just a matter of…	257
Overloaded Vehicle	185	Transitions	271
Blood Run	187	Epilogue	273
The Padlock	191		

<<< Warnings! >>>

Because I feel more comfortable in doing so, in this book, I capitalize common nouns a lot. Here's why...I took a lot of pride in my career as a State Trooper *(You see, I just did it. Now what's wrong with that?)* As I continued to write, I found myself capitalizing other job titles, like "Waitress" or "Garbage Collector," because the way I feel about it, anyone who works for a living should also be proud. Then came "Patrol Car." Well, I feel the same way about that. For me, it was a major part of my life and although I know it's not human, I sometimes felt it was alive. I'd even sometimes catch myself talking to it, encouraging it to go faster, or stop, or hang onto a curve. Maybe it listened, I don't know...But it sure took me for one helluva ride! So have no concern for the nouns that I've capitalized. It's for the ones that I haven't, that you need to watch out.

Don't be surprised. Levi has not enhanced all of these stories. But then again, I didn't include all of the tales that I would like to have. In all fairness to him, you and the publisher, as I requested, he drew his cartoons in color. But they were reduced to black and white in this book to make it more affordable.

There comes a point when the best thing to do is just stop. So that's what I did. But if you'll just take the time to read it, I think you'll agree...It's a far cry from a flop. And something else...

This book may be easier to digest if you just read a story or two and then just sit back and think for awhile. There's a lot of emotion in here! Seldom will my stories flow together and sometimes they change drastically from one story to the next, so it may be more than you can handle in just one sitting. But that was the nature of my job...Constant changes happened like that. Even my work schedule changed a lot...It changed from morning shift to late shift every damn week. And it was years after retirement before I my body became accustomed to normal and healthy sleep patterns again.

If my Career and my Working Schedule were both people, and together they went to see a Head Doctor, they'd both be labeled as manic depressive and placed on extremely high dosages of lithium, and receive frequent shock treatments. I loved the first one anyway, but always hated the second.

Ole Man on the Porch

Introduction

Timing is everything and the time is right. Winter is setting in and I find myself unfettered by many of life's normal distractions. Yes, the time is perfect. I will now take the bull by the horns and concentrate on this project that I have been putting off for far too long.

I have decided on this title, not because it is descriptive of me but because that is the vision I want you to have of me, as you read these events of my life. Time has had a wonderful affect on my memory. The unpleasant periods have faded and the good times have risen to the surface.

As absurd as this may sound and as ridiculous as I feel for even saying it, I'm convinced that I've survived because of the prayers of friends, relatives and especially, my Parents. If you want proof, I can't give it to you. It's just this gut feeling I've always had…I could always feel it! It was never an overwhelming feeling. It was always very subtle, always in the background and although my Parents are long gone, that feeling still remains. I didn't intend to, but now I've got to tell you about them.

My Parents were simple folks. My Mother was a Farmer's daughter, didn't have a high school education and never drove a car. Her whole life was centered on raising her two sons, my younger brother and I…And we were her life! My Father was a Methodist Preacher and we moved a lot, starting from the Outer Banks. He was the most religious person that I've ever known…He lived what he believed. I don't think Dad ever requested much of God for himself, but I do feel that I was a beneficiary of their relationship. Someone or something has been watching over me, protecting me and to some extent, guiding me. I've never felt *"called"* or *"led"* to do anything and I've never had any major spiritual awakenings, but I do feel that I have lived for a reason and have been blessed with many good friends and a loving family.

As a child, I remember the frustration and disappointment I felt for having to move so much. Making friends and then having to move away was always devastating, but my Brother was always there beside me to ease the pain. We became each other's best friend. In later years, we even double-dated.

Frequently changing locations was surely not the wishes of our Parents either. During his career as a Minister, Dad had to move twelve times and preached at forty-seven Churches, and I could see the anguish and sometimes the anger that he felt. He may have been bitter inside but after he'd calmed down some, he'd try to comfort us with *"Its God's Will"*...But that that didn't help much, our Mother still cried a lot. She became very withdrawn. I don't remember, maybe she always was, but constantly moving certainly didn't help her mental health much.

When my Bro and I became teenagers, she got to the point of not even unpacking much of our stuff, because she knew we'd soon be moving again. When that empty nest came, she didn't complain much because she knew it was coming, but she held on to us just as long as she could. The best way she could deal with us leaving home was with heavy medication. If her Doctor wouldn't give her the pills that she wanted, she'd go back to an old one who would. From the time that Bro and I left home until she died, she was mostly in a prescription drug stupor. As with most cases, the drugs didn't cure anything, they just relieved the hurt a little and covered up some of the symptoms.

Dad dealt with his frustrations differently. He talked to God a lot. After Mom died, I'd constantly catch him singing hymns in the middle of the night...But his dealing with stress went much deeper than that. I'm convinced that he received much of his enjoyment in life from helping others around him and from performing simple tasks. Bro and I could always tell how much stress he'd been under by the size of his woodpile. When his burdens became heavy or he got mad, he'd go get his axe and generate a brush or woodpile. In no time, he'd be content and I'd hear him start singing again.

I didn't inherit much of his goodness, but I've learned that the simplest manual tasks are the most rewarding and that anything given with love will be returned many times over. I've found it to be exactly as he said...

> *"Son, I just can't give anything away,"* he'd say. *"It just keeps coming right back to me."*

That was a mighty powerful declaration, especially for a poor man like him to say. Even now, I find that simple statement to be true. Don't get me wrong! I'm not suggesting that we give it all away...But when I give something without expecting anything back, it seems that almost immediately, something better takes its place.

All of us are unique. Each of us has traits that make us special. When I was younger, I was labeled by some as being immature. It felt like a putdown then, but now that I've become wrinkled and gray…Hearing descriptive terms such as that just brings a smile to my face and I just lean back in my chair and start remembering…

Yes, I've pulled a multitude of pranks, but it was not just the attention I craved. It was also the immediate benefit I received of creating delight from the ordinary and generating excitement. I must admit, it was always a thrill to walk into a gathering and hear the hushed voices of *"That's the guy I was telling you about!" "You'd better keep your eye on him!"* and *"There's no telling what he'll do next!"* This book will shock many, but others will say…*"That damn Bryan! I knew he'd do it!"*

When I go back to my old stomping grounds, I constantly hear the same complaints of…*"Things aren't like they used to be,"* and *"We don't have fun anymore."* I can't put it off any longer! These happenings must be recorded. Otherwise, they'll be forgotten and lost forever. I've received too much joy from life not to share it. I intend to relate these incidents using my best and most straightforward recollection, and without much effort in cleaning up the language.

Originally, I intended to immortalize all those involved by including their real names, but finally made the decision not to take too big of a gamble. I really don't want happy homes to be broken up or children disowning their Parents or Grandparents.

Maybe I should've taken life more seriously. Who'll be the judge? I do know that I've been happiest when bringing excitement, joy and laughter to those around me or when making their lives a little easier.

Sometimes, I think of life as a garden which flourishes when ample manure is applied. I've become convinced that when spread with care, bullshit can make life more interesting and actually fuel morale. Be assured. There will be many examples of it in the following pages.

This has not been an easy task. Writing does not come easy for me. I've had to fight with every word. Regardless, it's time to get on with it…So I present these memories to you and for those generations to come, to know where this ole man has been and just a hint of the enjoyment he has received.

Here, put my shoes on. Go where I've gone. Do what I've done. Now let me find my chair and I'll rock while you read.

"The Trooper"

Preface

From this book, I want you to receive a better understanding of why I chose the profession that I did, why I stayed with it until retirement and how I received so much pleasure from it. I want you to see what I saw and feel the emotions that I felt…All of them!

I don't remember seeing a Police Officer until I was about 10 years old. On the Outer Banks where we lived, there wasn't much need for law enforcement…There was no crime! Everybody knew everybody else and besides that, there was no place to flee…The Ferry was the only way off and on Hatteras Island. Most tourists hadn't found us yet and everybody just left their doors unlocked. I remember going to the grocery store quite often when the owner wasn't even there. He'd leave a note on the door and leave the cash register wide open. We'd get our groceries, make our own change and go home…No big deal. The only problem I can remember was a drunk I'd occasionally see stumbling down the road. Before long though, somebody would stop, throw him in the back of their truck and take him home.

My first encounter with a North Carolina State Trooper was a very colorful experience. We had moved inland and I was a newly licensed driver, driving my Dad's car on a lonely country road. It had just turned dark and I was in a hurry to see my girlfriend. The dash lights weren't working and I wasn't sure how fast I was going, and didn't really care. I was eagerly anticipating female companionship…It was an emergency! I was clipping along pretty good and not another vehicle was in sight when all at once, there appeared a large Christmas tree with a siren in my rearview mirror. It was a State Trooper, who had been following me with his lights off and he had just turned all of his resources on at the same time…I almost had a heart attack! I was so greatly frightened that I drove off the roadway and out into a tobacco field. He casually walked up and introduced himself and then he told me why he'd stopped me, as he checked my car for damage. There was none. He was kind enough not to laugh in my face, but I caught a glimpse of his sense of self-satisfaction as he wrote my ticket. I suppose I was impressed by the professionalism he displayed and the joy he must have felt inside. I don't remember his name, but in more ways than one…He had me!

Now, I'm a retired North Carolina State Trooper who lives in Pennsylvania.

The North Carolina State Highway Patrol renders the image of highly trained, polished, professional and polite Law Enforcement Officers. It offers one of the best training programs and facilities for Police Officers anywhere. It is a very proud organization representing a very proud state, but behind the scenes we can get kind of rowdy, with one another and with those close to us. If you'd like to formally meet a polished North Carolina State Trooper, drive 100mph through North Carolina…But if you want to take a behind the scenes view, come with me and I'll give you a tour of my experiences. To get things started, I'd better set the stage. I hope the following information will help you understand the rest of this book a little better.

- In North Carolina, blue lights are used by Police Officers and no one else.
- North Carolina State Troopers normally work alone without riding partners.
- We were issued a new Patrol Car every year or so, which we drove home at the end of our shift each day. This vehicle could not be used for off–duty driving. These vehicles were serviced and bodywork was done at centralized Highway Patrol Garages. I was a frequent visitor and was the recipient of much of their handiwork. They were and still are, good! One would be hard–pressed to find better work done anywhere.
- Our Radio Dispatchers were located in the same area. Our lives depended on the information they gave us and the manner with which they gave it. We worked on different frequencies than other Police agencies, but our Dispatchers could relay needed information. They assigned calls to each Trooper, so I made it a point to suck up to them.
- Radio repair is also done in the same general area and Technicians maintained our electronic equipment. We couldn't do without them.

Unless otherwise mentioned, I always drove a marked Patrol Car. The colors were always black and silver and to me, those colors always looked good. For years, North Carolina State Troopers won awards for being the best-dressed and best-equipped in the Nation. Yes, we were a proud bunch! Wouldn't you be?

A Trooper writes tickets or makes arrests for violations that are "clear-cut and substantial." *(That's where the individual Officer's judgment comes into play)*

Our policy of impartiality has always been a main ingredient of the respect that the organization still enjoys. I've never known of a Trooper who was told by a Supervisor…*"Don't give, so and so, a ticket."* Regardless of how powerful the defendant might be, the Highway Patrol would always back the Trooper.

Persons arrested are usually handcuffed and placed in the front passenger seat of the Patrol Car. A Trooper either learns how to be diplomatic or he has a lot of fights. You might call it diplomacy…I'll call it bullshit. Since I greatly prefer loving to fighting, I've spent my whole life honing that skill. Sure, I've had many close calls and I count myself fortunate indeed not to have had to kill someone to survive. Granted, it is a dangerous job and ample caution must be taken when constantly dealing with unknown characters, but an abrasive nature in a Police Officer only compounds the problems.

I've always tried to look at it like this…Lawbreakers weren't breaking the law because they didn't like me, so why should I take it personally. Nothing inflamed me more than to see another Officer abusing a prisoner. As far as I'm concerned, we all came out of the same pot…We're all family and I wouldn't treat a family member like that.

Before you get in too deep, heed my advice. As tempting as it may be for you to jump around and read these stories out of sequence, don't do it too much…You may miss some of the development. As needed, terminology will be explained and characters expanded as the stories progress. But if you slip up sometimes, that's OK too.

When I decided to remain a Trooper,
Without other ambitions or goals,
I focused on enjoying my livelihood,
As you'll see when these stories unfold.

Hold on for the ride of your life!   Have fun!!

Terminology
Just enough to get you through

Our Highway Patrol could be broken down into these basic areas…

- <u>District</u>—*normally, one county*
- <u>Troop</u>—*a group of Districts…normally six or seven*
- <u>Training</u>—*responsible for training and retraining all personnel*
- <u>Command</u>—*oversaw complete organization…including Internal Affairs and most all other areas of operation*
- <u>State Legislature</u>—*provided resources and funds for operation of organization*
- <u>Governor</u>—*designated all Command (Commissioned) Officers.* We all worked at the pleasure of our Governor. Whenever a new Governor was elected, chances were, new Command (Commissioned) Officers would be appointed and many of the former ones would retire.

The basic designation of ranks was as follows…

- <u>Trooper</u> *(Trp)*—sometimes called "Road Trooper." The main working force of the Highway Patrol. Work schedules changed every week…One week of early shift, the next…Late shift. Shifts were nine hours long. About one weekend off every six weeks. Worked almost all Holidays.
- <u>Line Sergeant</u> *(L/Sgt)*—immediate supervisor of Troopers. Supervised a squad or shift of Troopers. Performed duties of a Trooper whenever possible. Constant shift changes also.
- <u>First Sergeant</u> *(F/Sgt)*—also known as District F/Sgt. Responsible for all District operations. Highest ranking, Non–Commissioned Officer. From this rank on up to the top, working hours generally became more stable.
- <u>Lieutenant</u> *(Lt)*—go–between connecting District Operations and Troop Commander. "Gopher" *(go for this…"gopher" that)* for the Captain. Lowest ranking Commissioned Officer. Worked whatever schedule the Captain designated.
- <u>Captain</u> *(Capt)*—also known as Troop Commander. Responsible for all Troop operations. Worked schedule as he saw fit, mostly weekdays.
- <u>Major</u>—*(Maj)*—also known as Zone Major. Responsible for a number of Troops

- **Lieutenant Colonel**—*(Lt Col)*—the Majors reported to him. "Gopher" for the Colonel
- **Colonel**—*(Col)*—Patrol Commander. Highest-ranking Commissioned Officer.

Other words and phrases…
- **Politics**—Any power source capable of influencing our advancement, our organization, or us. Could be **Internal** (within our organization) or **External** (any outside source).
- **Policies and Procedures**—the guidelines by which we operated and lived. They constantly changed with the times.
- I'll try to explain the rest as I go along.

The Waiting

Until my last six months as an MP in the Army, I had no clue as to what kind of career I wanted. I yearned for direction, but heard no voice from above that guided me. Time was slipping away. Soon, I would be out there in a harsh, unfamiliar world. What was I going to do? What was I going to do?

Instead of re-enlisting in the Army, I decided on taking up traffic enforcement on the state level and sent for brochures from fifteen states that had Highway Patrols. I was somewhat surprised to find that North Carolina was right up there at the top in wages, benefits, equipment and enforcement statistics. Since I'd been raised there anyway, and since I thought their Highway Patrol colors of black and silver would make me look good…I decided to apply.

This part was rather tricky. I had to make formal and personal application at the Highway Patrol Troop Headquarters from my area of residence in North Carolina. The problem was…I was still in Virginia. My parents had recently moved to Dublin, NC and I wasn't sure were my residence was. Anyhow, I took a chance and applied at the Troop Headquarters in Elizabethtown, NC, which was close to Dublin. Unlike some, I had no contacts…I knew no Politicians and I had no friends on the Highway Patrol. All I had going for me was my good looks and high intelligence…I had it in the bag!

As with a normal pregnancy, the screening process took about nine months. During this waiting period, I studied the North Carolina State Highway Patrol and found that…
- it came into existence in 1929,
- it's founding members were trained in Pennsylvania,
- it covered more than 78,000 miles of roadways,
- it had the primary mission of reducing collisions and making the highways of North Carolina as safe as possible,
- and that it promoted highway safety and provided presentations to schools, civic groups, or any other interested parties.

At last, I received notification of my acceptance.

Labor

The nine months of waiting had ended. Now the birth of a new person, "The Trooper," began. I would now receive the training to become a member of *"The Showcase of North Carolina"*...The North Carolina State Highway Patrol. It would be a painful, but joyful, experience.

In the Fall of 1969 our training began. At the Institute of Government, on the UNCC campus in Chapel Hill...We were greeted by our Instructors, our new Mothers. We were an eager bunch, filled with anticipation and dreams of glory. We were informed that so long as a Cadet had the will to continue, the Training Staff would support him. The law was laid down and our rigid timetable commenced.

Physical fitness was not an option...It was a must! Long before daybreak, we were roused from slumber by our over-zealous PT *(physical training)* Instructors and our long day began. We donned our sweat suits, ran to the workout area and began the day with strenuous exercise. We performed calisthenics until even the strongest ones could do no more. Just when we thought we were surely going to die and the vomiting had stopped, our Trainers would lead us out for our morning run. The weaker ones were allowed to fall to the rear, but had to complete the ever-increasing distance at their own pace. Some of us who were stronger would encourage and support those who were lagging behind. I remember running with one of my friends who was lagging behind and was making brief stops to throw up.

> *"I'm not gonna make it!...I'm not gonna make it!"* he kept saying, as I dragged him around the track.

He stayed with the Highway Patrol and retired as a First Sergeant. *(I must admit, there were times that I regretted encouraging him to stick with it)* Within three months, one Cadet dropped in waist size from 40" down to a 32". *(Regurgitation will eventually cause weight loss. If I ever finish this one, maybe I should write a book on "How to Lose Weight")*

Eight hours of classroom instruction began after our physical exercises. From Lawyers and Judges, we learned the law. With the guidance of Black Belt Instructors, we studied and practiced defensive tactics. We were taught the methods of inflicting tremendous pain without causing injury. We gained knowledge in the use of firearms and the guts to use them to protect life and liberty. We learned pursuit driving, accident investigation, first aid, court procedures and self-reliance from seasoned Instructors. We were taken to an abandoned airport in Maxton where we were instructed in high-speed driving. We were taught to find the capabilities and limitations of our vehicles by the craziest Troopers in the state. *(Well, that's the way it seemed to me)* We became so proficient with speed estimation and the operation of Radar and speed timing devices, that we were competent enough to tell a motorist why we had stopped him. We didn't have to ask…*"Do you know how fast you were going?"*…We could tell him! Our skills of observation were developed to the point that we could actually tell a defendant why we had stopped him, rather than having to ask the asinine question…*"Do you know why I stopped you?"* We were trained to be professional, polite, courteous and firm. We were taught that no one was above the law and to apply enforcement in an impartial manner.

Throughout our training, Patrol personnel, Officers form other counties and states, and unknown dignitaries, appeared on the sidelines to chuckle at our misery and to cheer us on.

The birthing process continued.

The Spectrum

Back then, discrimination was still obvious, but we were coming out of the dark ages. My class was the second one to have any Blacks. We had two. They were probably better qualified than most of the rest of us. One made it all the way to the top as our Colonel and I was glad for him.

Female Troopers back then…No way! When I see female Troopers now, it brings me joy. In general, females seem to have more compassion and understanding, and that's what this world needs more of. Maybe, *"The meek will inherit the earth,"* and besides, could they possibly screw it up more than we have? Enough of that, let's get back to the story.

Our class contained a spectrum of personalities as you'll find in most any large group. It doesn't take long and it becomes obvious to everyone. In short order, a brown-noser always comes to the surface. Let me describe this one to you and you decide. This fellow was built like Arnold Schwarzenegger and he was the superman of our class, or thought he was. When we were herded onto the bus to travel from one point to another, he had to be the last one on and the first one off. While the rest of us were seated, he would stand in front of the bus close to the instructor who was driving. He had to be first in everything! He always remained close to whoever was in charge…To relay instructions to us. He didn't even flinch when we called him "Green-Cheese." *(Hint…that might have something to do with his name)* Now I'm going to say something that could hurt his feelings. He tried hard, but I have run across greater brown-nosing giants. You will also, as you continue reading.

We had one Cadet who kept us awake with his loud snoring, but we helped him. We cured him! We made sure he had plenty of liquids to drink before "lights out" and then we let him go to sleep and start his snoring. We waited for about 30 minutes, then snuck into his room and filled one of his hands with shaving cream. We then gently moved his other hand into a pan of warm water. Someone then tickled his eyebrow and we hauled ass. He slapped himself in the face and peed all over himself. Warm water will cause that reaction. No doubt, he spent many sleepless nights after that, but he stopped snoring.

Yes, it was tough going, but we had some good times in Patrol School.

The Boxing Match

Well into our training and when we were all in peak physical shape, a morning was set aside for boxing. No one, except the Instructors, knew who the opponents would be. The basic rules were pronounced…

The names of the upcoming two adversaries would be called out and protective gear would be put on. They'd square off, touch gloves and commence boxing. After three minutes, a whistle would be blown. The contestants would rest for a moment and then the match would continue for another round. The match would last three rounds. We were ready! The matches began.

I'd been raised with tenderness and had never boxed before. We watched as at least half a dozen opponents entered the ring and fought. At the end of each fight a winner was pronounced. Up until now, the opponents had been fairly well matched and no real injuries were sustained. Oh No!!…What was that? They just called out my name!

I was paired with Bradley, a Cadet who had me by about 20 pounds. He was larger and stronger than I was but my arms were longer. We walked out into the ring and I held my gloves up to touch his. But instead of touching gloves, he knocked the hell out of me!…I went down. *(He'd been telling other Cadets he was going to do that, but the word never got back to me)* Even as I was going down to my knees, I forgave him. I figured he just wasn't paying attention to the rules. That's when he hit me behind the head and completely flattened me out.

The time for compassion had ended.

"*Get him Bryan! Get him!*" the crowd hollered.

For the first time in my life, I was really pissed off! I came up like a tornado and the ass-whipping began.

I gave Bradley a blow to the nose and ripped one of his nostrils. You could see the blood and one side of his nose flapping in the breeze. We fought and we fought. I was constantly listening and we were well past the three-minute limit, but the whistle never blew. I was getting in the better licks but neither one of us went down. We fought some more. Where was that damn whistle? After awhile, we both began to look like windmills that were slinging wet noodles at one another. Finally, we both just sat down. We were absolutely exhausted. But still, there was no whistle…Were our Instructors trying to kill us? No, I believe they just wanted to see what I had in me.

As we rested, I put my arm around Bradley and apologized to him for busting his nose. From then on, we were like "Mutt and Jeff"…He followed me around everywhere! Wherever I went, Bradley wanted to go. It had to be quite amusing to see…Big ole him, following little ole me. We had all learned a lot.

Graduation was drawing closer.

End of the Beginning

As the time drew near for our departure, we collectively decided to dish out some of what we'd been taking. During the night, we nailed all the windows shut in the barracks. We then prepared a reward for our ugly "Mothers,"…Our PT Instructors.

The next morning, we awoke early and waited for them to begin their wake-up call…We had a surprise for them. When they were about half-way down the hall, we all rushed out and subdued them. We pulled their clothes off and fitted them with nice, sexy purple panty hose filled with shaving cream. We all then ran out of the barracks and left them locked inside with an activated tear gas canister. After we'd let them suffer awhile, we carried them out to the swimming pool, which was filled with scummy, 40 degree water and then threw them in. This event signaled the completion of our birthing process.

Now something very unusual and unexpected happened that I had never seen happen before. One of my Instructors privately gave me a choice of duty stations…But the choice had to be made right then! Would it be Elizabethtown, from which I had applied, or would I prefer Gastonia? I was dumb-founded! Cadets were never asked anything…They were told! I asked him why I was given a choice. He said that the First Sergeant there had been watching me and would like to have me back there with him. *(Damn, that made me feel good…And I didn't even know him well)* Feeling somewhat uncomfortable starting out in familiar territory and having no knowledge of the latter, except that it was near Charlotte…I chose Gastonia.

We were all assigned our duty stations and issued excellent equipment. For the only time in my career, I was issued a used Patrol Car, a '68 Plymouth Fury 440. *(Damn, that was one hot car! It would run 158mph)* At last, we were on our way.

We graduated. Somehow, most of us were able to accomplish what we had come to believe was the impossible. Yes, we were a proud bunch…We were born together. We were convinced that we were now ready to live and die for one another and the public we would serve.

Regardless of which paths they take later on, any person who has ever made it through our Basic Highway Patrol School has my love and respect. We have the same raising. We are all family.

The Hard Ass

Fresh out of Patrol School in 1969, three of us were assigned to work in Gaston County. Upon arriving, more seasoned Troopers informed us that we were now officially within, "*The Asshole of the Highway Patrol.*" I found that description to be true because for the next five years, I lived in pure hell. But, believe it or not, I came to like it...I came to think that hell was normal until I transferred to another county. Now, the only reason I call it hell is because I had very, very strict supervision...To which I did not respond well. I enjoyed the area and to say the least, my stay there was exciting. But you could put your money on it...For one out of every six cars I stopped, the driver would either jump and run, I'd have a fight on my hands or a car chase would take place.

The District First Sergeant was Jack Mostella. He had retired as a Colonel from the Air Force and was one of the few surviving "founding members" of the North Carolina State Highway Patrol. Rigorous discipline was his guiding principle. If there ever was a "by the book" man, he was it...He was 100% Highway Patrol.

We turned in weekly reports on Sundays and he would call each one of us individually, beforehand, to advise us of our designated appointment with him at the Office. We were expected to have our weekly reports completed by then with all i's dotted and t's crossed. This meeting would last exactly 15 minutes and unless we were investigating an accident or arresting a drunk, we'd better make that meeting.

He tolerated no crap, whatsoever...Except from his wife.

All Troopers had a clothing allowance which he closely guarded and First Sergeant Mostella would always destroy the old before issuing new. For example...If a Trooper wanted more shoes, he had to present the old, worn-out pair to the First Sergeant beforehand, who would then cut the tongues out and then return them to the Trooper. When myself or other Troopers indicated desire to continue our education, this was his response...

> "*If the Highway Patrol doesn't teach it to you...You don't need to know it!*"

On our own time, some of us ignored him and went back to college anyway.

I'm tired of writing. Take it for a while, Levi.

He would even tell the story on himself…About the time he gave himself a ticket!

He had been driving his Patrol Car in a residential area, ran a stop sign and struck another vehicle in the side. The local Police were called to investigate. After the paperwork was finished, First Sergeant Mostella asked the investigating Officer…

"It was my fault! Aren't you going to give me a ticket?"

"No Sir," the Officer replied, "*I'm not about to give you one.*"

"Well, damn it," the First Sergeant said, "*I'll give myself one!*"

He did! And then went to Court and paid it off.

Once, he even attempted to write his wife up for speeding. That never got off the ground…She threatened his life! He referred to her as *"The Ole Battle Ax."* He would've given his own Mother a ticket, or tried to. I was a little different.

After becoming exposed to First Sergeant Mostella and many other Highway Patrol members, I began to see this difference more clearly. Mostly, because of my raising, I tended to be more forgiving in nature…But the Highway Patrol must've seen something in me that they liked and wanted, or they would've never let me on. I loved the work, but I wondered if I'd be able to make it.

On his behalf, I must say that First Sergeant Mostella had a very likeable personality with the general public. He didn't just pick on me…He was tough on all of his Troopers. I became notorious for wrecking Patrol Cars and he came to call me *"Hot Rod"*…And I upheld that reputation. I wrecked every Patrol Car I ever had.

He, and those who were hard-nosed as he was, created the reputation of impartiality that The North Carolina State Highway Patrol has enjoyed since 1929. Surely, he overheard the nickname that we called him, but I really believe First Sergeant Mostella was proud to be known as a Hard Ass.

Hard Asses are not necessarily bad. We all need at least one around to keep us straight.

Other Mother

At his first duty station, a Rookie customarily rides with a Training Officer for about six weeks to get his feet wet. Most of the time, the Rookie would do the driving and the Training Officer would just sit there, make sure he did everything right and give advice. Many of us referred to our Training Officer as our *"Other Mother."*

Jethro was my Training Officer and was about twice my size. He had trained scores of Rookies before me and many more would follow. Jethro loved to work…Jethro kicked ass! If anything illegal was going on, he found it. He was always at the top of the heap when it came to writing tickets and he was First Sergeant Mostella's only pet. As we rode together, he'd spot violations like a hawk and I'd never see them. He did his best to prepare me and I wanted so much to be like him, but I never truly succeeded. When my six weeks was over he cut me loose, but I wasn't ready…He was so good at it, and I was so scared.

After being out on my own for a couple of weeks, Jethro called me on the radio. He wanted assistance and I was not too far away. When I found him on a country road, Jethro had a car pulled over and its passenger door was wide open. The only other visible person around was the fellow cuffed and seat-belted in on the passenger seat of Jethro's Patrol Car. Jethro was mad and his head was as red as a beet. He was just like that.

There's no way I can put into print our conversation, because when he got excited, Jethro would start stammering and except for his cussing, I couldn't understand much of what he was saying. When I finally did get his meaning, I couldn't believe what he was requesting.

Apparently, when Jethro first stopped the vehicle for erratic driving there were two males in the front seat. Jethro arrested the drunk driver, then cuffed him and sat him down into his Patrol Car's front passenger seat…Without seat-belting him in. About this time, the other occupant of the stopped car, who was sober (?), began leaning out of the car window and waving and calling to Jethro. He was obviously trying to get Jethro to come back up to the violator's vehicle. Jethro stomped back up to the car to find out what the problem was. While he was thusly being distracted, out of the corner of his eye he saw a flash. Upon closer examination, he found that the handcuffed drunk driver, who had been in his Patrol Car, had just made a mad dash for freedom. This made him mad, because now the real culprit was getting away. Jethro felt this distraction was planned by the sober (?) passenger in an effort to give his buddy a chance to take off. Somebody was going to pay for this crap! Guess who.

The fellow who was now in Jethro's Patrol Car was originally the passenger of the stopped vehicle. Jethro wanted me to take him to Jail for public drunkenness. I hesitated.

> "*Jethro?*" I questioned, "*He looks fine to me and I don't even smell any alcohol on his breath!*"
>
> "*I don't give a damn what you smell or what you don't smell,*" he responded. "*I said take his ass to Jail and I mean it!*"
>
> "*Yes Sir! You're the boss,*" without further comments, I stated. "*Whatever you say, Sir.*"

With that, I loaded him up and headed for the Big House. In the meantime, Jethro was out beating the bushes for that original defendant who was still wearing his handcuffs. *(And I believe he's one of the few defendants to ever get away from Jethro)*

After arriving at the Jail, I walked my prisoner in and presented him to the Jailer, and then told him to lock the defendant up for Public Drunkenness.

> "*This fellow's not drunk!*" with some shock, the Jailer said.
>
> "*My Training Officer, Jethro, said he is…So he is!*" I confidently stated. "*I'm just a Rookie, so what do I know?*"

Yes we did! I can't say that I'm proud of it and he didn't stay in there long…But I still believe we put an innocent man in Jail.

And that concludes this tale of my Other Mother, as I remember it happening, a long time ago.

Sneaky Snake

We had another tough Supervisor in our District who was a Line Sergeant. This man was "by the book" also and knew the Motor Vehicle Law and our Patrol Policy inside and out. He was a perfectionist and everything he did was exact and organized. When he sat down to eat, he would take one precise bite of each item on his plate, in a clockwise motion, until his plate was clean…And not one crumb would ever fall. He was highly intelligent but he had an unapproachable air about him. He was always there to tell us how to do it right, but seldom there to help us out. If you asked him a question, he'd give you a long, sarcastic look before he uttered a word. He was addicted to nasal inhalers and he had the personality of a turd.

What really set him apart from all others was his sneakiness. Don't you just hate that? I disliked it so much that I'm going to relate several stories about him in this section. Behind his back, we called him Sneaky Snake…So that's what I'll call him now.

The Snake Killer

Sneaky Snake had a very powerful set of binoculars that he loved to use to spy on us. He'd sneak around and listen to us on our radios and when he'd found out where we were, he'd sit back in the distance and watch us with his binoculars. Then he'd ask us for our 10–20 *(location)*…Just to see if we'd lie. And if we did, he'd write us up.

Lying about one's current location was common practice and most all of us did it at one time or another. Who wants to take a wreck or some other involved project, and spend a lot of time on that, when they can be out writing a lot of speeding tickets or doing their own thing? As he'd done to the rest of us, he tried to pull this crap on Jethro. He should've known better!

Jethro was minding his own business, doing whatever he was doing, and no doubt…Working. On our radio, I heard Sneaky Snake break the silence.

"*What's your 10–20?*" he asked Jethro.

Without any hesitation whatsoever, Jethro came right back to him.

"A couple hundred yards from where you are, Sarge," Jethro boldly responded. *"Don't you know where that is?"*

Sneaky Snake didn't respond. For once, that shut him up…Because there was no manly response for a statement like that. I laughed until I about peed on myself and I'm sure everybody else who heard it did too. Sneaky Snake tucked his tail between his legs and silently slithered away.

The Gun Spring

Sneaky Snake was an absolute gun nut and he knew firearms inside and out. From scratch, he would often even build his own weapons, for personal use. The Highway Patrol used his knowledge and expertise wisely. Whenever needed, he held firearms classes. The following class was one of his most memorable. We were being issued new weapons…357 Magnum Revolvers.

The way I remember it, the class that he instructed me in had no more than thirty Troopers in it, but whenever I've been around any older Troopers and the subject of Sneaky Snake comes up…They all claim to have been there when this incident occurred. The only way that I can figure it is that this class must've been a lot larger than I thought…Every Trooper in the State *(more than 1000)* must've been there!

The class began. For the first hour he went over all the "Use of Force" laws. Sneaky Snake was so detailed in his instruction that no one asked any questions. Then, we took a short break and came back. For the next hour, we thoroughly went over all the other written material and studied the nomenclature and diagrams of our new equipment. Not until the next break was over and we were told to do so, were we allowed to even open the boxes and look at our new weapons. Now, we would be taught the proper cleaning methods. Complete disassembly was not required. We would only break them down enough to maintain them and clean them well. For us to tamper with any of the delicate internal springs and mechanisms was an offense that could get us fired…Only a firearms expert, such as himself, would ever be allowed to do that.

With our unloaded Revolvers lying there on the tables before us, in no uncertain terms, he made the rules plain. Without being instructed to do so, no one was allowed to even touch their new weapon…And under no circumstances, would we ever be touching any part with a spring. When directed, together, we would all painstakingly go one step at a time and to get ahead of the group would be an unforgivable mistake. After carefully going over all the rules, the tedious process began. It got every quiet. Only his stern voice was heard. Our butts were tight. We dared not cross ole Sneaky Snake.

In unison, we began the process. We removed the cylinder and its holding pin. Together, we then carefully removed the handle grips and gently laid them to the side. So far, everything was going just fine. Then, the silence was broken by a sound that was so soft, that it was impossible to tell where it was coming from.

"Sprong!"

In tense stillness, we all listened as that little high-tension spring ricocheted around the classroom. Sneaky Snake angrily looked around but not one word was spoken. Somewhere from the back of the room an unidentifiable slight snicker could be heard. We all just sat there…Bursting in silence. He must've known it would be fruitless to try to locate the culprit and as far as I know, that little spring was never seen again and the offender has never yet surfaced.

OK, just one more and then I'll let you go.

The Briefcase

One Sunday evening when we were all doing our paperwork around the long tables in the Patrol Office, with no Supervisors around, I noticed Sneaky Snake's briefcase sitting in an odd location. It was on the floor and was right in the middle of the area that we normally occupied. Sneaky Snake was not one to forget anything, especially his prized briefcase, so I wondered…*"What in the world is that doing here?"* I went over to it and noticed that a group of small holes had been drilled into the side of it, in a small circular pattern. And not only that, but an unusual button had been installed on the top near the handle. It was locked *(no big surprise)*, so to satisfy our curiosity, we jimmied it open.

You guessed it! There it was…A tape recorder. And voice activated too. We put it back together as it was and proceeded to put on a show.

For the next thirty minutes or so, we made up a bunch of lies and told them. Then we all started talking about how sorry people were who'd use tape recorders to listen in on others. We played loud music for him and even took that thing outside and recorded our Patrol Cars' racing engines and squealing tires for him.

He must've got his ears full when he listened to that tape, because that was the last we ever saw of that briefcase.

The End of Sneaky Snake

Eventually, he made more rank and ended up in a situation that he was well-suited for. Sneaky Snake spent his last years with us at our Training Center. He was in charge of the Armory there and basically, he worked, lived and quite possibly died…Alone.

Autoway Floyd

What in the world could that mean? Well, that's the real name of one of the first DWI defendants I arrested, and as unusual as his name is, so were the circumstances surrounding this incident.

On a hot, humid day I was dispatched to a 10–50 PD *(accident involving property damage)*. The scene was on a dirt road in the middle of nowhere and involved one vehicle that had cleaned out ditches on both sides of the road. The car had a lot of damage, but no one was injured. As I approached, I noticed about a dozen people standing around. One of them came up to me and identified himself as an ABC *(alcohol)* Enforcement Officer…He was in plain clothes, but was wearing a gun and huge badge on his belt. Then he stepped back into the gathering.

> *"What happened here?"* I asked, loud enough for all to hear.

One of the largest men I've ever seen in my life stepped forward and he was obviously drunk.

> *"When I was driving down the road…"* He started out OK, but then he started mumbling and making ridiculous, drunken statements.

I introduced myself to him, shook his giant-sized hand and he told me his name was Autoway Floyd.

> *"Autoway,"* I then said, *"it looks to me like you've had too much to drink to be driving."* That really got his attention.

> *"You're not gonna take me to Jail for no DUI!"* with all the confidence in the world, he said.

I didn't respond, but his wrists were so large that my handcuffs wouldn't have fit him anyway.

With that, out of the corner of my eye I noticed that everybody else, included my fellow enforcement officer in civilian clothes, was wandering off and positioning themselves a safe distance away. It felt to me like they were arranging ringside seats to see little ole young Trooper me get his butt kicked. This was my first

REAL test. Would I die on this isolated dirt road or would I develop an acceptable line of bullshit and possibly survive? With limited options, I gave it a try.

> "*Autoway, it's your car isn't it?*" I started out.

> "*Yes,*" was his reply.

> "*Well,*" I said, "*I've got to put something on this damn wreck report. Come on over here and help me fill it out.*"

I went around to the driver's side of my Patrol Car and sat down and then invited him to also sit down on the passenger side. He did so, but would not close his door. For the moment, I ignored him. We sat there for a few minutes while I pretended to fill out the report. *(I was scared to death but did my best not to show it.)* The spectators were starting to mill around now, eagerly awaiting the beginning of bloodshed.

> "*Autoway,*" I finally said, "*I'm about to burn up from the heat. How about closing that door so we're not air conditioning the whole world.*"

Ever so cautious, he did it...He closed the door. At the very instant he closed that door, I gave no warning...I threw her in gear, put the pedal to the metal and we were out of there. I was still petrified, but my career as a State Trooper was now getting off the ground. Our conversation went something like this...

> "*You little son of a bitch,*" he said. "*What the hell do you think you're doing?*"

> "*Autoway, you're under arrest for DUI.*" I firmly stated.

> "*I'll wreck us, you SOB!*" he threatened. "*All I've gotta do is grab the steering wheel.*"

> "*You could do that Autoway, but so long as my little scrawny ass is under this steering wheel, you can bet on one thing...The wreck will be on your side, not mine!*"

> "*Sooner or later, you're gonna stop and then I'll jump and run.*"

"I'd have to shoot you, Autoway! And I don't want to do that. There's no way I could fight you, you'd kill me!"

We kept talking and before long we became quite friendly…I even stopped for a few traffic lights without incident. But I must admit, I was continuously running my mouth like a sewing machine. When we arrived at the Jail, I got out of my side first.

"*Come on, Autoway.*" I then said.

(Our procedure then was to first present the subject to the Jailer and then go to the Magistrate's Office to get a warrant for him…Then return to the Jail and give the warrant to the Jailer for serving) Without uttering a word, this giant followed me like a lamb to the Jailer's desk. I made it a point to politely introduce him to the two Jailers who were present. I then left for the Magistrate's Office and when I returned about fifteen minutes later, there were four Jailers now…And they all looked like they'd been through a meat grinder. *(Being a Rookie, I didn't really know any of them well)*

"*Trooper,*" one of them spoke up and said. "*How the hell did you get that fella in here by yourself? Lucky for us it was shift change, because it took all four of us to get him into a cell.*"

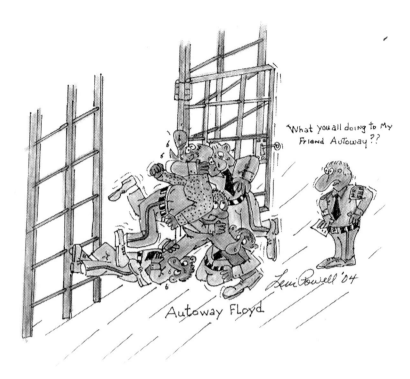

I never told them how…I just let them wonder. And thus began my good reputation.

Bribe to Survive

For the first six months, I lived in the Gastonia Fire Station. Rebecca and I planned to get married as soon as her divorce was final, but before long, I became a little too brave. I rented a house up on Spencer's Mountain across from the First Baptist Church and we moved in. We'd slip on wedding rings once in awhile to keep the natives happy. This kind of activity is no big deal now, but back then it was frowned upon, so I didn't broadcast it around to my Supervisors...I just told a few friends. Everyone on the Patrol knew we weren't married but soon would be.

All was rocking and rolling along pretty good until, on one of my days off, one of my Rookie buddies, Jim Brettan, excitedly called me on the phone.

> "Bryan!" he was almost out of breath when he said, "*I was just at the Office and overheard First Sergeant Mostella raising hell. Apparently, another Trooper has turned you in!*" Then he really got my attention with..."*Mostella's gonna have your ass! I just thought you ought to know.*"

Right about then is when my aging process really began. I didn't know whether to fish or cut bait. I did know one thing though, I wasn't going to hang around the house and wait for the knock on the door! I gathered up Rebecca and we took off.

I still had one more day off before I'd have to make an appearance at the Office and although my butt was mighty tight, my brain was still functioning. I had to find a place for my reputation to reside. We rode around and talked about it for a good while. Finally, we ended up in Charlotte and I bribed a clerk at the YMCA to give me a backdated receipt for a room there, completely covering the time we'd been living in that house.

Well, that long awaited day arrived way too soon. I put my uniform on and drove to the Office and sure enough, First Sergeant Mostella immediately called me into his inner sanctum. I've got to be honest. I wasn't real smooth. I was scared to death! It went something like this...

> "*I understand that you're living with this girl and you're not married,*" he started out. "*The Highway Patrol does not tolerate that kind of activity.*"

> "Sarge," I meekly replied, *"we've been working on the house a lot, trying to get it ready to move in."* Then I asked, *"Are the neighbors complaining?"*
>
> *"No, it's an internal complaint,"* he replied.
>
> *"Here's my receipt for a room at the YMCA in Charlotte."* I passed it to him with a sweaty hand, and then I continued with," *I've been staying over there."*

With that, his jaw kind of dropped. He knew I was lying but he didn't have me nailed down as well as he'd thought! I wasn't raised to lie, but I'd worked too damned hard to get on the Highway Patrol to just throw it away.

> *"How about...(specific date and time after dark),"* he was getting madder now when he said, *"your car was there and so was hers! What were you doing then?"*
>
> *"Sarge,"* I was getting bolder when I said, *"I believe that's the night we worked late, painting."*

His feathers were really ruffled now, but I was calming down.

> *"Well how about...(specific date and time in the wee hours of the morning),"* he continued. (He had all these times written down) *"Both of your cars were there!...And there were no lights on in the house! How the hell do you explain that?"*
>
> *"Sarge,"* I replied, (I had completely regained my composure by now) *"I can't be for sure on the date, but that must've been the night that we both worked so hard and late that rather than drive all the way to the 'Y'...I slept in my car."* Now I got kind of smart-assed when I said..."Did anyone think to check in there?"

He let me go that time, but he had to know I was lying. I was young. If I hadn't been such a smart-aleck like that, maybe I wouldn't have had so much trouble from him. From then on, he nailed me every time I turned around.

Months later, after he'd saved up a number of my screw-ups *(some of which I think he made up)*...He dragged me before the Captain and laid them all out.

As a result, I got suspended without pay for three days that ran consecutively with my normal days off. That gave me five days off in a row. I had to take my Patrol Car to the Office and turn in my badge and gun for that suspension. Rebecca was standing by to get me away from there. How embarrassing!

I had done some more thinking and Rebecca had helped me. Rather than spending those five days reflecting on my sins, we had decided we were going to celebrate and go to the Beach. We were married now. According to Patrol Policy, we had to fill out a "temporary address form" when we were leaving town. So I went back into the Office and filled one out the best I could, and then gave it to First Sergeant Mostella.

> "Sarge," I said, *"there's a spot on here for the phone number of the place we're staying, but there is no phone, so I've included the phone number of the Myrtle Beach Police Dept. That's the only way, I can think of, that we can be reached."*

First Sergeant Mostella's jaws were really tight when I left and those were five of the most enjoyable days I've ever had off…And by the way, when my next paycheck arrived, the difference in pay was only about five dollars.

Now there's one more area that hasn't been addressed. Who turned me in to First Sergeant Mostella? Upon reflection, I remember two different Troopers who kept coming by the house and checking on us and one, in particular, who I'd see riding by quite a bit, even though he wasn't working that area. He was also known as a brown-noser…But there's no good reason to go any further. Brown-nosing doesn't appear to have gotten him very far anyway.

I've had to live with the bad choices I've made, but there has never been a doubt in my mind…Some of my best spent money, was for that bribe to survive.

Old Man on the Porch

I don't remember if I had previously wrecked my '68 Plymouth or it was just at the Patrol Garage for service…Anyway, I was now driving a spare car which I was not that familiar with. It was a '69 Ford and this was one heavy car. As I headed north on New Hope Road near I85, suddenly, I became aware of the fact that I had a flat tire on the left rear. Knowing I would have to change it, I eased into a quiet residential area and out of the public eye. It was a beautiful day in the neighborhood.

I threw it in Park, got out and commenced changing the tire. After jacking up the rear bumper, removing the flat and positioning the spare tire under wheel well, I noticed that the whole car was, ever so gently…Creeping backward. If I didn't do something pretty quickly, that car was going to fall off of the jack! Overestimating my strength, I placed my right hand into the wheel well and tried to pull the car forward…Back into its original position. For a moment or two, it seemed to help some, but I had not been working out enough…The car fell! My right hand was now caught between the fender and the spare tire. I don't think I screamed out, but it felt like the weight of the whole world was on that hand! I began to feel a little dizzy and as I looked around for help, there he was, maybe a hundred feet away. He'd been watching me the whole time.

> "Help! Help!" without any pride, I cried to him.

He shuffled around on the porch some as he responded.

> "Eh?" (That means "What?"…To you folks who don't understand English)

> "Come Here! Help Me!" again I called out to him.

> This time he replied, "OK, I'll go call the Police," as he slowly rambled back into the house.

That was the last time I saw him, but I'll not forget him…That damned old man on the porch.

It seemed like an hour, but it was more like 15 minutes, before I saw another living soul. Finally…finally, a car pulled onto the street and a young couple drove up. This time, I was more dignified in my approach, but for the youthful observers, it had to look strange indeed.

Ahead of them was a State Trooper, standing outside of his vehicle and facing them, bent over with his right hand shoved into the left rear wheel well and he was gently waving his left arm over the trunk of his car…And all this with a crazy grin on his face. *(I was very happy to see them, because I had come to believe that I was the only person left alive on this earth)*

The car stopped about a hundred feet behind me and the couple cautiously got out. The young girl stayed behind as the boy bravely, but slowly, moved toward me. With all the patience I could muster, I waited until he was within five or six feet of me before I spoke.

> *"My hand is caught,"* I calmly said. *"Please jack up the car so I can get it out."*

He was anxious and scared. I had to detail every step of the process to him, because I knew exactly what had to be done…And he didn't. After the young man nervously jacked the car up, I removed my hand and together we put the spare tire on.

My hand had no feeling for awhile but I could still move my fingers. The impression of the tire tread was across my fingers and there was some blood, but not much. I began to feel queasy now and I didn't know whether I had broken fingers or not. I did know that I had no business driving and had to notify someone…So, on my radio, I called a brother Trooper I knew to be working nearby. After detailing the incident to him, he asked me if my hand was still stuck in the wheel well. If I could've reached across the radio and strangled him, I believe I might've tried. *(How could I have possibly called him on the radio, which was inside the vehicle, if my hand was still caught in the wheel well? We didn't have walkie—talkies back then)*

He kindly came and got me, then took me to the Hospital. No fingers were broken and I put on a few band-aids and went back to work.

Although he had very little to do with it, when I recall this incident, what sticks out in my mind most is…That %$@# old man on the porch.

Arrest of a Trooper

After I'd blazed the trail in Gaston County for a few years, along came a new Rookie Trooper...Joe Ikell. I felt sorry for Joe because he didn't have any friends, so I took him under my wing. *(Now wait just a minute...This is my story and I'm telling it)* We worked the same area and had the same Court days...Every two weeks on Thursdays. One particular Thursday morning, we got to Court a little early and my good friend was telling me what had just transpired.

Joe told me that a friend of his had called him early that morning.

> "Joe," he had said, *"you've got to help me...I'm in Jail!"*

This friend had previously been involved in a fight, had gone to Court and then been ordered by the Court to pay restitution of $250 to the other party. He had failed to do that, so he'd been locked up. Joe asked how he could help and the friend continued...

> "They won't let me outta Jail til I pay the $250 and I don't have the cash on me. The Clerk of Court won't take my check, but surely she'll take yours...You're a Trooper."

> "I can't do that," Joe said, "I don't have $250 in my checking account."

> "Tell ya what," the friend kept on, *"you go write a check to the Clerk of Court and they'll let me out of Jail. I'll run to my bank and get the cash, give it to you and then you can deposit it into your bank account...It'll be a breeze."*

They pulled it off...Well, almost. Joe had the $250 cash in his pocket and was waiting until our first break before making his deposit. Big Mistake!

Here I sat with all this information. My friend had written a bad check to the Clerk of Court! What was I going to do? I couldn't let something like this slide, so I did what any law-abiding citizen should do...I politely excused myself and went immediately to the Clerk of Court's Office. *(Betty Jenkins was our Clerk of Court then. She was all business and very professional)* I told her I desperately needed her help and then proceeded to squeal my guts out. *(Up until now, I'd never seen her laugh)* She asked me what she could do to help me.

> "Joe needs to be arrested," I told her. "If you'll sign a 'Capias Instanter' with $500 cash bond (That means, put his butt in Jail if he can't cough up $500 cash)…*I'll handle the rest.*"

She did. *(Betty had one of the most beautiful signatures I've ever seen)*

With paper in hand, I sought out and located the largest and meanest looking Deputy I could find, told him the story, recruited his help, gave him the "Capias Instander" and then made my way back into the Courtroom. All of this was accomplished in no more than ten minutes.

The Court was in full swing now. Joe and I were sitting in the front of the room and about twenty feet away from the Judge. The back door between us and the Judge was the one normally used for us to enter and exit. We had been there about long enough for me to catch my breath good when the door cracked open and the Deputy got Joe's attention. Joe quietly went to the door, stayed for a couple of minutes and then came back with a very pale face…He was looking mighty bad! I couldn't look at him. I had to cover my mouth with my hand to conceal that uncontrollable grin.

> "Joe, what's the matter?" being the caring person I am, I asked.

> "That Deputy's got a 'Capias Instander' to arrest me for 'worthless check'!" he excitedly whispered. "How the hell did they find out so fast?"

> "Maybe they normally run the checks through the first thing in the morning," I suggested. "What are they gonna do now?"

Joe was really worked up now. I didn't think he could stand much more, but I let it go on anyway.

> "That Deputy told me he'd let me finish my Court cases before they lock me up," he said. "Now what the hell am I gonna do?"

> ………I had to take a deep breath before this one………

"There's not but one thing you can do, Joe," I advised, "you've got to tell First Sergeant Mostella."

That about did him in. Joe's eyes were starting to glaze over and I could tell his whole life was beginning to flash before his eyes. If I wanted him to live, I had to nip this in the bud…Right now!! So I said…

"Joe, it's a joke. I pulled it on you."

"No you didn't," he replied. "This is no joke! You ain't got enough sense to pull anything like this and besides…That's Betty Jenkins' signature! And that Deputy out there?…He doesn't pull any crap either!"

There was nothing else I could say, because Joe wouldn't believe me. His health was steadily going downhill and this was developing quickly into a life-threatening situation. So I went out and found the Deputy and had him tell Joe the truth…Outside of the Courtroom and in the hallway. Not being a complete idiot, I made sure there was about fifty feet between us. Shortly thereafter, a chase of my life began.

We ran down the stairs and out into the parking lot…Around and around we went. I thought I was in better shape than he was, but every time I looked behind me, he was gaining ground. I ran back upstairs, came through the front door of the Courtroom and then walked briskly through it. I turned to look and Joe had never slowed down. Obviously he didn't care what the Judge might do to him for interrupting his Courtroom, because he was running full blast behind me. I have no idea how I escaped with my life, but here I am safe at last…And up in Pennsylvania writing about it.

Levi's good, isn't he?

Preacher's Kid

From a young age, I was gleefully harassed by my friends because my Father was a Methodist Minister. Whenever I pulled pranks or got into trouble, they'd say... *"We're not surprised, that's just what preachers' kids do."* Even into adulthood, this stereotype followed me.

We had been trained well in Patrol School and in the methods of properly testifying in Court, we were well-versed. But my real training in these matters came later from Defense Attorneys...It was from losing cases to them that I learned the most. While still quite new and inexperienced, I came to dread cases with high profile and expensive Lawyers. Just when I thought I had a very strong case, that's when I'd lose it on a murky detail.

I recall one of the first cases I had, in which one such Lawyer was representing a drunk driver I had arrested. I thought the DWI case I had against the defendant was pretty solid and apparently, so did his Lawyer, because he had to reach deep into his bag of tricks to come up with this defense. Somehow, he had discovered that I was the son of a Minister.

> *"Your Honor,"* he started out. *"I move for the dismissal of this case because I have discovered that Trooper Gregory is the son of a Methodist Minister and is no doubt, biased to alcohol in any form."* Then he continued with, *"I feel that for even the slightest odor of alcohol, Trooper Gregory would have arrested my client."*

Normally, the Judge would have either accepted this motion or denied it. But instead, his response was highly unusual.

> *"Trooper Gregory, approach the bench!"* he commanded.

No one else was invited...It was just the Judge and I. But in a voice loud enough for all to hear, the Judge leaned over and spoke to me...

> *"Is that true?"* he asked. *"Is your Father a Methodist Minister?"*

> *"Yes Sir,"* I nervously replied.

> *"Well, so is mine!"* he thundered!

For a good ten minutes, in open Court, we then carried on a conversation about where our Fathers had ministered, where we had lived and how we had come to where we were. We were smiling, laughing and having a grand ole time while the Defense Attorney sat at his table…Just cringing. It was obvious to him and everybody else that the Judge was rubbing it in. From the Courtroom came occasional soft bursts of snickers and laughter.

The Judge did not allow the motion for dismissal and after hearing the evidence, he found my defendant guilty. I don't recall having another trial with that Defense Attorney, before that Judge, ever again. As a matter of fact, I don't believe I ever tried another case with him. The Judge remained my friend.

This incident was a wake-up call for me. From then on, I would not have traded places with anyone else. It sure was nice to discover, that being known as a Preacher's Kid can have benefits too.

The Fickle Female

I was stationed in Gaston County for the first five years of my career. A female there had supposedly been having an affair with a Trooper who had moved to another county to get away from her. Upon Bill's *(Oops!)* departure, she began looking for another object for her affection.

What luck! She spotted me. I don't know whether it was a kind word that I gave her or she just thought I was pretty. Anyway, she couldn't help herself and she fell in love...And I couldn't get rid of her! Regardless of where I was or what I was doing, she would hunt me down and follow me around while I was on-duty. Whenever and wherever I was working, she was right there...There was no getting away from her! Once I even accelerated to 120mph and then crossed a median to escape her, but when I looked in the rearview mirror of my Patrol Car again, there she was, still on my bumper in her little green sports car...Flashing her headlights and blowing her horn. Although I had never laid a finger on her, this was no joking matter! Then it began getting even worse...She began calling my house! My wife wasn't taking it well and if this crap didn't stop soon, I might have to find a new spouse.

Then the clincher came...

One Sunday evening, we were all at the Gaston County Patrol Office completing our weekly reports, when one of my cohorts, Barry Williams, began hee-hawing and ribbing me about this girl following me around. He just wouldn't let it rest...He kept right on embarrassing me in front of my other Trooper friends. Everybody was laughing at me and hurting my feelings, and my reputation was going downhill fast.

Not long after this, she went to the Hospital and had a short stay there, for some unknown reason. After she came out, it's almost like she forgot all about me. Her affections were now completely focused on my ole buddy, Barry Williams. *(But I didn't harass him. As always, I remained a gentleman)*

Months passed and I had recently put in for a transfer to Mecklenburg County. One day, Barry and I were talking and he brought the subject up.

> *"Bryan,"* he began, *"I've never been able to figure it out...How that ole girl that used to follow you around is now doing the same to me. Help me out here...How did you manage to get rid of her?"*
>
> *"Don't you remember her going to the Hospital?"* I asked.
>
> *"Yes, I remember,"* he replied.
>
> *"Well, don't you remember sending that dozen roses to her?"* I innocently asked. *(I had bought and sent her flowers with a nice, loving card from him)*

After that, foul language and ugly, nasty words came out of his mouth that I don't have the vocabulary or patience to print here. Finally, I was gaining the respect I craved and developing a decent reputation.

The Air Conditioner

It was the middle of the week and well after dark. Joe Ikell and I had ended up at the Office together to complete some paperwork. I had parked my new '73 Dodge next to the large outside air conditioning unit, which was in the slot to my left and came out from the curb about four or five feet. This unit was protected at the two outermost corners by two large yellow poles, set in concrete. I guess this thing extended out to the back of my left front wheel and was about one foot away from my vehicle. We did our business in the Office and after awhile, we came out.

I was so proud of my new Patrol Car. Joe didn't have one like me. I'd already checked it out some to determine its capabilities and wanted to show him my new trick, the reverse turn-around. Joe was my best friend and I wanted him to be the first one to see.

This maneuver wasn't taught to us in Patrol School, but I had seen an older, crazy Trooper do it there on our Driving Track. I sure was impressed by how it looked and the way it was done. By now, I'd practiced it some and thought I'd learned. I guess I'd better explain it some…

For a Traffic Officer, after meeting and passing a motorist on a narrow road with no shoulders, this is the quickest way to turn around. It is dangerous, and it takes a lot of nerve and practice, but it can be done. First, bring your car to a stop in the opposing lane *(the left one)*. While looking to the rear, accelerate to a pretty good speed *(you'll know it when you get there)*, then slam on brakes and swerve to the right. Keep applying brakes, throw it in low range, turn the steering wheel to the left and accelerate all at the same time. When you've slid as much as you need to, release the brakes and take off. If you've done it right, you've never left the pavement, you've slid that car around, you're now headed in the opposite direction and you're quickly approaching the motorist you're after. If you've done it wrong, you may be dead or have killed someone else by now. Seldom did I ever use this trick, but in isolated areas, I did practice it from time to time. This was one of those times. I was not an expert! I just thought I was.

I figured I'd just show young Joe my short version of this maneuver. I jumped into my spanking new car.

"*Watch this!*" I proudly stated.

I revved it up, looked to the rear, held my foot on the brake, threw it in reverse, turned the steering wheel to the right and let her go! There were so many other things going on in my head that I forgot about that air conditioner.

BAM!! That's when I remembered…But it was too late! When I got out and looked, the whole headlight assembly was just barely hanging on and my bumper had been pulled out on the left…Not to mention what I did to that air conditioner.

It wasn't long afterwards that I was there by myself, because as my good friend Joe would put it…He got scared and left.

I had to call our First Sergeant at home and he was not a happy camper. I got a lengthy Office visit with him, a good chewing out and three days off without pay. I've learned, but as with many other lessons in life, I've had to learn it the hard way. Although I'm much older now, I've slowed down some and become a little smarter…But not much.

Blowing the Boss

Isn't this exciting? Now get your mind out of the gutter.

It was dark. Late on this night, there was very little traffic out as I headed north on I85. The median was very wide when I observed an unknown vehicle heading south. It looked like it may have been speeding about 10–15mph over the limit, but no big deal. I was bored, so I waited until it got out of sight and then crossed the median. I punched it out to about 130mph and when I was within sight of it's tail lights and approximately ½ mile behind it, I turned on my blue light. Normally, this would have given the vehicle plenty of time to accelerate and escape, but what he didn't know was…I was closing in at a tremendous rate!

Sure enough, at the sight of my blue light, the vehicle accelerated and by the time it had reached 120mph, I was right there…On its bumper. I could see it well now. It was a new, red 302 Boss Mustang, with two male occupants inside.

We just drove hard for awhile. When we'd come up on other vehicles and it had to slow down, I noticed that the Mustang would brake suddenly, then "pedal to the metal" again. *(Engines, especially new ones back then, would not withstand a lot of abrupt slow then go like that, at high rpm's)* For a distance of about ten miles, this happened 8–10 times. Since my First Sergeant was still upset about me tearing up my last car and I didn't need any more time off, I lay back just a little. But I kept my momentum up and let the Boss blaze the trail. We would be in South Carolina in another five miles, so if something didn't happen pretty soon, I would have to break it off.

Suddenly, there was a dense fog and I quickly slowed down. When I came out of it, there was the Boss Mustang on the shoulder. Only now did I realize it had not been fog…But smoke from the engine of that Mustang, as it "blew up." I pulled up behind it.

As the teenage driver sheepishly got out, I could hear the passenger say to him…

> "You dumb ass! I told you to pull over."

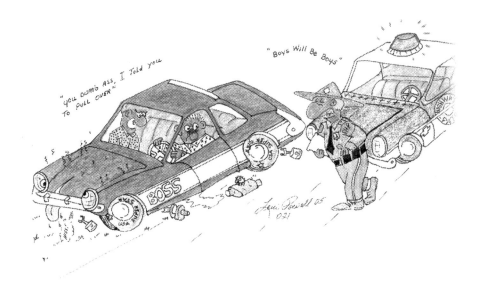

When the court day came, the young driver's father came to court with him.

> *"Trooper Gregory,"* he said, *"I don't care what you do to my son, but I'm taking his license til he's 21 and he's got to buy a new motor. One of the pushrods went right through the side of the engine block."*

The Judge socked it to him, but I did not go out of my way to make him look bad. Would you?

All Rise!

"Oh Yes! Oh Yes! Oh Yes! This honorable Court is now in session. God save...blah, blah, blah. Honorable, so and so, presiding. Be seated, please!"

This is the universal phrase used by The Court Bailiff to "call out" the presiding Judge and officially open Court.

"Baldy" Hinkel was the Bailiff in our Court and he was everyone's friend. He was an institution in Gaston County and had been "The Bailiff" since the beginning of time. Baldy kept strict order in the Courtroom and when outside noise became distracting, he'd step outside and calm it down. The Bailiff's chair was positioned right at the back door of the Courtroom... Where the Judge, Law Enforcement Officers and Court personnel went out or came in.

Baldy had but one weakness, that we all tried to ignore...He'd take frequent naps. On one particular day, it got to be a real problem...He even fell out of his chair! In an effort to help him stay awake, I came up with a plan. Here's how it came together...

I waited until he had dozed off and started snoring again. I then walked by him and right before exiting...I leaned over, poked him and then whispered to him...

"Call him out, Baldy!"..."Call him out!"

I continued, briskly, leaving the Courtroom. I could hear the commotion behind me as I left the area. Baldy stood up, right in the middle of a trial, and boldly made his normal opening declaration.

From that time on, Baldy never dozed again…Not if I was anywhere around.

King of Beers

A Police Officer's work is not always exciting. Matter of fact, there's a lot of down time, and when there's not much going on it can get pretty boring. Sometimes, I had to create my own excitement. That is the case with this incident.

It was really dead. It was shortly before midnight and the middle of the week. There was very little traffic out as I had made my way to the Orthopedic Hospital parking lot on New Hope Road. This parking lot was up on a hill, and from it, I could discretely observe any nearby traffic. I also had a clear shot of the 7Eleven convenience store below.

Eventually, a vehicle pulled into the 7Eleven and two young men got out and went inside. I whipped out my binoculars and took a look. I watched as they went to the beer cooler.

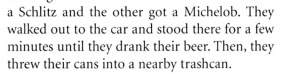

I could see that one of them got a Schlitz and the other got a Michelob. They walked out to the car and stood there for a few minutes until they drank their beer. Then, they threw their cans into a nearby trashcan.

After a few minutes, they left.

They eased out of the parking lot and headed south on New Hope Road. I let them get out of sight and then pulled out behind them. I followed, out of sight, for several miles and then accelerated and came up on them fast. I turned on my blue light and siren when I was right behind them. When they pulled over, I jumped out and walked up to their car.

"What's the matter officer?" with astonishment, the driver asked, "What did we do wrong?"

I sniffed the air a little.

"*You boys have been drinking, haven't you?*" I said.

"*No Sir, we haven't had a drop!*" they both replied.

I stuck my head slightly inside and took a short sniff.

"*Don't lie to me!*" I forcefully said, "*You've had a Schlitz!*"…another short sniff…"*And you've had a Michelob!*"

With utter shock, they looked at each other, then at me.

"*How the hell did you know?*" they both exclaimed.

"*I've been trained to distinguish different beers by their odor,*" I told them, "*but from the smell, I can tell that you've only had one beer apiece. Now get out of here and don't ever lie to Police Officers again!*"

I strongly suspect that they have both passed this story on to their grandchildren and further enhanced the image of The North Carolina State Highway Patrol…For generations, yet to come.

Loud Mufflers

Before I start out on this one, I've got some explaining to do. As you already know, each state has laws that are a little different from the others and these laws are constantly changing. Sometimes there are laws that a normal person wouldn't be aware of, and sometimes the reverse is true…There's no law against actions that an average person might assume is illegal. The latter is true in this case.

One lovely Summer afternoon, I was cruising west on Wilkinson Blvd, a divided highway with three lanes in each direction. I was receiving pleasure from the moment and had my windows rolled down. Traffic was very light. In the distance ahead of me, I could see a motorcycle in the center lane. The rider appeared to be conversing with the occupants of a station wagon that was running parallel and in the right lane. I accelerated and somehow managed to slip up behind them all. *(The motorcycle's exhaust was a little loud, but I didn't get too excited. Damn, they all are, aren't they?)* Low and behold, a passenger in the station wagon passed a beer over to the guy on the motorcycle. *(At this time in North Carolina, there was no law forbidding drinking beer and driving…You just couldn't have been drinking too much)*

I eased up into the left lane and all of our vehicles were now almost side by side. To my surprise, the male on the motorcycle turned up the beer can and began drinking…I couldn't believe my eyes! When he was about halfway through, I hollered over to him…

"Hey Fella! How about saving me a swallow!"

That's when he turned and saw me. I never even turned on my blue light, but he just sheepishly glided that cycle off onto the shoulder and before I could say anything, he spoke up.

"*Officer,*" he said, "*you sure got me that time…I'm guilty!*"

"You sure are!" I replied. "Now the next time I see you, you'd better have that muffler fixed."

With that, I drove off and continued enjoying the afternoon.

You guessed it. Levi's got a good one for us. Come on in here, Levi.

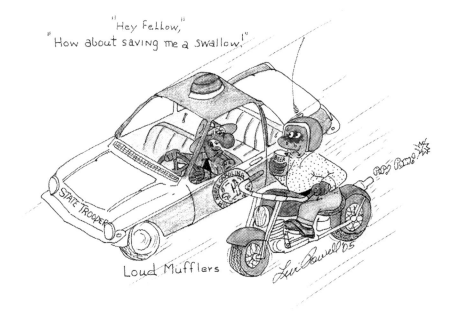

Advantage or Disadvantage?

I'm not sure how I first met him. Maybe it was at Johnny's Wrecker Service, I can't be for sure, but I became friends with a young man who just happened to be paraplegic…He'd lost his legs in Viet Nam. He was an excellent mechanic and had a great disposition. Just being around people like him has always lifted me up…All my little problems just seem to disappear.

Many times, I've seen him roll his wheelchair up to the front of a car, pop the hood, scramble up onto the top of an engine and sit on the carburetor as he worked on the motor. It was no big deal to him, but it sure was an interesting sight, watching him up there. He was more self-sufficient than many other folks and his Muscle Car was set up with all the hand controls needed for him to drive it…And drive it he did! He loved to hot-rod that thing around, and I'd stopped him a couple of times and just given him a warning.

> *"The next time, I'm gonna write you a ticket!"* I finally told him.

It didn't take long and that time came…I gave him a ticket for speeding 64mph in a 45mph zone. This was an offense that would have taken his driver's license and Court appearance was required.

The Court day came and he was sitting in the back of the Courtroom, in his wheelchair, when the District Attorney called out his name. He began wheeling up the aisle towards the front of the room.

> *"Trooper Gregory, what have you got this man charged with?"* the Judge then asked in a professional tone.

> *"64 in a 45mph zone, Your Honor."* I responded.

I could hear a few scattered chuckles erupt around the crowded Courtroom. For a few moments, the Judge just sat there.

> *"That's pretty good for a wheelchair,"* he finally stated. *"Not Guilty!"* he then proclaimed.

(You're right! I said he didn't have any legs and Levi drew him with legs)

He got away that time, but it wasn't long before I nailed him again. I know he ended up losing his driver's license at least once.

I sometimes wonder whatever happened to him and if he's still around. We weren't all that close, but I always considered him a friend of mine. He was one of those rare people who had taken a great difficulty and literally, turned it around.

English Bobbies

I had gone home for supper, taken my gun and holster off, and laid it all up on top of the refrigerator. Sometimes it gets uncomfortable, carrying all that hardware around. After mealtime, I went back to work and it was probably a half an hour later when I stopped a hot rod Chevy for speeding. Out of both the driver's side and the passenger side windows, hung arms as big around as my legs. When I got out of my vehicle to approach them, my arm fell to my side. That's when I became aware of the fact that I had no holster or weapon…I'd left them at home on the refrigerator!

Too late! I was already committed. So I walked up to the car and pretended nothing was wrong. I introduced myself to the driver, told him why I'd stopped him, and asked for his drivers' license and registration. He looked at me.

"*Where's your gun, Officer?*" he boldly asked.

"*The Highway Patrol is trying something new.*" I calmly replied. "*Some of us have received extensive training in defensive tactics and we may, eventually, do away with weapons altogether…You know, kinda like the Bobbies in England.*"

From then on, all you could hear was "*Yes Sir*" and "*No Sir*," and I continued the contact without further ado. Afterwards, I immediately went back home, changed my pants and got my weapon.

A Better Door Lock

Many of us had been summoned to the Warren County area…This was a big deal! An extensive manhunt was underway for five escaped murderers from Pennsylvania, so Troopers from all over our State had been called in. We had been beating the bushes all day and after our shift ended, we headed for the Holiday Inn.

Joe Ikell had been assigned a room by himself and next to mine. Both of our rooms were on the bottom floor. My adrenalin was still high and I needed to let some steam off…I had been planning for this moment for quite some time. I made it a point to arrive first and then back my Patrol Car into the slot right in front of Joe's door. I knew Joe's habits well enough to know that he would head straight for the bathroom and stay there for a pretty good while. Sure enough, Joe jumped out of his car and ran inside. *(Have I mentioned before that Joe has brown eyes?)* I waited for a minute or so, then got out and tied a rope from my back bumper to the doorknob of his room…I then cranked my car and tightened her up.

I wanted to allow him time to do his thing in the bathroom, so I waited about 15 minutes before I called him on his room phone. In the meantime, I made sure there were plenty of other Troopers in my room, to enjoy the show and to provide lots of background noise.

> "Hey Joe, come on over," I invited, "drink a beer and play some poker with us."
>
> "All right," he said. "I'll be right over!"

Well, he didn't show and he didn't show. Before long, he called me back and began stretching his vocabulary to the limits…He was not kind! *(He had discovered that he was locked inside his room with no way out. All he had to do was look out of his solid plate glass window to see that rope tied to my Patrol Car)* I patiently listened to his ranting and raving for a few minutes.

> "Joe," I then calmly said, "*your heart's not right. Now calm down! You just stay in there for awhile and think about your attitude…Then call me back and apologize for all those ugly names you've been calling me, and maybe, just maybe…I'll let you out.*"

He never called. He never apologized. I waited an hour or so and then snuck out and cut him loose. The next day, he got me back.

During the night, he had popped the hood on my Patrol Car and put sardines on the manifold. For awhile, they put out quite an odor. But that was OK. I didn't mind. I still had that grin on my face.

Do your thing, Levi.

Donkey Basketball

The Gaston County Jaycees *(Junior Chamber of Commerce)* had no Law Enforcement members until I came along. I was approached as a candidate for membership. When I mentioned the subject of joining to First Sergeant Mostella, I could tell that he was not keen on the idea at all...So I decided to join.

As time permitted, I became involved in Jaycee activities when I was off-duty. Then came the fund-raiser...Donkey Basketball. This event was planned to take place at the local Armory on an evening when I was scheduled to be working. Try as I might, I could not get my work hours changed so that I could be off and I really wanted to participate. It sounded like fun! So I took a big chance.

I went on my meal hour, while in uniform, and had a Trooper buddy "listen out" for me to cover my butt. When I arrived at the Armory, the game had already begun and the stands were packed. The bleachers had been somewhat retracted, to where the bottom row of seats were about head high, to keep the donkeys from jumping up into the stands. There was but one donkey left. The other Jaycees had apparently already tried him, didn't like him and left him for whoever came in last.

If you've never seen Donkey Basketball, you should know that there's really no game at all. Donkeys have a mind of their own and will not conform to game rules. It's just a spectacle of riders trying to stay on their bucking animals without getting hurt.

In uniform, I got on the back of this little, insignificant-looking animal and immediately...All hell broke loose! Although my feet were almost dragging the floor, together, we put on quite a show! Time after time, he threw me off...I'd get back on and he'd throw me off again. The crowds went wild! They sure were getting their money's worth!

I remember falling off and onto my left elbow once and the pain shooting down my arm...But we continued. After awhile, he became too tired to throw me, so he'd just rub me up against the bleachers or crash me into anything or anyone else he could find.

When it finally ended, my left arm was killing me...So I went to the Hospital to have it checked out. My elbow was broken. The Doctor said I would have to have a solid cast put on from the wrist to the armpit, and I would have to keep that arm elevated and in a sling for six months.

"*No Way!*" I told the Doctor.

I couldn't afford to be out of work that long and I knew that if First Sergeant Mostella found out, he'd kill me!

When all was said and done...I had a half cast put on, keeping my arm rigid, with a slight bend at the elbow. While working, I kept the arm elevated as much as I could without being too obvious. Since we wore long-sleeved shirts all year around, I had my shirts tailored to cover the cast and somehow, managed to keep it hidden from my Supervisors. There was only one side benefit I can think of.

About two months into wearing that cast, I got into a scuffle with a drunk and clobbered him with my cast...I almost knocked him out! He was impressed! He thought I had muscles of steel and even after he sobered up, whenever he'd see me around, with respect in his voice, he referred to me "Super Trooper." I never told him any different.

When the time came to take it off, I was ready…It came off. I'd had enough fun! Donkey Basketball is not a game that I'd recommend for any Police Officers in uniform, anywhere. How I escaped without being detected for six months, I'll never know. As with many other episodes in this book…I guess it just wasn't my time to go.

Deep Cover

I liked driving marked Patrol vehicles. With bold markings and blue light racks on top, they were easily identifiable…Even from a great distance. They demanded more attention and compliance with the traffic laws than an unmarked vehicle. Other motorists would, more than likely, give me the right of way when I was dealing with an emergency. I preferred marked cars, but from time to time, I was temporarily assigned an unmarked one.

During the 70's, the NC State Highway Patrol used a "floating" unmarked car. This vehicle would only remain in one county for about a month. Different Troopers would drive it and then it would be moved on to another county, before local residents became accustomed to it. The average person would never identify this vehicle as a Highway Patrol vehicle. It was a light blue '69 Ford LTD with a black vinyl top and red ring tires. *(That was the current fad)*

On a Saturday morning, I had arrested a drunk driver and was transporting him to the Gaston County Jail. We were eastbound on Franklin Blvd and were both in the front seat…He was handcuffed and seat-belted in. This area was a four lane divided highway and had a traffic light at every intersection. Numerous fast food and ice cream parlors were in the area, and it was a favorite place for the younger crowd…And they were out in force today, everywhere.

While in the left lane, we stopped for a red light. A teenage male, in a hot rod, pulled up beside us in the right lane and revved his engine. Without even looking in his direction, I revved mine too. He took off like a rocket and beat me to the next light. I couldn't believe it…*"Was he trying to drag race with me?"*

As we were stopped at the next light, I leaned over in front of my drunken passenger.

"Hey fella!" I hollered over to him, *"is that the best you can do?"*

I already had one customer and wasn't looking for another. I didn't have my hat on, but surely, he could see my uniform and would back off. We were now in front of a major teenage hangout and all of the kids were looking our way.

This time, he smoked his tires as he took off. In the meantime, my passenger was having a ball.

"*Get him Trooper! Get him!*" he kept laughing and saying.

I let him get ahead of me and then turned on my blue light and siren. As he pulled his car over to the shoulder you could see him slither down in his seat.

He was so embarrassed. I charged him with reckless driving, piled him into my vehicle also, and took him to the "Big House" to post a bond.

My first customer was elated.

"*If you need a witness, I'll be glad to come testify for you,*" he kept saying.

I didn't need one. Matter of fact, I'd didn't have to say much at all in Court. That young man came in and confessed all to the Judge and even went into greater details than I would have.

Drunk at Church

Around lunchtime, on a Sunday, I was cruising in the Springwood section of North Belmont, known as "The Slide." I came up behind a vehicle that had one occupant, the driver. He was driving slowly ahead of me and was weaving all over the road. When I turned on my blue light and siren, the car did not pull over immediately…It continued slowly for about ¼ mile more, before stopping right in front of a large Church. Church services had obviously just ended because the congregation had just begun exiting the Church.

I walked up to the car. The driver never looked at me, but quickly locked his doors and rolled up his windows. He just sat there, with a look of drunken smugness, staring straight ahead. From my commands for him to open the door, all I could get from him were negative shakes of his head. Then…

"You're not gonna take me to jail," he said.

I felt like an idiot as I stood there for a few minutes, trying to reason with this guy. No luck! The most he would do is to roll his window down about an inch. The well-dressed worshipers were casting inquisitive eyes in our direction and they had to walk around us to get to their cars.

It just so happens that I had been well-trained in dealing with situations such as this…But I never dreamed I'd have to use this knowledge, especially in front of a Church. Once again, I tried to talk him into unlocking the door. He just slid down in his seat some, put his hands behind his head and relaxed as he smiled. He thought he had me. That's when lighting struck!

With my blackjack, I broke out the window. *(Don't worry, it was safety glass)* Without ever opening the door, I reached through the window with both arms, twisted his head around and pulled it out of the window…His body eagerly came out behind. He was cuffed and stuffed in no time.

I hadn't been paying attention to the Church members but as I left, I could see them as they stood there in amazement. Unlike me, they had not been prepared for an event such as this at their Church, on a Sunday. I'll bet they had a huge turnout for the next worship service…And I've often wondered what that sermon was about.

Let's take a look at Levi's interpretation.

Bubba & the Drag Race

Bubba Thomas. We called him Bubba because that's what he called everybody else. As far as he was concerned, all males were named Bubba. Bubba Thomas was a tall and lanky Trooper who loved his work and was good at it. He was easy-going, rarely got upset and he always had something good to say about everybody. Bubba was one of those Troopers who all the others looked up to…He was tall, too. It seemed like he'd been on the Highway Patrol forever. He knew it. He loved it. He was an institution.

I'd just finished supper and was heading south on Robinson Road. In this area, the road was fairly straight with a few dips and mild curves. Dusk had just turned to darkness. As I topped a slight hill, I noticed two sets of tail lights on the next ridge, but didn't think too much about it. After all, traffic was always light on this road and visibility was good…But I picked up my pace. As I arrived at the location they had been sitting, I was in for a surprise. The roadway was filled with smoke and there were two parallel sets of wide rubber marks. I could smell the rubber and see the two cars about ¼ mile ahead of me. I notified the Dispatcher and other Patrol Cars.

It wasn't until later that I learned this, but now is as good a time as any to throw it in. These cars had been built and geared for a short drag strip. They were mighty quick on the take-off, but not much on top end.

As I quickly approached, they had apparently slowed down to compare notes. Neither of the cars had hoods on them and their motors were humongous…No registration plates whatsoever. I turned on my blue light and siren. One of the vehicles immediately gave up and pulled over onto the shoulder…The other took off. That's the one I wanted! I didn't even slow down for the first one, but set my sights on the one trying to get away. The road was becoming much more curvy now and I could catch up to him in the curves, but he'd walk off and leave me on the straight-aways.

Bubba let me know he was trying to get into position at the end of Robinson Road, where it "T" intersected with New Hope Road.

For a couple of miles, we played the game of him leaving me, then my catching up to him, until we got close to the intersection. I could see Bubba sitting on New Hope Road and off on the right shoulder, with his blue light on, as we approached. The car slowed some because he was going to have to make a turn one way or the other. As he slowed, I put my front bumper on his rear one and shoved him into the intersection. He was now trying to turn right and I was shoving straight. He lost it. I backed off.

Bubba was a one-man welcoming committee. That's all I needed.

There was no other traffic out and I watched as Bubba chased that car around in a circle for a few laps. Suddenly, it slowed and the driver's door flew open. The driver jumped and ran. Both Bubba and myself bailed out of our cars and ran after him. We left the one passenger in the car…Just sitting there. The fellow had a pretty good jump on us and we couldn't really see him, but we could hear him thrashing around in the bushes as we ran after him. Before long, I came up to a barbed wire fence with a lot of briars behind it. I could see the movement back in there and knew that's where he'd gone. I wasn't going to chase him through that mess and Bubba wasn't excited about the idea either. We caught our breath and walked back to our cars.

When we got back, our cars were still sitting in the roadway with their blue lights going *(We'd taken our keys. We weren't that stupid!)*. As we approached the car we'd been chasing, we noticed a large man standing beside it.

> "*Officers,*" he said, "*I live in that house over there and heard all this commotion going on out here, so I came out to take a look. While you were out running after your suspect, I walked over here and told this teenage passenger to stay right where he was. He did!*"

We thanked him. After talking to the young man for a little bit, he told us everything…So we called for a wrecker and let him go. An hour or so later I went to the address of the young fellow who'd been driving the car. His father answered the door and said he wasn't there. I let him know why I'd dropped by and told him I'd be back the next day.

When I came back at the appointed time, the young fellow and his father were waiting. That boy had scratches and cuts all over him from the thicket he'd gone through. With his father beside him, he honestly laid it all out. He ended up paying dearly for his mistakes, but I'm convinced he learned more from this event than most kids do from college.

Everybody screws up, but that's not important. It's what we do after we screw up that carries more weight.

Flying Shit

You just couldn't wait…Could you?

I know, I know! Surely, you're wondering…*"Can't he clean it up a little?"* and *"Does he have to be so graphic?"* Well, I did give this topic a lot of thought, and contrary to my warning in the introduction, I did put a lot of effort into cleaning up the language of this subject. I tried many other descriptive words and phrases but nothing else captured the true meaning of this episode…Nothing else seemed to work. As disgusting as it sounds, it is an element of life. It is what it is, and this story is truly about shit. Besides, you've already bought the book. Onward.

I was in the process of investigating a traffic accident involving property damage and personal injury. The driver had been transported to the Hospital and the only other occupant, a public drunk, was still sitting in the wrecked vehicle. Back then, just being drunk in public was against the law. He had already been checked for injuries, there were none, and he was extremely drunk…Almost ready to pass out. I had let him remain in the vehicle because he had shit all over himself and I didn't want to put him in my Patrol Car. It was a stinking, runny, diarrhea that ran down both of his pants legs. I just let him sit there.

Without being called, another Trooper arrived at the scene to offer his assistance…The Rookie, John Penney. John had just finished his six weeks of ride-along training and Charlie had trained him. John was always around to offer his help. He was eager to learn and he was sharp. When John arrived, I was busy directing traffic and taking measurements. His timing could not have been better! I was just winding up at the scene when John asked if he could help me out.

> "Sure," I said, *"you can wait for the wrecker, then arrest that drunk sitting over there and take him to Jail for me. I need to run to the Hospital to check on the driver. When I get through there, I'll meet you at the Jail."*

The deal was made. I stuck around long enough to watch Rookie John get the drunk out of the car and stand him up. I'd had enough…I had passed one off on him! I put my sunglasses on and laughed all the way to the Hospital.

I hurriedly did my business at the Hospital and arrived at the Jail some forty-five minutes later, but John and his drunk had not yet arrived. Thank goodness, I certainly didn't want to miss this show. Charlie had obviously heard us on the radio, because just about the time John pulled in, here came Charlie in his Patrol Car. Charlie still felt like John's Mother because he'd trained him, and he wanted to make sure John did everything right.

From the doorway, I watched them as they got out of their Patrol Cars. I thought to myself…*"Hey! Where's the drunk?"*

John had been very creative…I'd never seen this done before! He walked around to his trunk, opened it and then together, he and Charlie got the drunk out of it. It was a pitiful sight. That poor ole drunk was wrapped in a raincoat, stinking and shitty.

> *"Did you search this fellow?"* I could hear Charlie ask John.

> *"Well no, not exactly,"* John replied.

Charlie stepped in, spread-eagled the stinking fellow and began to frisk him for weapons. After spreading his legs, Charlie simultaneously ran both his hands into the drunk's trouser pockets. *(These pockets had large holes in them)* Upon withdrawing them, he didn't have weapons in them…He had two handfuls of, you guessed it…Shit!

Levi! Help me out here!

John and I just stood there, cracking up with laughter. Charlie wasn't laughing…He was mad! He went off on the two of us.

Afterthought…

At this point, I should probably let it rest, but I won't…I just can't! There's an unhappy addition that needs to be addressed, so let's get on with it.

John was turning into a really decent Trooper. Who knows, he may've even ended up like me…But he didn't last more than about eight years. Maybe John just had bad luck.

One day John was out playing golf and he was behind a comrade who was teeing off. As his friend took an unexpectedly long swing, John was struck in the eye by the club. Not only did he lose his eye, but he lost his career as a State Trooper. In an instant, all of his hopes and dreams for the future were suddenly shattered!

Way too soon, he was put out to pasture. He had bills to pay! He had a family to support! He had to find another way! If anyone has ever had reason for deep depression, he did. I've always admired John, because in spite of all this, he's loved our organization even though, in my opinion, we let him down. Even now, after all these years, he still shows up at many Highway Patrol functions with a smile on his face.

For the Road Troopers, there was no haven for the sick or disabled. No desk job! No nothing! Once sick leave and vacation time were exhausted, that was it. John was only one of the many friend's I've had who were forced into early retirement because of disabilities that were sustained both off-duty and on. Maybe some of this has changed now for the better…I certainly hope so.

If you bought the line that I originally gave you for the use of such a vulgar topic word, then I've made it "fly"…Thusly, flying shit.

To my way of thinking, even the afterthought relates to the title of this little story.

Gully Washer

For about a week now, we'd been having steady rain. It was a very cool November night and the rain had slowed some...Just a light drizzle was falling now. As I headed north on Wilkinson Blvd, my attention was drawn to the traffic ahead of me...Something out of the ordinary was happening up there. The light had just turned green for the traffic in front of me and the vehicle in the right lane began fish-tailing as it accelerated on the wet road. As it pulled away from the intersection and left the other traffic, I caught up to it...But still, its pace continued to increase to well above the posted speed limit. This was a very slick road!

When I turned on my blue light and siren, the driver made no attempt whatsoever to back off, instead, he accelerated his Malibu even more. By now, I was right on his bumper and he couldn't leave me...So he swerved into the left lane, and without giving any signal, he made a quick U turn at a median crossover and then headed south. Again he accelerated, but I didn't go anywhere...I was still there.

Suddenly, he pulled over onto the right emergency lane and stopped. We were now at the bottom of the hill and directly across from the Holy Angels Convent. His driver's door flew open and he bailed out. As he ran towards the front of his car and vanished into the darkness, I was a few steps behind him...And for a brief moment, I paused on the shoulder where he had disappeared. It was dark. It was foggy. It was still.

As I began running into the darkness behind him, I suddenly realized...My feet were not even touching the ground! I was falling, and where was he?...Beneath me somewhere?

Splash!...That was the next sensation I felt. I had fallen about fifteen feet and it was wet, it was cold, and when I came up, it was about waist deep. I had landed in a culvert that rapidly moved water underneath the highway, but still...Where was he?

As I thrashed around trying to regain my balance in the current, it was so dark that I couldn't see him, but I knew he was there...I could hear him just beyond me as he also thrashed around. Once in awhile I could grab him, but he'd then jerk away. Out came my blackjack. I swung that thing around a few times and let him listen to it, as it whistled in the air.

> *"Boy!"* I called out to him, *"you'd better give up now, before I knock the hell out of you!"*

He didn't respond right away so I kept on swinging. My eyes were adjusting more to the darkness now and directly, that blackjack found some meat.

> *"Thump!"* it went.

> *"OK! I give up,"* he frantically hollered.

Without any further trouble, I got the handcuffs on him and told him what he was under arrest for. He was pretty well lit, but even with his handcuffs on, I made him pull me up and out of that ditch.

> *"You got me down here,"* I told him, *"now you can get me back out of here."*

We were both soaked. To help warm him up some, I got my raincoat out and wrapped it around him. Then, after getting him into my Patrol Car, and even after the heat came back on again…I shivered most of the way to the Jail.

Although we had both given each other a hard time, he was impressed by that small gesture of mine…And once again, before we reached Jail, I had accomplished much more than just arresting a drunk.

Down in that gully, I had found a new friend.

The Cattle Prod

We moved to Belmont and into a mill house in the Imperial Mill Village. John was a Belmont Police Officer who lived not far from us and he'd come by our house once in awhile with some of the neatest gadgets. He'd keep them for awhile, until he got tired of them, and then he'd trade with me. He and I didn't use money much...We just traded. Some of these items were designed to be used by Police Officers but were not condoned for use by the Highway Patrol. Matter of fact, I could've been fired if I'd been caught with them while I was working, but I thought I could get away with it...So I went ahead and took that risk anyway.

One gizmo that I ended up with was a black plastic club about a foot long. This insignificant looking little club was filled with flashlight batteries, had two small metal electrodes on the tip end, and had a small button on the handle to activate it. When held near an object and turned on, it would shoot out blue flames about four inches long. For all intents and purposes, it was a miniature cattle prod...The fun was over if this thing zapped you! I stuck it in the trunk of my Patrol Car and waited for a chance to try it out...And time passed.

One night I arrested a drunk driver near the Diane 29 Drive-In Theater, on US 29 South and near Edgewood Road. He was extremely intoxicated and was too drunk to give me much trouble. *(Our "Policies and Procedures" dictated that when we arresting someone...We were to handcuff them with their hands behind their back)* He begged me not to, and he was so fat that to put the handcuffs on him, as I was supposed to do, might have pulled his arms out of their sockets. So I decided against the handcuffs. I escorted him to the passenger side of my Patrol Car and opened the door for him, but...He wouldn't get in! He placed his hands up on the roof of my car and just froze there. I couldn't believe it...As nice as I'd

been to him and he was now balking. This was the opportunity I'd been waiting for. It was now time for me to try my new toy.

Wanting a witness, I called my ole buddy, Joe Ikell, to come and view the proceedings. He was close by and in no time at all, he got there. After he arrived, Joe offered to help me stuff the fellow into my car, but I declined.

"No, I've got a better idea," I said.

I popped my trunk, whipped out my new plaything and walked around behind the defendant.

I pushed the button and stuck that thing to his rear end...That got his attention!

He jumped into my Patrol Car and then in one continuous motion, he scrambled all the way through the car and out of my driver's side door he came.

We had to start all over again and put him in the conventional way.

This time, he didn't need any persuading. This time, on his own...He got in.

Scratch My Back

Although this happened to me many, many years ago, it's been coming back to me now as if it was just yesterday. This story and the next one are two of the most important…These are a couple that I won't forget! The next one takes up where this one leaves off.

I'd been working the southeastern section of the county for a year or so by now. One day, as I was cruising through his little town, a young local Police Officer flagged me down…He was very frustrated and mad! He told me that a local fellow *(I'll just call him John Doe)*, who owned a small catering company, was driving around everyday with his driver's license revoked…And getting away with it!

Every morning about 5:30am, John Doe would take off in his "Lunch Wagon" catering truck. *(You've seen them…Those small trucks with square stainless steel box beds and flip-down sides on them)* He'd ride around to different construction sites and businesses, stop, flip down the sides of his truck, and sell the folks snacks and such. John Doe had been driving around like this for six months or better. On several occasions, this local Police Officer had stopped him, but John Doe didn't care. Apparently, he thought he had diplomatic immunity, just because he was also a big supporter and campaign worker for a prominent long-term State Senator *(I'll just call him Senator Joe Blow)*, who also lived in the area.

Once, the local Officer had tried to arrest him and take him to Jail, but when this had happened, John Doe had said…

> "You'd better check with your Supervisor! You're about to make a big mistake. You'd better leave me alone…I'm a strong supporter of Senator Joe Blow!"

Sure enough, after checking with his Chief, the young Officer was told…"*Lay off!*" At the end of his wits, he had come to me.

> "*Don't worry further about it,*" without reservations, I said, "*I'll take care of Mister John Doe!*"

Although I wasn't scheduled to work until 9am the next morning, I came out early...Then found and arrested that political workhorse, Mister Doe. Just as I'd been told, he was out in his Lunch Wagon, driving away. He tried to pull the same crap with me.

> *"Check with your Supervisor!"..."Big Mistake!"..."blah, blah, blah."*

Without hesitation, I took him straight to Jail.

I knew he'd just post a bond and be released soon, but to my amazement, before I'd even finished my paperwork...He was gone! *(Apparently, the results of a phone call to Senator Joe Blow)* The Court date was set for about a month off.

When I got home that evening, I'd just had supper and settled down some when the telephone rang. *(Troopers' home phone numbers were most always published in the local white pages...We weren't hard to find)* It all started cordially with a caller who identified himself as Senator Joe Blow.

> *"Good Evening,"* politely, he said, *"I'm Senator Joe Blow and I understand that you've arrested a good friend of mine, John Doe. Is there anyway you can help him out?"* he then asked. *"I'd certainly appreciate it and I'd consider it a personal favor to me."*
>
> *"I understand your concern,"* I calmly replied, *"but John's been driving with his license revoked and that's against the law. It's pretty much cut and dried. I'm not gonna overlook that!...And besides, I've already made the charge against him. It's for a Judge to decide now. I'm sorry, but there's nothing else I can say or do!"*
>
> *"Trooper! Don't you know who I am?"* he was much angrier now, *"I'm Senator Joe Blow!"*
>
> *"I don't know who you are!"* I stormed back. *"You could be anybody! I can't see your face and besides, it's out of my hands now. It's for a Judge to decide!"*
>
> *"Trooper, all you've gotta do is go talk to a Solicitor* (They're called District Attorneys now) *and have it dismissed. As I said before, I'd consider it a personal favor. Surely, you want to move up in rank. That's how the system works! You scratch my back and I'll scratch yours."*

> "I don't know who you are," I said. "For all I know, you could be Santa Claus, calling me on the phone like this, and besides…I don't give a damn who you are! The charge stays!"
>
> "Trooper! You're making a big mistake…"

Those were the last words I heard from him then, because I hung up the phone.

A few days went by. He called again! My response was about the same. As the Court day drew closer, the calls became more frequent and more threatening. I remained steadfast!…The Judge would decide.

The Court day came. I was preparing to go to work and head for the Courthouse when once again, the telephone rang!

> "Trooper Gregory!" an unfamiliar voice erupted from the other end…(I'll just call him Big Ben) "My name is Big Ben and no doubt, you've heard of me. I'm the Commissioner of Motor Vehicles and right beside the Governor…My picture is on your Highway Patrol Office wall."

The Commissioner wasn't an elected official. He was an appointed administrator who oversaw us all. He was a very powerful figure who could create and control career changes with the simple drop of a hat. He continued…

> "Today, I want you to back off on your case with John Doe! I'd really appreciate it and I can really help you get ahead in your career. I can make you or break you," he said.

I would not be swayed. I remembered my training. I would not be intimidated by political pressure. I would professionally perform my job. Neither John Doe, Joe Blow nor even Big Ben, was above the law! I let him know that it was now for the Judge to decide, and if someone like him could take my job, he could have it…It wouldn't be worth having anyway! I said my piece and then politely hung up the phone.

From here on out, everything became rather fuzzy. It all became…

Smoke & Mirrors

At 8am, I checked on-duty and then headed straight for the Courthouse. It was Thursday, remember?...I had morning Court that day.

The Courtroom was packed and yes, the Judge on the bench was a friend of mine, the Preacher's kid...Remember him? The docket was read by the Solicitor. When John Doe's name was called, his attorney spoke out...

"Not Guilty, Your Honor!"

After this, normally the guilty pleas were taken first. But today, we would not have normal court proceedings. Today we would have smoke & mirrors...Today we'd have a Magic Show! There would be no trial for my defendant, Mr. John Doe. Before the Solicitor could call out the first case, the Judge called one out himself...

"In the case of State vs. John Doe...I hereby declare it dismissed!"

And just that quick, the show was over! In the blink of an eye, the magic had been preformed.

It didn't take a genius...Anyone in the Courtroom could look at me and tell, I was really, really, pissed! Then, immediately thereafter, the Judge called for a fifteen-minute recess. He stepped down from the bench and walked straight over to me.

"Trooper Gregory," he said, *"I want to see you in my Chambers!"*

Everyone else in the Courtroom just sat there with astonished looks on their faces. They must have been wondering..."*What has just happened here? Court hasn't even started good and here we are taking a recess!*" He led me out into the hallway. We never made it to his Chambers.

"Bryan, I had to do it!" as soon as we were alone, he said. *"I just got a call from the Commissioner of Motor Vehicles, and had I not dismissed your case, you would've lost your job! I knew you wouldn't back down, so I did it for you. I think the world of you and I want to keep you around!"*

Somehow, that did not make me feel much better. Did he really think that much of me, or was he just buttering his own bread? Anyway, that ended that!

I don't know whatever happened to Mister John Doe, and don't honestly care. Believe me, I looked for him, but I never saw him on the road again…I'm either losing my mind or he was laying low. Not too much longer after this, I transferred to Mecklenburg County, but it wouldn't surprise me in the slightest to know…That he is now representing us in some government capacity, somewhere.

That good Senator, Joe Blow, maintained his position as Senator for many, many, years because…Well, we kept voting him back in! He was a professional politician! He knew the value of "scratching backs." He took care of his supporters…He took care of those who took care of him.

And the Commissioner of Motor Vehicles, Big Ben? Well, he kept his position in Government until the other Party came in and then his head came off, another Appointee took over, and here we go…It's started all over again!

These are the types who make it to the top! These are the folks we choose to represent us…And it's not all their fault. We don't check them out! We don't screen them! We don't test them! We don't have time, so we often end up with the weak ones! We give them the power! We don't keep an eye on them! We let them make up their own rules, make up their own salaries, give themselves far better pensions than they'll get you and I and then provide themselves livelong healthcare. They line their own pockets, take care of their own and if we start complaining, they'll throw us a bone. It's the special interests that are hidden. It's what's under the table that we don't see. The fat ones keep getting fatter and there's less for you and me. We ought to be stripping them and searching them when they go in and then doing the same when they come back out again…I wonder what they'd have in their pockets that's ours. They're our servants, not our lords! They're our representatives! We don't demand better! We put them there and then forget about them! It's our fault…Yours and Mine!

Want to see more smoke & mirrors?…Just turn on your TV and watch them talking. And when you get a puzzled feeling *(like those spectators in the Courtroom, in this story)*…You've probably just witnessed another Magic Show.

By now, you're thinking I hate politicians, but to be honest, that's not really the case. I believe that most start out well-intentioned, but when they get there...The Power's already in place.

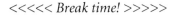

<<<<< Break time! >>>>>

Now don't get me wrong. There's no doubt in my mind. The Highway Patrol would've backed me...But I'd still be out of a job. Those without uniforms had control of us! That's just the way that it was. I don't know how it is now, but I would put my money on it...To some degree, it will remain the same.

Did I just make the mistake of a lifetime? Did I just throw away my ticket to success? Did I just miss the boat? These were the questions I've asked myself, but they weren't so important now...They were now in the past. I had more important issues to deal with that were still on the table! Now, I had to decide...Would I succumb to political pressure? Was I ready to become beholding to others?...or...Would I just stay down here and make do?

They surely didn't mean too, but these politicians had done me a great favor...They'd opened my eyes! They'd helped me decide which career path I'd pursue on the North Carolina State Highway Patrol. Now, my choice was much easier. Now, I could sleep better at night. My happiness would not be controlled by prestige, money or pressure. These games weren't for me! I just wasn't raised that way. Let others play.

I couldn't help but wonder...How many promotions had been made or rejected because of influences like little ole John Doe? I'd rather stay at the bottom level with some sense of pride, than to take that which wasn't deserved and step on the backs of those below.

I'm sorry. I didn't mean to be so heavy-duty. It just worked out that way...The more I wrote about these folks, the more I had to say.

Better than Most

We've all met people who look down their noses at us. They just have that air about them…The way they talk, the way they walk and the way that they carry themselves. They leave the impression that they're just a cut above the rest of us, and we can't stand to be around them much. They seem to believe that they're above all the rules…Rules are for us, not them! Sometimes, we can look through that shell and see their insecurity and loneliness. But Police Officers don't deal with the cause much, we deal with the symptoms.

In the early afternoon, when Joe called me on the radio, we were working at opposite ends of the county. He was calling to tell me that he had just given a ticket to a lady, in a black Cadillac from Georgia, for speeding. She had angrily wadded it up, thrown it out her window and then took off again, speeding 80mph in a 55mph zone and this time…She wouldn't stop for his blue light. She was mad! Joe was excited and confused.

We switched our radios over to a more private channel to continue our talk. Joe was still a Rookie Trooper and was not sure what to do…But I did.

> *"We'll stop her again and arrest her for littering and failing to stop for an Officer,"* I said. *"We can't let her get away with that!"*

Since the Cadillac was heading north on I85 and towards me, I stopped all traffic right before the McAdenville exit. Quite soon, Joe called me back to let me know she'd had to stop for the traffic jam I'd caused. He'd caught her! I released the traffic and proceeded vigorously in his direction. By the time I got there, he'd already cuffed and stuffed her. Fancy jewelry was hanging everywhere and she was kicking, screaming and raising hell! We called a wrecker for the Cadillac and took her straight to Jail.

The Gaston County Jail was in the Courthouse building and while Joe was making her lodging arrangements, I went upstairs to see if the Judge was still there. He was, just barely. The Judge was winding it down when I got his ear.

"Bring her on up here," he said, *"I'll take care of this matter right now!"*

After patiently listening to Joe's side of the story and then her ranting and raving, the Judge made an observation of his own…

"Lady, you've just made a complete ass of yourself," he sternly proclaimed. *"That'll be $500 and costs!"* Then he said, *"after spending the night in our Jail, you can leave tomorrow morning."*

Most likely, one single night did not make her a new person. But there's no doubt about it…For this incident, she received an overdue attitude adjustment.

Mud

It was a foggy and the rain was gently falling when I got back into my Patrol Car after supper. At once, I received a call from my Dispatcher, sending me to an accident on Wilkinson Blvd just west of NC 273…A pedestrian had been struck! In that area, Wilkinson Blvd was a multi-lane highway, divided by a very low concrete median. The accident had occurred at a long median crossover on a gently sloping hillcrest. I came in from the opposite direction that the vehicle involved had been traveling.

About ¼ mile ahead, I could see the Rescue Squad vehicle facing me and stopped at the crest of the ridge. Its emergency lights were activated and I could see a small gathering standing in front of its headlights. To my left, I noticed a vehicle pulled over onto the shoulder, with no occupants. *(That was the vehicle which had struck the pedestrian)* I jumped the median in my Patrol Car, turned around and then stopped behind that vehicle. I left my blue light on and then started walking towards the probable origin of the accident.

As I walked, I swept my flashlight beam around to look for possible evidence and there was mud on the wet blacktop. As I drew closer, I could see a covered body lying in the passing lane. The roadway became more muddy now, but I walked right on through it. *(I figured construction traffic entering the highway had caused it)* The mud was caking up on the soles of my shoes and I stopped briefly to wipe them off on the concrete median. When I reached the body and the small group, a middle-aged man came forward and identified himself as being involved in the accident.

> *"Officer,"* he said, *"several other vehicles and myself had stopped at the traffic light about ¼ mile back. When we took off, I was in the left lane. Because of the heavy fog, we were all going a good deal less than the posted speed limit. Upon reaching this hillcrest, I saw an object in the roadway, but I couldn't go left, because of the median and I couldn't go right, because of the other cars…So I hit it! It wasn't until I came back to see what it was, that I realized that what I had hit was a person."*

I pulled the blanket back and looked at the body. It was a middle-aged man and most of his head was missing. There were no personal belongings or wallet whatsoever on the body…No watch, no rings, no nothing! I investigated this accident for more than two weeks. Finally, my First Sergeant ordered me to stop and turn it over to the SBI *(State Bureau of Investigation)*. Based on the evidence I found and the persons I interviewed, this was the most likely scenario.

John Doe was an alcoholic and he couldn't see much without glasses. His driver's license was revoked and he just walked or hitched rides to wherever he wanted to go. He didn't drive and he lived alone. He frequented a bar about three miles away in Mecklenburg County. He'd just won a bet on a baseball game and had a large amount of cash in his possession on the night of this incident…And, he'd been flashing it around at the bar. The bartender told me that a couple of shady characters had been helping him get drunk, had given him a ride and had probably rolled him.

Near the scene of the accident, there was an unused logging path that went back into the woods from the median crossover. About four hundred feet down this path…I found his wallet, ID card and his personal belongings strewn all around. His glasses were also broken and lying there.

After being robbed and probably beaten, John stumbled towards the highway without his glasses. He made it halfway across the highway but just couldn't go any further. He stopped and either sat, or squatted, in an area that he probably thought to be safe…The median. In fact, he was in a median crossover area and because of the lane structure there, he was really in the passing lane for eastbound traffic.

When the car's bumper hit him, his head exploded. I had not been walking in mud at all…It was John's gray matter.

I threw this one in just to balance it out. Fun and games was not all it was about.

The Silo

Back when I was there, South New Hope Road was a long, straight and lonely road. The blacktop surface was just like new. The lanes were wide. The shoulders were quite ample and gently sloping too. Right out in the middle of nowhere, stood an old tall concrete silo. In years gone by, it must've been used for grain storage by a local Farmer, but now it just silently stood there surrounded by woods. Off the road and to the left it stood, as one headed south on New Hope Road. It was the local landmark. Even when our Dispatchers would give us a call for anything nearby, they'd simply say... *"Near the Silo."*

I had just been issued a new Patrol Car and was eager to check it out. So just after dark, I headed for my favorite proving grounds...That isolated area, near the Silo.

There weren't any houses anywhere around, probably within a mile or so, and I was having a really big time...Just me out there, tearing up the road. I'd been bootlegging it around from the left shoulder and then I'd tried a reverse turnaround or so. I was really eating up the rubber, but I wasn't worried...How could anyone know? I was right in the middle of high-speed turnaround when my Dispatcher called out on the radio...

> *"Gaston County car working New Hope Road! Speeding and Reckless Driving reported!...Near the Silo!"*

Nervously, I looked around. Not another soul was in sight! I sure didn't want to answer that radio. Just for the heck of it, I did one more turnaround and then I didn't wait for the grass to grow…I got out of there! Again the Dispatcher called. And this time there was no ignoring him. Without beating around the bush, he called me specifically…

> *"H-140!* (my call number) *10–20?* (What's your location?) *Check for speeding and reckless driving, at or near the Silo!"*

I don't recall all the details, but I can tell you this. I didn't give my true location and as far as my Dispatcher was concerned, I was unable to locate any violations down there.

But for a stroke of luck, I would never have known the whole story…Of that night, long ago, near the Silo. More than fifteen years later, I stopped by to see an old friend of mine. When I'd last seen him, he was a Gaston County Rural Police Detective. Now, he'd taken on the position of Chief of Police in a small Gaston County town. As we sat there reminiscing, somehow I began talking about that night I was trying out my new Patrol Car, near the Silo. As I spoke, his eyes got bigger and then he told me…He was also there, at the same place, at the same time. Matter of fact, he'd called in the complaint!

Back then, he was single. He'd hooked up with his girlfriend *(they were married now)* and they were back in the woods, in his Patrol Car, near the Silo. All the squealing tires and burning rubber distracted them, and not being willing to stop whatever he was doing to check it out, he'd simply called the Highway Patrol Dispatcher to have it stopped. It worked!

"Hurry up, Levi…We're waiting!"

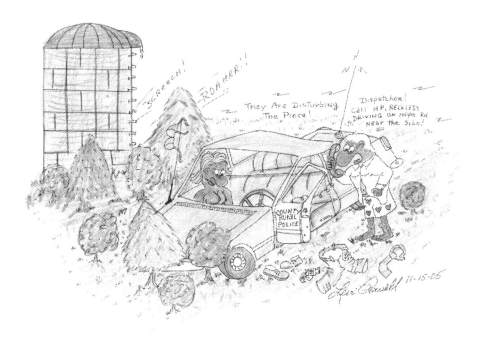

It took us years to get together. It took us years before we'd know. But there was one who saw it all. Yep! You got it!…That lonely ole concrete Silo.

Unanswered Prayer

It was such a beautiful day and I was in no hurry. It was a sunny, lazy, Sunday afternoon. With windows rolled down and arm out the window, I made my way up the narrow, winding road with no shoulders known as Crowder's Mountain Road. Today, I felt of it as my own private road. It didn't normally have a lot of traffic and right now, I just wanted to take it easy and enjoy the scenery. I wasn't looking for any trouble.

Before long, I rounded a curve and came up behind a traffic jam. Five or six cars were barely idling along. The roadway was divided by double yellow lines and the lead car was obstructing traffic. There was no place for the vehicles behind it to safely pass, because the road was full of blind curves. I lagged behind for a few minutes, but the situation didn't improve. Finally, I made my move to the position directly behind the root of the problem. It was a well-dressed man driving slowly and erratically, as he enjoyed and pointed out the beauties of nature to his family. I gave him a little slack, because I understood. We passed several places that he could've pulled off onto the shoulder, but he didn't. Wasn't he aware of the train behind him?…And didn't he see that State Trooper on his bumper? Finally, I'd had enough.

I turned on my blue light and he pulled over. As I casually strolled up to his car, he got out. As I stuck my hand out and introduced myself, we agreed on what a fine day it was and then I asked him to accompany me to the rear of his car…I didn't want to embarrass him in front of his family.

> "Sir," I started out, *"I stopped you because you've been impeding the flow of traffic. There were half a dozen vehicles behind you that couldn't pass."* I went on with, *"From now on, when you want to look at the scenery…How about just pulling off onto the shoulder when you want to look around."*

At this point, my intention was to just verbally warn him and let him go.

> "I have you know I'm a Man of God!" he boldly proclaimed, *"I'm The Reverend so and so, of such and such, good-sized Church, and I have you know…I don't break any laws!"*

Well, I wasn't ready for that! I had found myself blessed and in the presence of, someone better than most everyone else.

> "Well Sir," I replied, "None of us are perfect! I know I'm not! And this time, you were wrong by holding up the traffic behind you! I'm just gonna give you a warning ticket to remind you not to do it again."

I'd changed my mind now! A verbal warning just wasn't going to get it.

> "I can't accept that," he angrily stated. "I've never had any kind of ticket in my life! I've never done anything wrong! You are absolutely mistaken!"

He continued working himself up into a sweat and before long, he even began cursing! His religion was wearing mighty thin and I'd had enough…That did it!

> "Sir, I'm charging you with Impeding the Flow of Traffic." I then calmly said, "I'll be right back with the paperwork."

I walked back to my car and wrote out the ticket… The Big One. As I was writing, it astonished me to see that he had now dropped down on his knees in front of my Patrol Car, God and everybody, and begun praying. When I returned, I could hear him as he audibly prayed for me *(that I would realize my mistake and correct it before it was too late…blah, blah, blah)*. As I explained the ticket to him *(costs, optional court date, etc)*, he would not be distracted from his prayers…But I ignored his charade. I stuck the ticket into his shirt pocket, got back into my Patrol Car and backed up so I wouldn't run over him when I left. Then I drove off.

His performance continued until I was almost out of sight, and I watched in my rearview mirror as he finally jumped up and angrily stomped back to his car. Yes, for anyone watching, he had put on quite a show.

His Church members, I didn't care about, because they had an option…They could get up and leave. I just felt sorry for his family and the daily hell they must have had to go through…Simply living with this man.

And I wondered how God felt.

My God

I can't say that I know where my God is,
                        I'm not even sure of his sex or his name,
        But I believe he looks over my shoulder,
                        And loves me, just the same.

I know I don't go to Church as you'd like me,
        But if you do, you're on the right track,
                I'd just rather use what I've got to help others,
            Than to feel I must pay a kick-back.

                    Yes, I'll take a drink when I feel like it,
                  Might even, find a woman or two,
But I don't think I'll be banned from Heaven,
Just because I don't believe as you do.

                    There's no need for me to kneel at your altar,
            In an effort for me to impress you,
        My God already knows that I love him,
        And if you live as you should, yours will too.

Friend of an Angel

Rather than tease you with the title, this time, I'm going to come right out with it. The main character in this story was the Boss of the Angels in our area…The Hell's Angels. He was Carroll Armstrong. Fate brought us together. It was meant to be.

It all started with an old abandoned shack on Union Road near the South Carolina state line. I worked that area and noticed that on several occasions, a large group of Angels would appear…They were fixing up the place! They were accomplishing much more than just hanging out and drinking beer.

There was a small grocery store nearby, but not much else. One day, when I stopped by to buy a soda, the Grocer told me what was happening. The Hell's Angels had bought that shack and were converting it into a motorcycle repair shop. Their efforts were showing too! By now, they'd put up new siding and cleaned it up pretty good. Soon, they'd be ready for business.

I drove by the place one afternoon and noticed that they'd just put in a gravel driveway and small parking lot…No one was there. Today, I decided I'd slip down into South Carolina, just to check out the connecting roads to my area. I could've been fired if I'd been caught down there without permission because we had no jurisdiction in SC, and the law and Patrol policy was very clear on that.

I was probably about five miles inside South Carolina when I turned around and headed back. I came up behind a yellow Volkswagen that was weaving noticeably. Maybe he was drunk…He sure drove as if he was. Knowing that I couldn't stop him in South Carolina, I passed him and kicked it. As soon as I got back into my State, I started looking for a place to hide until he came by, then I'd check him out. There it was…The perfect place, the unoccupied motorcycle shop.

We'd had a pretty good rain several hours before, but that never crossed my mind as I made a quick left turn into the driveway on my side of the building…Big mistake! That new gravel was like ice! My Patrol Car slid into the front left corner of the building and I tore up the right front of my car…And the new shop didn't fair much better, several rows of siding were demolished. I backed up and hastily made my way to the other side of the building, and hid there until the Volkswagen came by. Even after it was long gone, I sat there like a whipped puppy. What was I going to do?

I'd already wrecked more than my share of Patrol Cars and really didn't want to go through all the hassle of a report again…Especially now, under these circumstances. I knew what I had to do because I'd done it before. My working shift was about over, so I drove to Austen's Wrecker Service. Austen's had a fellow working the night shift who was good at bodywork. We slaved on my car all night long, knocked all the dents out and then repainted it. When daylight came, my car was in good shape again.

During the following days, I'd regularly go by the motorcycle shop to see if anyone was there…Nothing, there was no activity at all. As more time passed, my conscience began to bother me more, because I'd damaged someone else's property. Sure enough, about a week later, I drove by and noticed a crowd of Angels there, banging on boards and drinking beer. I recognized Carroll right off. He was tall, with long black hair. I'd seen him before, but we'd never met. I'd written a couple of his members tickets, but they'd never given me any grief…They'd always shown me respect. Their guns, their tattoos, their gypsy leather and their Harleys intimidated a lot of folks, but to me, they were just fellow human beings. I drove my Patrol Car right into the middle of them and parked it.

They were shocked! They weren't expecting company…Especially a State Trooper! One or two of them started heading for the woods…I ignored them. I walked straight up to Carroll and introduced myself.

> "You fella's have got this place looking pretty good," I boldly said. "What happened to the side of your building?"

> "Well," Carroll replied, "*we had a party here last week and one of these turkeys got drunk and drove into the side of the shop, but nobody will fess up to it.*"

> "Carroll…Don't give em too hard of a time because I did it," I confessed. "Whatever the damage is, I'll pay for it."

Then I told him the whole story about what I'd done.

"There's really not much damage at all," with shock in his voice, he said. "All that was messed up were a few boards. No big deal at all."

"Regardless, I'm gonna pay for the damage," I forcefully said. "After you get it fixed, give me the costs and I'll pay for it."

I gave him my card and home phone number and then left.

A week or so later I came by after all repairs were made and the shop had opened. He was there. I asked for the costs of damage and he refused to give me a figure. I threw fifty bucks down on the counter and walked out.

I didn't hear from him again right away, but every once in awhile, he'd call me on the phone for advice. Sometimes, he'd call just to say Hi. Occasionally, he'd give me tidbits of information on illegal activities. He never squealed on his own, but the info he gave me was more than I could handle, so I passed it on to other government agencies that could, with his blessings. We were never public friends, but we came to be somewhat fond of one another.

From time to time, I'd read an article about him and his Angel's in the newspaper. Carroll didn't live to see old age. A few years later, after I transferred to Mecklenburg County, he was killed by gunshot at a clubhouse.

I knew he wasn't perfect, but I sure was proud to be…The friend of an Angel.

Bottomless Pit

Joe was a lot bigger than I was, was Lebanese, and everybody gave him a hard time. *(Have you ever seen anybody with mustaches under their eyes?)* After getting out of Basic Patrol School, Joe started putting the weight back on and he's been fighting his weight ever since. As I've mentioned before, Joe Ikell didn't have any friends and I felt sorry for him. We worked the same shift a lot and I hung out with him to keep him from being so lonely.

Now wait just a minute! I've told you before, this is my story and I'm telling it. Excuse me, I'll be right back. Let me go get another drink.

Late one evening, while working, Joe and I met at one of our favorite hangouts...The Howard Johnson's on US 321 at I85. It was mealtime and Joe had put himself on a strict diet. He ordered a small salad and I ordered up a nice big juicy steak with all the trimmings...Yes, I was his only friend. Joe flirted with our Waitress, Nancy, as I sat there in awkward silence. *(You don't believe that for a minute, now do you?)*

Our orders arrived and I dug in while Joe began picking at his salad. I made it a point to let him know how much I was enjoying this wonderful meal. I was just about to order dessert when our Waitress came walking up with a humongous steak platter.

That steak was hanging off the sides of the plate. Somebody else had ordered it, got tired of waiting for it and then left before it arrived...She didn't want to throw it out.

"*Can either of you handle this?*" she asked, as she gave Joe the eye.

It was obvious she liked him and unlike me...He was available. Joe was strong! He declined.

"*I'm watching my weight.*" he said, as he sucked his belly in.

"*Yes, I'll take it,*" I faked it out when I said, "*I'm still hungry!*"

For another forty-five minutes we sat there while I elaborated over every morsel. Joe was still playing with his piddly salad when I finally ordered a large dessert. I was about to burst when we left…But tucked it in, grinned and bore it.

Take it away, Levi!

Joe ended up marrying Nancy and they had a long and happy marriage. We weren't prepared for her passing and she's dead now. We miss her!

The Trash Collectors

Just when we think nobody's looking and we think we won't get caught, that's normally when the axe falls…And our greatest lessons are taught.

It was the middle of the Summer and the days were long and hot. Although I was working the evening shift and was heading home for my supper hour, it was several hours until dark. As I deliberately made my way up the winding road to Spencer's Mountain, I came up behind a pickup truck. This truck had just entered the roadway ahead of me and almost immediately, I saw a bottle come sailing out from the passenger side. That really made me mad, because this area looked like a trash dump…Discarded items were scattered everywhere! I knew I shouldn't take it personally but I couldn't help it, I did…I traveled this road at least four times a day because I lived in this neck of the woods. I stopped them.

I got out of my Patrol Car and briskly walked up. Two young fellows, I'd say they were in their early twenty's, were in there. When I told them why I'd stopped them and the possible consequences, they were somewhat surprised. Even back then, a littering charge was high. Because the driver had control of the vehicle and it was registered in his name, although he hadn't thrown the bottle out, he was legally guilty of the same. Of course, they just wanted me to warn them and let em go…As a matter of fact, they begged and pleaded that I do so.

> "Please, Officer…Let us go," the passenger said. "The fine is so high and we don't have the money. We promise! We won't do it again. Just let us pick up trash for awhile."

I had a weak moment now, so I wrote down their driver's license and registration information…They seemed like pretty good kids and I knew where they lived.

> "Tell you what," I started out, "I'm going home for supper now, but I'll be back by here in about an hour and a half. You can either load that truck up with trash or, if you decide to take off, I'm gonna go have warrants drawn up for the two of you for littering."

Excitedly, they agreed. You would've thought it was Christmastime. I left and took my meal hour, and maybe a little bit more. Back then, there was no such thing as compensation time and we continuously worked well over forty hours a week. This was normal…It wasn't written down anywhere, but we were expected to. For most of us, it was no big deal. We just took long breaks when we could and either turned the volume up on our radio or listened to our scanners inside of our homes.

When I returned to their location, I was in for a surprise. Those boys had the back of that truck loaded down. I pulled over onto the shoulder close to them and watched. I sat there and did paperwork while they worked, just to see how far they'd go. It was starting to get dark and although the pile was well beyond the height of the rails now, they went on. Finally, I got out of my car.

> *"I think that's enough, Fellas,"* I then said. *"I don't think she'll carry anymore! Let's take that load to the dump and you can go home."*

Only when I said that did they stop, and they had barely cleaned up between two telephone poles. I followed them to the dump and watched them unload.

Several days later, when I was off-duty and out mowing my yard, two visitors arrived. It was those same two boys, in that same pickup truck, carrying another load. They were so proud!

> *"Trooper Gregory,"* one of them said, *"we're on the way to the landfill with another load."* Then he went on, *"we just stopped by your place to let you see. Thank you, Sir…For not writing us up."*

Maybe I didn't write as many tickets as some other Troopers did...But how could they possibly feel better about themselves than I now did?

The Fox Drive-In

This is the only incident in the book that I was not involved in, but it's too good to leave out. It occurred in Charlotte right before I transferred there but fallout from it was still descending. I did, however, make a video production of it for display at Eddie Scummings Retirement Dinner. So I think you'll enjoy it. Here it goes…

The Fox Drive-In was one of the few drive-in theaters left anywhere around. It was especially unique in that it only showed X-rated movies.

Sunday evenings were always active at the Charlotte Patrol Office. That's when those Troopers working congregated and completed their paperwork and then turned it in. It had come to be routine that after turning in reports, some of the guys would load up in an unmarked Patrol Car and head for the Fox Drive-In. After a stressful weekend, I suppose this was a cooling off period for them. Anyway, that's what had happened on this occasion. Several Troopers had finished their reports early and then loaded up in Johnny Mac's unmarked Patrol Car and gone to the Drive-In. The remaining Troopers at the Office knew where they were…But the Supervisor didn't.

Before long, the Office phone rang and the Line Sergeant answered. *(We all loved this Sergeant, but he got excited easily. We referred to him as "Jumpin Joe", so that's what I'll do now)*

> "I live over here near the Fox Drive-In," the lady said, "and I'm getting sick and tired of watching Troopers go out and in. There's a carload of them over here right now!" she complained. "Does the Highway Patrol condone these activities?"

One of the Troopers in the next room was listening in on an extension. Jumpin Joe didn't say much, but it was obvious to everyone there…He was hopping mad!

> "I'll investigate that right now!" he told her and then he hung up the phone.
>
> *Trooper Scummings! Drive me over to the Fox Drive-In,"* he hollered out. *"Now!"*

Scummings had the only other unmarked car, but he damn sure didn't want to take the Sergeant there to catch his friends. Reluctantly, he left with Jumpin Joe in his car. As soon as they left, everybody else got busy. They tried to contact the culprits on the radio...No luck. They tried to call the Drive-In office...That didn't work either. All they could do now was just sit there and wait. Meanwhile, at the Drive-In, those Troopers were having a really big time...But they didn't know that Jumpin Joe was now on the warpath.

Jumpin Joe made Scummings park on the shoulder just outside of the Drive-In. Then, he went stomping out among all the cars in there with his flashlight, searching for that unmarked Patrol Car. *(I can only imagine all the sights he saw on the way)* Finally, he found it! It was an ugly scene.

It was warm outside. Those fellows had the car doors open and were eating popcorn and hot dogs when the light hit them. *(Now comes the really stupid part)* As soon as he spoke and they recognized him, they slammed the doors shut and took off in that unmarked Patrol Car...Leaving Jumpin Joe standing right there with a puzzled look on his face and that silly flashlight.

Eventually, all parties involved ended up back at the Charlotte Office. Maybe it was because he didn't want to go through all the paperwork, I don't know...But after a lot of thunder and lighting and a long cooling off period, Jumpin Joe let them go.

For years, Scummings was accused of turning those fellows in, or at least volunteering his services to complicate the fix they were in...I can't swear to that.

But I have wondered if it was Troopers in uniform, who really caused the demise of the Drive-Ins.

Railroad Tracks

Remember at the beginning, I told you that timing is everything and the time is right? Well, I'm convinced that a lot of things are just like that...They're just meant to be. They are going to happen and the best we can do is just go with the flow. These things can't be forecasted, because only God knows when. Oh, you'll get all kinds of arguments and some folks will just sneer...But that's the way it's gone in my life and a fine example is right here.

Our Country was on the verge of great celebration, July 4, 1976...Year 200 of Our Independence...The Bicentennial. For months, even years, The United States of America had been preparing for this event. Tonight the festivity would begin and we would rejoice together as we remembered the accomplishments of our Ancestors. In just a few minutes, the fireworks would begin high above the skyscrapers of Charlotte and we would then witness the most spectacular display of fireworks that most of us had ever seen.

Traffic had already slowed a great deal. Many vehicles had already pulled off onto the emergency lanes and stopped. By now, some occupants had pulled out their lawn chairs and blankets and begun lounging in the grassy areas. Although I was on-duty, I also anticipated the show. Yes, this would be a major event of my lifetime...In more ways than one.

As I headed south on I77, traffic increasingly became more congested and although I certainly wasn't looking for a drunk driver, there he was...Right in front of me. I wanted to watch the fireworks, damn it...So I forgave him for a few weaves in the road. But his driving didn't improve...It only got worse! When I turned on my blue light and tapped the siren, he tried to accelerate and make a run for it, but that didn't last long...There was no place he could go. By now, traffic had come to a standstill and he was stuck like a fly on flypaper. He reluctantly pulled over onto the right emergency lane.

Figuring he might try to jump and run, I ran towards the driver's door...I was waiting for him when he came out. He was a couple of inches shorter than I and the smell of alcohol was obvious, but there was something else unusual about him...He had a wild, paranoid look in his eyes.

As I introduced myself and told him why I'd stopped him, his eyes were constantly moving around. I'd seen that look many times before and I knew what he was thinking…He was looking for the best way to get out of there. As I told him he was under arrest, I grabbed him by the arm and led him around to the passenger side of my car. But his feet didn't want to follow his body…They wanted to head off in another direction somewhere. I spun him around and starting slapping the cuffs on him…That did it! He summoned all his energy and bolted like a jackrabbit.

The grass was wet and his feet slipped…I tackled him and got one cuff on. He bolted again! *"Where was he getting all this energy?"* I wondered. Again, I jumped on him and we wallered around on the hillside.

> *"Fella, if you don't give up, I'm gonna clobber you with my nightstick!"* I warned him.

Up until now, I'd been in all kinds of fights and altercations, but I'd never had to really beat anyone. But this day was special, it was The Bicentennial. For the two of us and everyone else…Now the fireworks commenced!

He ran again and I clobbered him on top of the head with my short plastic stick. *(It just so happens that for years now, I'd been splitting a lot of firewood, so I could hit the mark for which I was aiming…And that mark was the top of his head)* He ran again. I hit him! He ran again. I hit him! He ran again. I hit him! From his forehead to the backside of his noggin, I created a symmetrical set of railroad tracks. We went to the ground again and as we wrestled around, I could hear a male voice behind me.

> *"Officer!"* the voice said, *"Do you need any help?"*

I looked around. One of the many pedestrians had come to offer his help.

> *"No, I don't need any help,"* I responded, *"but this fella does! If you don't help me get these handcuffs on him, I'm afraid I'll kill him."*

Together, we got the cuffs on him and escorted him back to my car.

He was more cooperative now but didn't talk much. His driver's license and other credentials appeared to be in order. After searching him more thoroughly, I found a nickel bag of marijuana in one of his socks. I searched his car…Nothing much there. I locked his car up and called for a wrecker, and then put a bandage and cold pack on top of his head. It was now time to get him to a Hospital. He was hurt bad!...Jail would have to wait.

By now, most traffic had pulled off to the shoulders and all were enjoying the spectacular display of skyrockets. We made our way to the Charlotte Memorial Hospital. What luck!...One of the best Plastic Surgeons in the area was working the Emergency Room that night. I knew he was good...He'd sewed me up a few times before. He wore a bow tie and he was a friend of mine. It was obvious my customer needed attention, so he took us right in.

> "Trooper," the Doctor ordered, *"you'll have to remove the handcuffs from your defendant."*

> "Doctor, I don't think that's a good idea," I replied. "You can see what I had to do to him to get him here."

> *"Take em off!"* he insisted. *"I can't work on him like that, with his hands cuffed behind his back."*

> "OK, Doc!...You're the boss," I reluctantly said.

The cuffs came off and his feet started moving again. Once again, I tackled him and tried to subdue him...But that wasn't enough! For a second time, the stick came out and I clobbered his head...Right there inside of the Hospital and in front of everybody! We got him restrained again and now, the Doctor understood...The handcuffs stayed on. Now, the defendant began cussing both myself and the Doctor. He would live to regret it...The good Doctor got mad!

In no time flat, the Doctor had him sewed up. In places, the stitches were an inch apart.

> *"That'll give him something to remember,"* the Doc proclaimed. *"I only put in 26 stitches where he could have used four times as many. He'll remember this incident every time he looks in a mirror."*

We left the Hospital and I took him to Jail, and he stayed there until the Court day. About two months later, when that day came, he pled guilty to the charges I'd made. His driver's license was revoked, a large fine was levied and he was sentenced to six more months in Jail. Although the top of his head had healed up pretty good, it still looked like it had been through a meat grinder. Time passed, but that is not the end of this tale.

More than two years went by. A lawyer called beforehand and then met me at the Charlotte Office. He asked me if I remembered that incident.

> "*Certainly!*" I said. "*It happened on The Bicentennial.*"

> "*I represent the twin brother of the defendant you arrested,*" he continued. "*They're identical twins.*" (The lawyer then showed me their photos and birth certificates) "*My client tells me that his brother had stolen, and had been using his driver's license…Because his was revoked. The person you arrested was found guilty and served six months in prison…Using his brother's name. We don't know where he is now. Do you think you can look at my client and tell if he's the one you arrested?*" he asked.

> "*I don't know, but I'll give it a try,*" I replied.

The following day, we all met at the Charlotte Office. The lawyer's client looked exactly like the one I'd arrested. I told him to bend over and let me check out the top of his head. He obliged and I carefully looked it over. That was not the same head that myself and the Plastic Surgeon had worked on…No evidence of any previous head trauma was there. He was not the same man.

We had his record cleared…Because there were no railroad tracks on his head.

Hot Foot

The Highway Patrol became responsible for our Governor's security. At his request, a group of Troopers were trained and assigned to work at the Governor's Mansion. Their function was somewhat like that of the Secret Service. When he traveled, at least one of these Troopers was always with him. In key metropolitan areas around the state such as Charlotte, a few select Troopers were trained and assigned to act as point. *(Go in first and prepare the way)* Before the Governor made an appearance in that area, one of these local Troopers would meet his entourage and then lead the way. Only the best-looking and most intelligent Troopers were selected for these positions. Of course, Executive Security became one of my duties.

I received notice that the Governor would soon be coming to Charlotte, and detailed itinerary was included along with the name of his attending Trooper. This Trooper was new and I didn't know him…So I checked around to see if anybody else did. One of my cohorts came forth and confessed that he knew him, and then proceeded to tell me the following story about him…

> A couple of months ago, he had gone to some southern beach with another male Trooper. They had taken a long walk on the beach. After awhile, they noticed that something was not quite right. Upon closer inspection, they noticed that the other males in the area were holding hands, etc…And that they had wandered onto a gay beach. Not wanting be a party to any of that, they immediately made their way to the road and ran all the way back to a more favorable area…Barefooted and on the hot asphalt.

Well, the big day came for me to meet the Governor and his contingency at The Sportsman's Club of the Charlotte Motor Speedway. After meeting them there, I would lead them into Charlotte and guide them through his appointments there. In a nice suit, I walked in and observed the Governor and a group of his supporters sitting to the right. The Trooper, also in a suit, was sitting alone and to the left, at a table and on a semi-circle seat. I slid in beside him and introduced myself.

"*My name is Bryan Gregory,*" I said, "*damn, you look familiar.*"

I'd never seen him before in my life.

"*I'm...whoever,*" he replied, "*you look familiar too.*"

That was a lie. He was just being polite. He didn't know me. We sat there for awhile, just carrying on casual conversation and eating.

"*I think I know were I've seen you before,*" with a focused look on my face, I said. "*Were you at the beach a couple of months ago?*"

"*Yes, I was,*" with some surprise, he said.

"*That's where I saw you!*" I excitedly said. "*A friend of mine and I were lying on the beach, and you and a friend of yours came walking by.*" Then, as I gently reached over and touched his leg, I said, "*you know, you've got a nice butt.*"

He immediately pulled away and didn't want to be friends anymore...And had it not been for the Governor and the situation we were in, I may have received the thrashing of my life.

Man with the Plan

Back before cell phones, CB radios were the trend. "Smokey and The Bandit" was the hit movie and a lot of motorists had "ears." It was during this time that Troopers, who wanted them, with the blessings of the Highway Patrol, installed CB's in their Patrol Cars. These little radios were quite useful and many Truckers still use them today…To inform one another of road conditions and to keep the Smokies *(State Troopers)* at bay. These radios were not good for great distance, at the most twenty miles or so, but they allowed total strangers to talk to each other as if they were best friends. Even a little runt could look mighty big…On that CB radio. Nobody ever used their real names. Everybody just came up with a "handle," and used that to identify themselves.

After installing my radio, I listened to it some to learn the lingo. I noticed that most other Smokies used a handle with "Bear" in it, or something like that. They wanted everybody to know who they were. Of course, I had to be different…Anything with "Bear" in it, just wouldn't get it. So, after much thought, I made myself known as "The Man with the Plan"…I liked that. *"That'll keep those Truckers guessing,"* I thought. And sure enough, it did.

Needless to say, when a Patrol Car appeared on the highway, that Smokey became the talk of the day. Seldom was there anything better to talk about than finding out where he was. When I had my ears on, there was never any doubt in my mind…I knew how important I was! Even in the dead of night and when the CB was quiet, the first time that a Trucker spotted a Smokey…That radio came alive. Sometimes, I would hear those Truckers talking about me for hours, after I got off the Interstate.

Most Smokies with ears didn't talk much…They'd just sit back and listen. Me? I was what they called a "ratchet-jaw." I'd talk to almost anybody and on that radio, I could become their friend. I kept a CB in my Patrol Car for many, many years. As did other Troopers, I even caught numerous reckless drivers and drunks with it…Other CB'ers would often tell us about them. One incident that I remember is the drunk who turned himself in to me. Here, let me tell you about him.

Steve and I were just winding up our supper hour. I was still picking my teeth with a toothpick, when I got back into my Patrol Car…Steve walked around and sat down on the passenger side. We hadn't finished our conversation yet, so we continued with that. Even before I could crank my car, we heard that drunk on my little radio.

"*Break 19, for a radio check,*" with slurred speech, he said.

The CB had 40 channels, and channel 19 was the channel that most all motorists used.

No one else responded. Nobody wanted to mess with a drunk. So once or twice more, he broke the silence like that. He wanted so much to find someone to talk to. Finally, I spoke to him.

"*You've got the Man with the Plan here,*" I came back to him with, "*I'm over here on East Independence near Albemarle Road and you're sounding good to me.*" "*What's your 10–20?*" I then asked. (That means "Where are you?")

I don't recall his precise words, but without hesitation, he told me what he was driving and exactly where he was…He wasn't far away either, no more than a mile or two off. He was so excited. He thought he'd just made a new friend. Little did he know that there were two State Troopers now…Who really wanted to meet him.

Steve jumped out of my car and headed towards his. Oops! What's that? My car wouldn't start. After frantically trying several more times, it still wouldn't crank! I waved for Steve to take off without me. I stayed behind. Off he went.

Although there wasn't enough juice in my battery to crank my car, I could still talk on that radio. So for the next few minutes I kept that drunk busy…We kept ratchet-jawing away. As Steve was getting closer to him, that drunk kept telling me where he was…And Steve was listening to the both of us, on his little radio. During breaks in our conversation, I pulled the jumper cables out of my trunk and found someone to jump me off. That drunk was still talking to me when Steve pulled him over…Right in his own driveway.

Even to this day, that drunk has never figured it out. While he was talking to me on his CB, he thought he'd found as good of a friend as anyone can. But he didn't know who he was dealing with. He didn't know…"The Man with the Plan."

I could go on forever, about fun that I had with that CB. But there's a lot more ground that I want to cover now…So for the time being, we'll just let it be.

Obscene Gestures

Just ask anyone who's worked in an Emergency Room or has been in law enforcement for awhile. Strange things happen on a full moon. That's when people seem to take the greatest risks. That's when they perform the most unpredictable and stupid acts. That's when they seem to be the most violent. That's when they seem to go absolutely crazy! I'm not superstitious by nature and you may think it's a bunch of bull, but some folks just go nuts when the moon is full.

This episode is so weird that it's even hard for me to believe it happened…But it did! It was broad daylight, but as was the case for many of the incidents in this book, you guessed it…There it was! The moon was full.

On I85 South, about ½ mile south of Harris Blvd, I had just stopped a motorist for speeding. I'd been running my car pretty hard to catch him and I didn't even think of it at the time, but my brakes were hot. Back then, brake pads weren't that good. After they cooled off they'd be OK, but right now, they were pretty well shot. I had just approached the driver and told him why I'd stopped him, when a car with two young females pulled in behind my Patrol Car. They both jumped out and came running up to me, waving their arms.

> "*Officer,*" the first one frantically said, "*a fellow has been harassing us on the highway! We finally passed him and got away from him, but he's still back there and he's coming this way!*"

> "*He's been hounding us for about twenty miles and won't leave us alone,*" the other one broke in and said. "*He's been making obscene gestures at us! He was exposing himself!*"

They were both jabbering at the same time and I've always had enough trouble understanding just one female, much less two at the same time. The first one became very graphic. I won't quote what she said, but in no uncertain terms, she let me know with just three descriptive words…That this unknown character was satisfying one of his basic needs, by himself and in their presence, while he was driving down the road. Then one of them hollered out…

> "*There he goes!…Right there!*"

There were a good many other cars out there, but they both excitedly pointed him out.

> "There he is…In that little car right there!" "Get him, Officer! Get him!" they both stammered, "Get him! He's getting away!"

"Not if I can help it." I thought to myself. "I'll rescue these fair maidens and suck up on their gratitude."

Quickly, I told the fellow I'd stopped for speeding "This is your lucky day," and then I hurriedly jumped into my Patrol Car and I was up, up and away. As I was taking off, the two girls could hear me say…

> "Don't worry girls, I'll get him. Just pull in behind me when I've got him stopped. You'll both have to testify in Court that I got the right one."

With relief in their voices, they both agreed…"OK."

It was on! I punched that '78 Plymouth out as fast as it would go. Just ahead, there was a slight bend in the Interstate to the right and just beyond that, the long ramp to Sugar Creek Road. I was running well over 120mph when I rounded the curve. Where was that little car? He certainly wasn't on the Interstate ahead. There he was…I saw him! No, he'll not get away! He was now stopped behind traffic, in the right lane at the red light, up on that long ramp to Sugar Creek Road.

When I hit the bottom of the ramp, I had slowed to about 100mph, but that wasn't enough…I'd have to do much better than that! When I hit my brakes, it was like stepping on a sponge…There were no brakes left! I'd used them all up on the last car I'd stopped. Damn! What a predicament!…And Sugar Creek Road intersection was coming up fast.

Up there, the traffic on Sugar Creek Road was moving…It had the right of way and all of the traffic lights for the ramp were still red. I aimed for the two lanes to the left because the right one had the only stopped traffic in it…Including that idiot who'd caused all this mess. There he casually sat, behind all the others…That damn bubblehead!

I revved the engine up and downshifted to low range, but was still going way too fast…It just wouldn't go. I slammed on the emergency brakes. That helped some, but not much. Again, I revved the engine up. This time I maxxed it out. Finally, it went down into low, but still...That wasn't enough! By now, I was almost at the top of the ramp. I had to do something...Now!

The traffic was heavy on Sugar Creek Road and I was right before hitting something! Easily, I could've wiped out half a dozen cars, but I had one last straw...I swerved to the left and broadsided that car. Sure enough, that slowed me down more, but still not enough! I slid sideways into the traffic. The right corner of my rear bumper wiped out the whole right side of a westbound-moving car. We were all lucky. No one was hurt.

The startled driver jumped out of his car. By now, I was out too. I ignored him and headed straight for the one I was after...That damn bubblehead. There he sat, still hung up in traffic back there.

Before he could blink, I was on him...I jerked him out of his car. There were some mighty funny looking stains, running down the side of his door. The next thing he knew, he was handcuffed and in the passenger seat of my car. I looked around. Those two female witnesses should've been here by now.

There they were. *"Hey! Over here!"* I shouted in vain. There they went...Straight down the Interstate. Couldn't they see my blue light? Didn't they see me waving my arms? Did they have tunnel vision? Didn't they even notice all the commotion up here on this ramp? *"Damn women,"* I thought. *"Well, maybe they saw me and they'll turn around and come back."*

There I was...Suspect in custody and he wouldn't talk. He may have been dumb, but not stupid...Without witnesses, he wasn't about to confess to something like that. Like a complete idiot, there I sat.

Now I spoke with the driver of the car I'd just hit. I calmed him down some and called for the Line Sergeant on-duty, to come out and investigate all of this. When he arrived, he listened, but didn't have much to say...He was too busy laughing.

For almost an hour, we stayed there...Investigating, measuring and filling out reports...And waiting for the return of my alibi, the fair maidens. I never saw them again, so I had no choice...I had to let bubblehead go. The Sergeant only half-way believed my story anyway, so he wasn't surprised when they didn't show.

My formal statement of this incident was not very interesting. For Highway Patrol purposes, simple was better.

There's one part of this story that I've never gotten over. For the harassment I've received and the ruckus they caused…Those girls have never once called, or sent me a card or a letter.

A Normal Speeder

It was a normal day. With my speed-timing device, Vascar, I had clocked a motorist speeding 74mph in a 55mph zone. It was an ordinary stop. I introduced myself to the well-dressed, middle-aged man and told him why I'd stopped him. He was quiet and polite, and complained very little as I wrote his ticket. The charge that I'd made against him required a Court appearance and I set that date for approximately four weeks away.

The Court day came and when the District Attorney called his name out, no one responded. This was not unusual, it happened all the time. I had other cases that were being tried and I forgot all about his.

Directly, one of the Clerks came over to me and handed me a note from a Parole Officer.

> *"I just received word of this,"* the note began. *"Please advise Trooper Gregory that the defendant in this case, (his name), will not be appearing in Court today. He died of a self-inflicted shotgun wound about an hour ago."*

Apparently, conviction of this speeding ticket would have been a parole violation and he did not want to take the chance of going back to prison. Maybe he would have, but probably he wouldn't.

Do you feel what I felt?

Levi can't help me out this time. You'll have to deal with this the best way that you can.

That's what I had to do.

The Biltmore House

A young Rookie had been assigned to Charlotte. In everything he put his hand to, he did his best. He had a farming background and became known as a very hard-working Trooper. He was rather quiet and maybe a little shy, but was always available to help anybody do anything. Somehow, we became friends.

His lovely little wife began working in the Driver's License Office, which was in an adjacent part of our building. When she took her breaks, she'd often slip into our Office and work on her needlepoint or read at one of our tables. I'll just refer to her as "Sweet Thing."

One day while she was taking a breather, several of us Troopers were sitting with her, just shooting the breeze, and she was longingly gazing at a brochure of The Biltmore House *(a large tourist attraction in Asheville, NC)*. In came her young Trooper husband. He did his business in the Office, tried to ignore us and never even spoke to his wife. *(This was normal for him. He was just that way…But we all knew that he loved her)* He was well within earshot now.

> "Boy," I started out, *"this little wife of yours wants to go to The Biltmore House. Why don't you take her up there on your days off?"*
>
> *"I can't,"* he replied, *"I've got to work in my tobacco."* (He had a fairly large tobacco crop on his farm, about 200 miles away, which he was constantly tending)
>
> *"Well, damn it! If you don't take her…I will!"* I then volunteered.

His face became flushed and I knew I'd hit a nerve…I'd found his soft spot! Now, all we Troopers proceeded to reel him in. We all began harassing him about ignoring his wife, how pretty she was and how he ought to spend more time with her. At one point, I even threatened to leave my wife and family, just to give her the attention she deserved. We were really getting to him. Then I took over.

> *"I think I'll just start calling you my 'Husband-in-Law',"* I said, *"because you're married to my girlfriend."*

He was torn up when he left, and to this day…I've called him my Husband-in-Law and survived.

About a month passed without further ado. Then it came his turn to go to our Training Center *(a good distance away)* for a week. Sweet Thing was going to be without his protection for a whole week.

I started planning and spoke with her about what I was scheming. She smiled timidly and consented. After he'd been away for a couple of days, I rounded up a picture postcard of The Biltmore House, addressed it to him at the Training Center and hand-wrote a nice note on the back that read…

> *"Having a wonderful time at The Biltmore House…Bryan & Sweet Thing"*

To make sure that it was properly postmarked from that area, I had the card discretely relayed by Patrol Cars all the way up to the Asheville area, where it was then mailed by a trusted cohort.

I'm sorry. Levi hasn't been feeling well…But I think you get the picture anyway.

Little Black Book

RV was a Trooper whose mild temperament was powered by his religious nature. He was trusting and trustworthy. He took his work and his life, very seriously. RV had his act together pretty good and he didn't need any adjustments from me, so I concentrated my skills in other areas. He stayed awhile…Then transferred to Union County.

Before long, new meat arrived in the form of Darryl…RV's brother. Darryl had been on the Patrol for awhile and was not one bit like his brother…Darryl didn't trust anybody! It seemed to me that he was always looking over his shoulder and was in constant fear that somebody was going to sneak up on him. He was twitchy and he talked a lot, but never said much. Darryl needed medication.

Rumors had it that one of our single, female Dispatchers had been keeping a little black book and was telling all. Supposedly, she'd been seeing an array of Highway Patrol personnel, of all ranks…Married and unmarried. Somebody had recently broken it off with her and she was out for revenge. The word was out…Internal Affairs was on the warpath! Many butts were tight!! These rumors had been flying for a week or so. One day, Darryl approached me. Although we were the only ones around, he refused to talk above a whisper.

> "Bryan, RV told me that I could trust you and that if anyone can help me, you can. Will you find out if my name is in that little black book?"

"*Damn*," I thought, "*If he were involved with her, surely he'd remember. And besides…How did I obtain a good reputation like that?*"

After I had picked his brain some, I formed the opinion that Darryl had not been involved with the girl except casually. I promised to investigate…Yes, he could trust me.

It wasn't long…Maybe a day or two, and I found an excuse to head up to the Dispatcher's Office. I then located one of the big wheels there.

> "Is Darryl's name in that little black book?" I asked him.
>
> "*No,*" he replied.

I then told him the whole nine yards about how Darryl had approached me.

> *"Let's just add his name in there,"* I then said, *"or at least make him think his name is in there."*

He agreed. We pumped up the rumor mill to include Darryl and then told everybody.

As soon as I got home that night, Darryl was calling me on the phone…Because he knew where I'd been. I told him I wasn't for sure, but I thought his name was in there. For weeks, Darryl ran around like a chicken with his head cut off, and we were all right there behind him…Pumping him up.

Whatever happened to all those people in that little black book?…You ask. I can't swear to it but shortly thereafter, they all got promoted…All except Darryl.

The Head

It was nice and warm. It was a beautiful Spring day. Our youngest son, David, wasn't born yet. He was still on the way.

A Mecklenburg County Officer and I had hooked up and we were checking driver's license on a good-sized country road. Traffic was light but we'd written a good many tickets. We were getting some work done and were enjoying ourselves at the same time.

Rather rapidly two Farmers in a pickup truck approached us. As we stood there in the middle of the road, the truck pulled up. The driver leaned out of his window.

> "*Officers,*" he excitedly said, "*we just found a skull lying in the middle of one of these back roads! Follow us and we'll show you where. We don't know what it is. It looks like something we've never seen before!*"

We formed a caravan and made our way back through the country. We drove down Allen Black Road and then made the turn onto Union Road...I'd never even been on this little road before. We were almost at the Union County line when we pulled over onto the shoulder. Sure enough, about 100 feet ahead of us, was a round object lying in the middle of this desolate and lonely road. When I got up to it I could tell...This was not a skull. It was a head!

Maybe an animal had dragged it there. The smell was horrible! The insects were going to town on it and it was hard to tell what kind of creature it had belonged to. Its features were not very clear. A feeling of horror began to creep over me. This was not the head of your run of the mill farm animal. Neither had it belonged to a normal forest creature...It was just too perfect and round.

No! No! It just couldn't be! This must be the head of that missing little 5-year-old girl. She'd been missing for more than a month now. Yes, this must be the partial remains...Of that sweet little Neely Smith.

I could feel it! I could feel her desperation! As we walked through the woods searching for more evidence and remains...I could just feel it. I could just tell she'd been there. She was so little. She must've been so scared! The tracking dogs led us to her scattered bones and clothing. She must've looked so precious in blue. A monster had kidnapped her, then dragged that innocent little thing back here and had his way with her…Then killed her, so she wouldn't tell. She was still here. He was long gone.

The crime scene Detectives came and taped off the area. They had it covered and I had no more business there. I wiped the tears from my eyes and got back into my Patrol Car. My shift wasn't over yet. I had other obligations. I had more work to do.

Her killer has never been charged. The prime suspect in this case was later found guilty of killing another little girl, Amanda Ray…Two years before Neely's death. There's lots of similarities between the two cases. Both little girls had lived in the same neighborhood, about 15 miles away from here…But Neely's folks didn't know about Amanda's death, they'd just moved there! He was still lurking. He lived in the same apartment complex as Neely. He didn't go anywhere.

Fred Coffey is completing his life sentence. He's already pled guilty to nine counts of taking indecent liberties with children in Caldwell County. He's eluded the death sentence twice! He's come up for parole ten times and will continue to do so every year, until he either dies or is released. He's been lucky. He'll probably be out before too long. Are you ready to welcome him to your neighborhood? Shucks, maybe better scenery will help a pedophile…What do you think? Personally, I think he's had enough chances. I think he's already seen more than his share of sweet things.

So don't count me in with those who'd give him another chance. I've been there. I've seen! I'll not forget about that little child's head.

The Young Marine

Although each incident a Trooper deals with is different, the majority are routine. But just when I'd start getting comfortable, that's when I'd run across someone like this young Marine.

Traffic was fairly heavy. I'd been sitting up on a major ramp watching it and operating my Vascar *(speed-timing device)* from there. Alone, he came whizzing by at about 90mph. I don't think he saw me, because when I fell in behind him, he didn't slow down. There were five lanes going in our direction, and he was using all of them to pass other traffic. The time had now come to pull him over and I had a message to deliver. In this neck of the woods, he was not the King of the Road…I was!

When I turned on my blue light, he reluctantly pulled over to the right shoulder and stopped. As I walked up to his car, he got out. I introduced myself and as normal, I told him why I'd stopped him…For speeding and reckless driving. He was fresh out of Boot Camp, had his well-pressed fatigues on, and it was all *"Yes Sir!"* and *"No Sir!"* as he spoke. But then, I began to smell the strong odor of alcohol on his breath. Without giving him warning, I slapped the cuffs on him and searched him, and while doing so, I told him why…The charge was now DWI and we were going to the Big House. Abruptly, his attitude changed.

There were no more military manners. From now on, I was one sorry SOB and he cussed me with all the words that his Drill Sergeants had taught him. But he didn't stop there…Then, he threatened me!

"You sorry bastard! You take these handcuffs off me and I'll kick you ass!"

This went on for awhile. He was no real threat to me now, so I just let him run his mouth. After about ten minutes of verbal abuse, finally, I'd had enough.

"Boy! Where are you from?" I started out.

"I'm from Pageland, SC…You son of a bitch!" he replied.

"Pageland, SC?" I went on, *"that's funny. I used to live in that area too. How old are you?"*

> *"I'm twenty-two years old,"* he replied. *"You GD SOB! What about it?"*

It was obvious…He was drunk and my questions were irritating him.

> *"Twenty-two?"* I calmly restated. *"You know, that's about the time I lived in that area…When you were born, 22–23 years ago. I was single then."* I paused for a moment and then said, *"You know something?...I might be your Daddy!"*

He flew hot!...And for a few more minutes, his language became worse. But I didn't care…I'd already gotten in my two cents worth. He was really upset now and I was having fun. I just sat there with a smile on my face and every once in awhile, as he cussed me…I'd call him *"Son."*

When we got to the Jail he was nearly worn out, and as is the case with most drunks who run their mouths, when the cuffs came off…The threats stopped! He may have been young and I may have been old, but from then on, he followed me around and politely did as was told.

Once again, it was *"Yes Sir!"* and *"No Sir!"* Once again…

If I was going somewhere with this, I forgot where.

The Secret Supervisor

The main character in this story is not doing well. Since word first got out that I was writing, he has become depressed and has been dealing with constant bouts of diarrhea. Relax and take a deep breath, Randy…I'll try to make it fast.

The Highway Patrol was in the beginning stages of forming a team of Troopers to concentrate on interstate highways, called the I-Team. Young Trooper Randy and a handful of others had been assigned this duty. They had been issued high-speed performance vehicles and were temporarily working out of our Charlotte Office…That's where they did their heavy-duty paperwork and kept their filing cabinets. Their cubbyhole message boxes were also there. A supervisory staff had not been fully established but was soon expected.

Randy was ambitious, but his youth and inexperience was showing. I was beginning to worry about him, his career and the rest of us, because if he didn't straighten out soon, he might even end up hurting someone. What he needed most was guidance, direction and strict supervision. Being the kind and caring person that I am, and without telling him, I took on that responsibility…And I began by keeping a close eye on him. The evidence was building against him.

Randy had recently been interviewed by a small local newspaper called <u>The Leader</u>. He and his Mustang had proudly appeared on the front page and he was quoted as saying…

> *"I might give someone a ticket for a lesser speed even though I clocked them going faster,"* he had said, or something like that.

Whatever he said, it was stupid! We were all amazed that he didn't get into trouble for publicly making such a ridiculous statement. At the time though, he had no one to directly supervise him. It was becoming obvious that Randy needed direction. More evidence was also showing.

One of my spies had just told me that Randy had moved out of our county and that he was telling his neighbors that he was married, when in fact, he wasn't…He was living with his girlfriend out of wedlock! *(What's this world coming to?)* Realizing that Randy was getting out of hand, I decided to get his attention.

First of all, I created a cubbyhole message box from an available vacant one, to be used by a believable Line Sergeant who could only be identified as…H-521. Then I created the following fictitious letter, put it in an envelope and placed it in Randy's message box. Although I wasn't there, I made sure that others were there when he read it…To give him moral support, to seek medical aid if the need arose and to give me feedback.

(The date of the day)

Trooper Randy,

It has come to my attention that there are some drastic discrepancies between your behavior and Patrol policy. You made such a fool of yourself and the Patrol in that recent <u>Leader</u> article that I have accepted the task of giving you the personal supervision that you so obviously require.

You have been separated from your spouse for some time now and it is obvious to me that you have moved to Cabarrus County to escape the strict supervision that you are in such dire need of.

I have received complaints from some of your neighbors that you are shacking up with some little hussy and then lying about it…You're telling everybody over there that you're married. Make up your mind! What's it going to be…Adultery, untruthfulness or both? Our policy is not very clear on fornication, but untruthfulness is a Type 1 violation covered under 9C-4(.0006). Have you considered other employment?

I will give you a limited amount of time to correct all these lies you've been telling on your own, and I also expect you to go to your First Sergeant and tell him everything. I'm sure he'll help you.

You can expect me to formally begin the disciplinary process with form HP-307 if you find yourself unable to get your head out of your ass and straighten out this mess. In the meantime, write out a complete statement for me and leave it in my box so I can have the information ready to proceed with the charge sheet.

(Unreadable forged signature)

Your Secret Supervisor,
H-521

Upon reading it, I understand that he became weak-kneed and had to be supported by those around him...He just couldn't withstand the pressure for very long. Shortly thereafter, he had to be told the truth...

"It's a joke! Bryan Gregory did it," or we may have lost him.

As a result of this incident, Randy has become a much stronger and more careful person. He may yet amount to something.

The Door Knob

To say the least, this incident was one of my most painful.

The time to go to work was drawing closer, and I'd already cleaned up and put on my uniform. There were still a few minutes left before I needed to jump into my Patrol Car and check on with the Dispatcher, so I decided to take care of some unfinished business at the house. Yes, that's what I'd do…I'd change the air conditioner filter.

To perform this maneuver, I normally used a small stepladder, because the filter return was on the ceiling. But on this occasion, the stepladder was not readily available, so I grabbed the closest object I could find that would suit my needs…A ladder back chair from the kitchen. This chair had a unique design that I would soon become more familiar with. You've seen them before…With two long spears bordering the backrest.

I stepped up onto the seat of this chair and immediately became engrossed in changing the filter. It was a tricky process! The filter cover was bent and I had to re-bend it…Finally, I finished. With the back of the chair to my rear, I stood in the seat for a moment longer to admire my handiwork. For that split-second before descending, my brain was thinking stepladder, not chair, so I came down in that manner. I briskly took the weight off one leg and stepped down…There was a problem! Instead of a lower step, there was now a long spear lodged in very unfamiliar territory…My rear end. This area had never been used for entrance purposes, just exits, and believe you me…I removed that unwanted object in no time at all.

I know I didn't, but it felt like I dragged that chair all over the house…Damn, it hurt! My religion was really kicking in now, but that just wasn't enough. I began to get light-headed and dizzy, and the throbbing pain was killing me! I knew I had to have medical attention…Fast! What was I going to do?

I had to figure out a way to get to a Doctor as soon as possible, but there was also something else to consider…My reputation. *"Damn,"* I thought, *"I can't go around telling people I stuck a chair up my ass!"* Surely, if word got out about this, I'd be the talk of the town for generations to come. Although my butt was killing me, my brain finally began to function again. Slowly but surely, I began to formulate a plan. Here's how it all came together.

I limped out to the Patrol Car, checked on and headed for the Charlotte Office. (*Normally, Troopers just go to the Office to get gas, do heavy-duty paperwork, turn in reports, pick up Radars or harass fellow employees*) I drove this trip very carefully. I didn't hit a single pothole and made no aggressive moves whatsoever…I drove like a little ole lady. The pain was tremendous!

Upon reaching the Office, I didn't mingle much…I simply wasn't in the mood. I just hung around the sidelines until all the clamoring had subsided. Finally, I was there alone. As soon as the other Troopers were out of sight, I called my Line Sergeant on the radio and asked him to meet me at the Office. When he got there, I fed him this line of bull…

> "Sarge, I've gotta go to the Hospital!"
>
> "What's the matter, Bryan?" he compassionately asked. I didn't have to fake it…He could see the pain on my face.
>
> "Sarge," I continued, *"I was in the Office getting a Radar unit and on the way out, after I'd opened the door to leave, I dropped a piece of the unit."* (These Radar units consisted of three awkward components and all were linked by a spaghetti of cables) *"While I was bent over to retrieve that fallen piece, somebody came through the door* (a very heavy, steel, spring-loaded door)…*And the door knob hit me in the ass."*

For a moment, he just stood there with a flabbergasted look on his face.

Please be gentle, Levi. It hurt bad enough the first time…

"Bryan Gregory," he then said, "*that's gotta be the craziest story I've ever heard!...But it must be true, because I don't believe anybody could make up anything like that.*" "Go ahead," he continued, "*Go on over to the Hospital* (which was two blocks away and one of the best around)*...And when you come back, don't forget to fill out the Workman's Comp form.*"

He was chuckling when I left, but I thought to myself…"*If you only knew the real story.*"

At the Hospital, I got the same treatment and it was once again, very embarrassing. I had to fill out a form stating my reason for being there…That damn door knob. *(Can you imagine having to fill out paperwork for the real reason? It's not even fun to talk about, much less put on paper)* When all was said and done, I had broken the very tip of my coccyx *(tailbone)*. Since that's an area that's impossible to splint, they gave me some pain pills and sent me home. I didn't stay out of work long, maybe a day or two…And when I did come back, I had to put up with all the hee-hawing for years to come.

If they had known then, as you do now, the REAL story…I would probably have had to retire in disgrace, early.

Ice Cream & Cake

Coming home after work was refreshing. Especially when I worked the early shift…When I got home at three o'clock or so in the afternoon, there was still a lot of day left. After dealing with accidents, law-breakers and the court system all day, it was just normal…I became more relaxed, the closer that I got to our house.

Our street was quiet today. It was the middle of the week, it was summertime and it was hot, and the neighbors were either inside or at work. As our house came into sight, right off the bat I could tell…Something was not right there today. There were clothes and toys, sheets and pillows, and even pieces of furniture, thrown out into our front yard. All of this mess was directly underneath the boys' room and their upstairs window. I quickly got out of my Patrol Car and made my way into the house.

"*Honey, what in the world is going on here?*" I called out to my wife.

The boys were sitting at the kitchen table and she was feeding them large portions of ice cream and cake.

"*You're going to be so proud of them,*" she called back. "*Just come on up to their room with me. You've got to see what they've done.*"

Without saying much, I followed her upstairs and looked with her. Sure enough, for a change, their room was immaculate…Everything was cleaned up!

"*Honey,*" I quietly said, "*I think you need to come outside with me.*"

She had no idea what I was talking about and without explaining much more, I led her out the front door. She was shocked!

"*Those boys!*" she was mad when she said, "*I told them to clean up their room and look what they've done…Instead of cleaning up as they were told to, they just threw all their mess out of the window and here I am…Rewarding them with ice cream and cake!*"

When we came back inside, our sons were still sitting there at the kitchen table with big glowing grins on their faces…Still stuffing their faces with ice cream and cake. They were so happy and proud! They had cleaned up their room as she had told them to and were now reaping the promised reward…Ice cream and cake.

She was very upset, but I chuckled. They were so small and so young, and there's no way that I was going to correct them for something like that. Before long though, she got over it and we all began laughing. After all, our sons had done exactly as they were instructed…Just in a different way than was meant.

I guess life is sometimes like that. Although we know it's not the best way, sometimes we do whatever it takes…To get our ice cream and cake.

Pop Quiz for Police Officers
(This section is for Police Officers only)

Imagine yourself stopping a motorist and upon approach, you ask… *"Do you know why I stopped you?"* or, *"Do you know how fast you were going?"*

List logical responses you should expect:

1. _____
2. _____
3. _____
4. _____
5. _____
6. _____

List ways you have now damaged your image as a professional:

1. _____
2. _____
3. _____
4. _____
5. _____
6. _____

Unless your eyes are recovering from a recent glaucoma exam, list reasons <u>for</u> leaving your sunglasses on while making a contact:

1. _____

<u>Against</u>:

1. _____
2. _____
3. _____
4. _____
5. _____
6. _____

(Use next page if more room needed)

(Additional room for responses)

How to Stop Smoking

I've smoked cigarettes since I was 18 yrs old and I didn't go out looking for them…They came looking for me. Nobody that I know of, on either side of my family, smoked.

When I was a kid, TV was just becoming popular and about all of my screen heroes were smoking. They were so cool! I wanted to grow up and be just like them. My Parents didn't approve and as long as they lived, I never smoked around them…But as soon as I moved away from home and started going to college, I started smoking.

At first, it was kind of scary being away from home…I needed a crutch! It began as just an effort to look cool like my childhood heroes. I figured I'd just light one up when I was around my peers, just so I'd look more like a "real man" and fit in better. My plan failed miserably and it didn't take long. That first pack came in such a neat little red & white box and it lasted me about a week…But after the second pack of short Marlboro's I was completely hooked.

I never dreamed they'd be so addictive! It just wasn't fair! They hadn't been honest with me! My heroes, who were on TV, in the movies and on the billboards, never told me that. I sure wish I could get the tobacco companies to pay me back for all the cigarettes that I didn't intend to smoke…I'd be rich like them and their lawyers.

If you'll notice, the title is "How to Stop Smoking"…not…"How I Quit Smoking." Even now, I'm smoking like a chimney. But these cigarettes must be better for me, they're lights. And besides, what's so bad about smoking anyway? Who's done more research on smoking than those good people at the Tobacco Institute have? If it were that harmful, surely they or our representatives in government would've caught it right off and shown concern for our health, many years ago. What's the price of honesty? Can we trust no one but ourselves anymore?

Excuse me. Let me take a deep breath…While I still can.

Anyway, I've tried all kinds of methods to quit and they all work…For awhile. The bottom line is, I crave nicotine…I'm an addict! I guess I had the best luck with Zyban, because with that, I stayed off of that wonderful, nasty weed for more than six months. When I started using Zyban to stop smoking, except for my family, I didn't broadcast it much...I just kept it to myself. However, if somebody brought the subject up, I'd tell them the truth...Except for Darryl.

This little upcoming story will tell you how to stop smoking. I'm not going to try it, but if you're game...Go for it!

Although all evidence pointed to the contrary, for some unknown reason, Darryl still believed what I told him. I'd been off tobacco for about four months now and most of my buddies already knew about the Zyban. It was the beginning of the evening shift and the Charlotte Office was crowded. Darryl Key, a heavy smoker, walked in.

> "Bryan, have you quit smoking?" he asked me.
>
> "Yep," I casually said.
>
> "You used to smoke like a blown motor," he continued. "How'd you do it?"
>
> "Darryl," I replied, "I've tried everything in this world to kick the habit. I've tried patches, chewing gums, hypnosis and about all the prescribed pills, and I've even combined the different strategies. I've tried everything and nothing worked til now. Finally, I've found something that works. It's not expensive and I'm still keeping the nicotine level up there pretty good. I use up about one cheap cigar a week...I use it as a suppository."

Darryl looked me dead in the eye...I didn't flinch. Then he looked around at everybody else...They all gave solemn nods of agreement. He slowly rambled out of the Office, shaking his head. We held it until we heard him crank his car and open up his four-barrel. Then came the explosion of laughter.

It's probably as good a solution as any other, but especially since that chair incident, I just haven't had the gall to try it.

Special Ingredient

The fields and woods at the northeast corner of Harris Blvd and Tryon Street were being cleared. Soon, it would all be developed into the commercial properties that are now known as University Place. The Developer had given Ralph and I any and all of the trees we wanted…If we would just get them out of there. Since we both used firewood to heat our homes and we were both off on the same days, we decided to get what we could.

So, we set out fairly early. All morning long we slaved away with our chainsaws, cutting up trees and throwing the wood into the back of my old pickup. We'd made several trips back and forth, loading and unloading. Around 11'oclock, we'd gone about as long as we could without eating, so we headed for our old hang-out at the bottom of the hill…The Park Drive-In.

We were much too filthy to go inside, so through the drive-in speakerphone we made our order. I ordered up a couple of hot dogs and Ralph got two hamburgers. In a few minutes, they arrived and we began woofing them down. After wiping out the first hot dog, I rolled the paper off the second one and noticed a large cockroach…Gazing up at me from the chili.

Without saying a word, I gently removed him, laid him over to the side and then continued eating my hot dog. Apparently, Ralph had noticed this too.

> "Bryan Gregory," he said. *"How in the hell can you do that! How can you keep eating after finding that damn cockroach?"*

> "Ralph," I calmly replied, *"it's really no big deal at all. At least I found mine, where's yours?"*

With that, Ralph threw down his remaining hamburger and jumped out of the truck. I don't know what he was doing, but he stayed outside, bent over, for a pretty good while.

Maybe Levi knows.

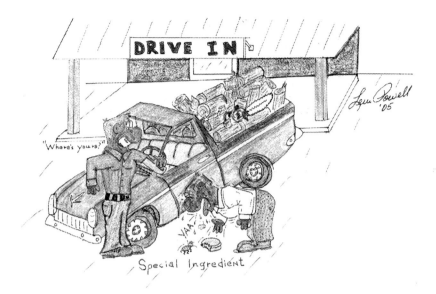

A little dirt, grease or foreign objects won't kill you. They just help keep your immune system strong.

Never There

How many times have you asked yourself…*"Where are the Police when I really need them?"* Then you'll angrily say to yourself…*"I'll bet they're out drinking coffee or taking a break somewhere!"* Well, I just want you to know that I've been in that same situation also. There have been times when I've needed the Police too and they didn't show. You might as well take the load off. I'm going to tell you my story. Here we go.

Dusk had just arrived and I was off-duty. My wife and I, and our two small boys, were riding around in our car. I don't remember exactly how we ended up there, but there we sat…In the parking lot of a large discount fabric store. It would just be a short visit, my wife promised. She would only be in there for a minute, she said, and then she'd come right back out.

"Do any of you want to come in with me?" she politely asked.

The three of us had no interest in fabric…So while she got out and began walking, we prepared ourselves for the long wait in the car.

As we watched her walk into the store, I glanced around the parking lot. There, not too far away from us, was a man changing a flat tire. He seemed to be handling it pretty well on his own, and I wasn't going to leave the children to go help a grown man. So he continued doing his thing out there, while the boys and I goofed off in the car.

After a few minutes, I glanced in his direction again. Something didn't seem quite right over there…He had now moved on to another tire. So I cranked our car and drove around closer to him, and when we were about ten feet apart, I stuck my head out of the window.

"Hey fellow," I called out. *"Do you need some help over there?"*

His English was not very good and I didn't speak Spanish. From the feverish rate at which he was working, and from the way that he was ignoring me…I felt that he really didn't want me anywhere around. I told the boys to remain in the car and I got out and then walked the few steps to where he was.

> "*Hey fellow,*" again I addressed him, "*I see lots of lug nuts laying around, but if you're going to rotate your tires out here in the parking lot, you're not going to have much luck without a jack…Especially in the dark. Now what in the hell are you doing out here anyhow?*"

By now he had almost removed all of the lug nuts from the passenger side of the car. He had no flashlight and lug nuts were scattered everywhere, and it appeared obvious to me that he had no intention of putting them back on.

He spoke very nervously and I couldn't understand much of what he said. But he could obviously understand some of the words that I spoke, because he did let me know that this was not his car at all…But that it belonged to some other unknown person, somewhere…blah, blah, blah

"*Enough of that garbage,*" I thought, "*I'm not sure what is going on here, but whatever it is doesn't look legal at all. Whoever owns this car will certainly not make it very far with lug nuts that are missing from the whole right side of their car.*"

So I pulled out my badge and showed it to him, and then I identified myself to him as an off-duty State Trooper. As I requested some identification from him, his feet began moving…Up he came and he began running! I had halfway expected something like that. I didn't hit him, but in short order, I jumped on top of him and pinned him to the ground. I reached into his hip pocket, got his wallet out and pulled out his driver's license. (*Being off-duty, I didn't have handcuffs with me. And especially with small children around, I never was one to carry a gun*)

> "*Papa,*" our oldest son, Trip, nervously called out, "*why are you holding that man on the ground?*"

Damn, what a dilemma I was in. It looked like, quite possibly, not only might I have a fight on my hands, but I would also have to calm the boys down. For the time being though, I had control. In as peaceful of a voice as I could muster, I spoke to my oldest son.

> "*Don't worry, Son…Everything will be just fine. Just go find your Mama and bring her back out here.*"

Then our youngest son, David, who had just learned to talk, piped in.

> "Papa! I'm scared and I want to go home!"

For their sake, I tried not to make a big deal out of it...But in short order, Trip had gone inside and brought his Mother back out.

> "Honey," I said to her, as she stood there with a look of shock on her face, "Go back inside and see if you can find out who owns this car. I'm not sure what this jerk is doing, but this car isn't his, and look on the ground...There are lug nuts everywhere. And while you're in there, call 911 too, and get the Charlotte City Police Department out here right away."

She quickly made her way back to the store. Now the fellow I was dealing became much more nervous. I still had the upper hand, but he was getting much harder to handle. It may have been ten minutes, but before long, she came back again. She said that she had called 911 and that the Police were on the way, and that she had looked all over the store, but that nobody knew who owned that car.

Finally, while I still had a hold on him, I let that man get up on his feet. While I still had him somewhat restrained, I gave her his driver's license and had her write down his information and name. Still, he was not forthcoming with information that would explain his taking those lug nuts off. He was becoming even more high-strung now...He really wanted to leave and I didn't want him to go anywhere. Dealing with him became much harder now, so I wrestled him back down to the ground. This tussle went on, and on, and on.

While we a waited for the Police to arrive, she went back inside and called 911 again. Yes, they were on the way, she was told, and it would only be a few more minutes more before they got there. Again she looked for the owner of that car with no luck at all. More time passed and I began to think more about the situation I was in.

The boys were very quiet now, but surely, after watching their Papa in this long wresting match, they were petrified. Barbara held her composure well, but surely, she also was terrified. I had all the information on this fellow that I was holding down. His driver's license was valid on its face...It had been issued fairly recently and his address looked pretty good. What I mean to say is that I felt that he could be located at some later date. Now, at least twenty minutes had passed since they were last called, and still...The City Police had not arrived. All in all, it had been more than a half an hour since 911 had first been called. *"Had that car with the lug nuts removed, just been abandoned there,"* I wondered, *"and was this really a crime that had been committed here, or what?"*

Finally, I'd had enough of waiting for the Police to show and I became doubtful of my role there…So I let him go. Off into the darkness he ran. Sure enough, it was almost as soon as he vanished that the Charlotte Police showed up. And yes, shortly after that, we found the owner of the car.

The girl who owned it worked in the fabric store. During the two times that my wife had tried to find her, she had been busy elsewhere…Taking out the trash. And what brought all of this on?…You ask?

Well, the young woman had just ended an affair with the fellow who was messing with her car. She had gone back to her husband now and had tried to dump him, but he would not hear of that. It was too late for him…He was in love and he wasn't taking this breaking up business very well. In the past month or so, on several occasions, he had vandalized her car. Once, while her car was parked at her house and she and her husband were inside, he had even broken out her windshield with a baseball bat!

I checked on her and her husband quite frequently after that, and as far as I know, neither of them ever saw that jerk again. I'm not sure where this story ends, but I can tell you this…I spent many hours when I was working, trying to serve warrants on that Spanish-speaking fellow. Even to this day, I don't know where he is. As far as I know, no one has ever seen him since. He's probably now living somewhere down in Mexico.

I do know this. As you may have felt before, when I needed them most…The Police didn't show.

Weak Bladder

I've got to spend a little time setting this one up, because it's the first of more to follow. So bear with me for a minute.

Back in the mid eighties, our leaders in government decided to investigate the possibilities of placing a nuclear waste dump in a rural area of North Carolina known as the Sandhills, and near the town…Hamlet.

Normally, the local folks were easy going, and by no means, was this the wealthiest part of the state. Many of them felt that they were being taken advantage of, because they didn't have a large voter base. On the other side, the whole State of North Carolina had a problem…How would we handle our nuclear byproducts and waste?

Finding a suitable location was a must! Scientists, Geologists and Core Drillers were called in to determine the compatibility of the earth crust. Surveyors operated in teams to plot and document every inch. Biologists, Botanists and Bird-Watchers were on hand to evaluate possible impacts on nature. This was a major undertaking and not taken lightly by anyone, especially the local population. They were upset!

The Protestors protested and the Newscasters came.

A Command Post was set up on about two acres. It was surrounded by rolls of barbed wire atop a chain link fence…To protect the personnel, equipment, mobile office units and portable toilets that were inside.

The Governor ordered the Highway Patrol to provide security, so that's exactly what we did…Troopers from surrounding areas were pulled in and assigned this duty for a week at a time. I ended up going there three times. Instead of our regular uniforms, we wore black jumpsuits and ball caps. We would line up in our 4x4's, normally Blazer's, two Troopers per vehicle and outside of the main gate. Whenever a Team went out, one of our units would escort and stay with them.

The demonstrations began peacefully and were well organized…But before long, acts of vandalism began to occur. *(For example…Roofing nails scattered on roadways and boards with long nails sticking through them, buried in the sandy paths used by the unwelcome vehicles)* Most natives didn't want a dump like this in their back yard, but they needed work!...So some took positions as Security Guards.

Those who took this employment found themselves in a dilemma. Whose side were they on?...Possible government take-over, or their friends, neighbors and even relatives? These Security Guards normally escorted only one person at a time...Usually a Supervisor from inside the compound who needed to go out and quickly check a site. We Troopers could hear their radio traffic, but they couldn't hear ours. At even the slightest suspicion of trouble, they'd back off and call in the Big Dogs. You guessed it! They called for us...The North Carolina State Highway Patrol.

This story is about one of those native Security Guards. He was good-natured and he was a nervous, wormy fellow. Like the rest, he stayed inside the compound until he was needed. Whenever one of the Wheels needed to go out and check something, he was right there. He would jump into one of those vehicles, normally a Suburban, and take them anywhere. The bigger the Wheel, the quicker he was. We called him "Flash."

From outside the fence, we Troopers could see well what went on in there. We noticed that as soon as he'd come back from a run, he'd head for the closest portable toilet...It was always the same one. Obviously, he was too scared to relieve himself out there in the woods, like the rest of us. He was too tense! There's no telling who could be hiding out there. They had calmed down a lot now, but in his mind, there were Protestors, Protestors...Everywhere! He wasn't about to take a leak in the bushes! Yes, he had a problem...And he also had a very weak bladder!

I was prepared. Knowing that we'd be there for a week, I brought along supplies. In my arsenal were stink bombs in small glass ampoules *(ammonium sulfide...No smoke, just stink!)* and string-pull party poppers.

The sewage truck came, emptied the toilets and then left.

While he was inside the main building and in the air-conditioning, I walked over to his vehicle and carefully placed one of these stink bombs under his gas pedal. Upon cranking and hitting the gas pedal, that thing should break.

It wasn't long. Soon, he came quickly out of the building and jumped into his Suburban. He and the Big Wheel took off.

They made it about ¼ mile…It must've taken that long for the smell to seep out. Suddenly, they slammed on brakes and the doors flew open! We laughed and watched as he jumped out and began fanning his hat! Big Wheel came out also…Just waving that passenger door back and forth. Shortly thereafter, we could hear Flash on his radio, as he called one of the other Security Guards.

> *"I don't know what's happening out here!"* he excitedly stated. *"Have you seen that sewage truck? It smells like he dumped his whole load in here!"*

After the odor finally died down, they got back in…And then continued their ½-hour run. I waited until they got out of sight, then took one of those string-pull party poppers and rigged it up to the toilet door that he normally used. When the next person opened that door, it would go off. Before long, they came back.

He jumped out of his Suburban and ran straight for the toilet. Obviously, he was under great stress. This time it was an emergency…There was no time to waste! He grabbed the handle and pulled.

> *"BAM!"* it went off!

He paused for a few seconds and then ever so slowly, he turned and started walking towards us. As he got closer, we could plainly see. His pants were wet from his crotch to his knees…That weak bladder, you know.

> *"Fellas,"* with confusion, he stated, *"I don't know what's going on here, but some mighty strange things are happening today!"*

Of course we laughed, even to his face!

The word got out! From then on, every week that a new crowd of Troopers came in, he would ask…

> *"Did that damn Bryan Gregory come back with ya'll this week?"*

The Best Shot

Although I've had a lot of training in the use of weapons, I've never developed an obsession for firearms. On a regular basis, all Patrol personnel were required to receive training at various firing ranges and maintain an acceptable level of proficiency in the use of issued weaponry. Other than this required training, that was it for me. As some would do, I didn't spend much of my own time and money to further develop my shooting skills. As a result, I couldn't stay on the porch with the big dogs, but I could always hold my own with the rest of the pack.

Steve Dredge was about as good of a shot as I was, and we began harassing each other about who was the best shot. We didn't hide it. Everybody knew about it. We started betting! Whoever had the best score won ten dollars from the loser. These bets continued for years. Most of the time I'd walk away with his money, but once in awhile, he'd take me. That's what had happened the last time we'd shot…He'd embarrassed me! In front of everybody, he had taken my money and then crowed about it. I got the feeling that he was sneaking off somewhere and practicing, but I remained steadfast and strong…I didn't. I relied more on my psychological skills.

The day arrived for us to go to the firing range again. The weather was nice and I was in a particularly rambunctious mood. Instead of practicing, I'd been doing some thinking. This time I had a special surprise for him. This time I had the edge. This time I had wrapped the handle of my pistol with white adhesive tape, for no other reason than to just blow his mind.

When we arrived at the range I never even mentioned it, but my goodness, who could ignore it…It stuck out like a sore thumb! Sure enough, it finally got the best of him and he walked over.

"Bryan, what in the hell have you got on your gun," he asked.

"It's nothing," I lied as I replied, "it's just something that I read in a shooting magazine to improve the grip, and I thought I'd give it a try."

We had a few minutes before training began and I laughed as I watched him running around, trying to find someone who might have some adhesive tape in his trunk. Low and behold, he found some! Now, in his mind, I didn't have the edge anymore…Because we both now had tape on our guns. The practice session began.

From the seven-yard line, we fired the rapid-fire rounds. As we picked up the empty shells from the ground and threw them in the buckets, we looked. I'd thrown a couple of mine into the white. *(That means…No points! You missed the target! You just screwed up! You idiot!)* Before everybody, Steve laughed at me. He rubbed it in and hurt my feelings! We continued shooting at increasing distances and positions until we'd shot up fifty rounds. Steve had beaten me…But for betting purposes, the practice didn't count. We began to make preparations for the upcoming qualifying round…The money round.

This was big money, ten dollars! And not only that, but our reputations were at stake…We'd been running our mouths! Everybody was watching us. While we waited for our turn to shoot, I did some relaxation exercises and some deep breathing. Then, more importantly, I made some arrangements with Ralph Smeth. Ralph agreed to take the lane to the right of Steve while I took the left. I had it in the bag…Steve would not take my ten dollars this time!

The firing commenced. After we'd emptied our weapons from the seven-yard line, I shielded my eyes with my hand and peered at Steve's target.

> *"What's that on your target,"* I asked. *"Looks to me like you've got a fly on your target, Steve."*

Steve just stood there with a flabbergasted look on his face. There's no way he could've thrown it in the white, because after all, he'd been practicing…Surely, his aim was better than that. We walked to the targets. Sure enough, way out in the white of his target was a wild bullet hole. Steve knew I didn't do it…He'd been keeping a close eye on me. He didn't know it, but Ralph had put it there.

From then on, my shooting got better and Steve's got worse. Every once in awhile, another "fly" showed up on his target. Every once in awhile, another wild shot appeared. He'd lost his confidence, but that was OK…I had enough for the two of us anyway.

After we finished blasting away from the fifty-yard line, we walked down to our targets again. Steve counted up all the holes in his. Damn, there were fifty-three holes in there…Where'd the extra three come from? Then he walked over and checked out my target. Yep, mine was OK. Mine had fifty holes in it, with all in the black. When the instructor came around to validate the scores, Ralph told him...

> "Oops! For those three shots, I must've accidentally shot Steve's target instead of mine."

Even with those three rounds not counted against him, I still beat him. Steve demanded a re-match, but that didn't go far...After all, we'd both qualified. His score was just lower than mine.

Yes, once again, I could hold my head up. Once again, I could rest easy at night. Once again, my reputation was intact, even if his was not. Once again, I was ten dollars richer. Once again, I could proudly say...I was the best shot.

Lying Eyes

For most of us, when we realize that our perception of something is wrong, it tends to remind us of our humanity...And we just accept that reality and go on. For Police Officers, this is especially difficult, because we are trained to trust our own instincts and judgment. When working alone, we have to reply on ourselves. We have to make instant and correct decisions. We have to depend on our senses. We have to believe what we see.

It was so nice outside. It was approaching the middle of the day. I was second in line at the red light on this country road. I had my arm out the window as I laughed at the John Boy & Billy Show on my commercial radio.

An older beat-up truck approached from the road to the left and made a left turn in front of us. Would you look at that! A beer can came flying out of the passenger window...But there was only one occupant, the driver. I thought it rather strange, but I'd seen it done before. I'd seen drivers sling trash out through an open passenger window before.

For the past few years, I'd seen that truck many times. The man who drove it was well thought of and was up in his seventies now. He owned and operated a small construction company. He specialized in heavy equipment. With his Bulldozer and Road Grader, he'd clear off the land and lay off the streets before the Developers came in. He lived about two miles from me and I did know his name was Mr. Potter, but I didn't know him well.

I turned on my blue light and he pulled over. When I walked up and told him why I'd stopped him, for littering...He denied it. That didn't surprise me much. A lot of people did that. He said he'd drank a beer at a friend's house about fifteen minutes earlier, but that he certainly had not thrown a can out of his window. I knew what I saw! I wrote him a ticket.

After finishing the ticket, I gave it to him. For sixty-five dollars, he could pay it off.

> "Trooper, I think I know what you saw," he then said. "I just left a friend's house and several of us were standing around drinking a beer. Now I remember! One of em put his beer up on the right rail of the bed of my truck, near the cab. He must've left it there. When I made that left turn, it must've fallen off. Could that be what you saw?"

Immediately, I knew I was wrong. The can that I'd seen sailing through the air was spilling beer everywhere, and come to think of it, I didn't think Mr. Potter would waste good beer like that. I told him that I couldn't tear up the ticket or void it out…There was too much red tape. Our tickets were numbered and each one had to be accounted for. As Troopers, we just didn't do that.

> *"If you'll come to Court on the court date I set,"* I said, *"I'll admit my mistake before the District Attorney, and the Judge if necessary. It'll be inconvenient for you, but that's all I can do. That should take care of that."*

That day came. He didn't show. When I checked the records, I was in for a surprise…He'd already paid it off! The very next day I stopped by his house and asked him why he didn't take it to Court.

> *"The money's no big deal to me,"* he said. *"Besides, I've screwed up before and didn't get caught."*

Several weeks passed. I was off-duty and slaving away, clearing some of the trees out around the new log house we were building. The Brick Mason was in the process of laying our foundation. Down the long path to our work site, I heard someone coming. Soon, an unexpected visitor arrived. It was Mr. Potter in that same old pickup, and behind it, he was pulling a large front-end loader on a trailer. It was a New Holland. I walked out and greeted him.

> *"Can you use this,"* he asked.

> *"If I knew how to operate it, I could,"* I replied, *"but I've never been on one of those things before."*

He was a man of few words. He said he didn't need it right away.

> *"I'd much rather you use it,"* he said, *"than to just let it sit at my house gathering rust."*

He backed it off the trailer, gave me about five minutes of instruction and then left. I could tell that the Brick Mason I'd hired was nervous. As I scooted that thing around the foundation he was building, I assured him that if I tore up his work, I'd pay him extra to repair it. Soon, I got pretty good at operating that thing. When I was off-duty, sometimes, I'd operate that machine day and night. For more than a month, I kept that New Holland. Once, I dug myself into a hole that was so deep that I couldn't get out. Mr. Potter came when I called him.

> *"It ain't no big deal,"* he laughed when he said. *"Just quit spinning your wheels and use the bucket to push yourself out."*

Sure enough, it worked.

Every once in awhile, I'd spin off a tire and have to go have it blown up again. Every few days, Mr. Potter stopped by. I refueled it once, but Mr. Potter got mad.

> *"I've got a tank of fuel on the back of my truck,"* he said, *"and a large tank of fuel at home. Save your money. When it needs it…I'll put it in."*

There's no telling how many thousands of dollars I saved by having the use of his piece of equipment. Mr. Potter was rare. He could very well have held a grudge and become an enemy, but instead…He decided to be my friend. He is just one of the many friends that I've had, and more folks have helped me out than I can put in this book. I've used him as an example to simply show you, that from thin air and even false perceptions, good things can arise.

And I may have never known him, had it not been for my lying eyes.

Wired

We all do it. When we meet a State Trooper on the highway, we keep watching our rearview mirror until he's out of sight...Just to see if his brake lights come on, and if we're caught.

I'd never seen another Trooper do it, but I'd heard of it being done...I rigged up a hidden toggle switch panel that I used to cut off those damn brake lights. And something else, I could turn off one headlight too. This panel was within easy reach under the dash and over the gas pedal. As I sat in my car, it was just above my right knee.

Boy, I had some fun with those switches. Especially after dark, I blew a lot of people's minds. Countless were the times that I'd meet a car at night, then after passing him, I'd hit the brake light cut-off switch and cut off one headlight. Then, I'd slam on brakes and boot-leg that Patrol Car around. After I got turned around, I'd just lie back there behind for awhile...To give the motorist a chance to make a complete ass of himself. If he did, right before I stopped him, I'd turn both headlights back on. They were always surprised.

> "*Officer, I didn't see you,*" they would generally say. "*Where in the world did you come from?*"

Sometimes, they'd ask me...

> "*Officer, did you know you have a headlight out?*"

I'd turn around and look at my car.

> "*To me, they both look OK,*" I'd then say, "*are you sure you haven't been drinking too much to be driving today?*"

Having these switches was something I couldn't brag about, so only a few trusted friends knew. We weren't supposed to modify our Patrol Cars...I could've been fired for doing that! I even knew of a Trooper who lost his job because he'd tampered with his catalytic converter, and I surely didn't want to meet that fate. Especially when I took my car to the Patrol Garage for maintenance, I had to be careful...I always double-checked to make sure they were in the "On" position. For years, I kept those switches. From old Patrol Cars to the new ones, I moved them. Then it happened.

I had transmission trouble. My Patrol Car had to be towed to Salisbury. And yes, I double-checked to make sure the switches were "On." When he came to pick mine up, the Patrol Mechanic brought me a spare car so I'd have something to drive. Two days later, I received word from the Dispatcher that my car was ready and to come to Salisbury, at my convenience, to pick it up. I wanted my car and my switches back as soon as possible, so I did just that.

When I arrived, the lanky, long-legged Mechanic who had worked on my car met me and commenced to chew me out. My beloved toggle switches were now gone and he had a few words to say about that.

> *"When I first got into your car, my knee must've hit your switches…But I didn't know. I didn't see em!"* He continued. *"Fixing your transmission was easy, but your car was about due for inspection so I did that too. All was going well until I got to the headlights. There was one out, so I replaced it. That didn't help, so I put in another."* He was getting hotter as he kept going. *"I have you know, Bryan, that I went through three light bulbs before I smelled a rat."* By now, he'd really worked himself into a sweat. *"I started looking around and noticed a strange wire to the headlight that wasn't supposed to be there, so I gave it a jerk. I just kept pulling on it until I got all your mess out of there."* Then he topped it all off with…*"I should've turned you in but I didn't. You owe me!…You Devil."*

From then on, I bore gifts when I stopped by the Garage. I missed those switches, but I survived. Never again did I go to work…Wired.

Mistaken Identity

In the middle of a Spring day, I was driving along on I85 South near Woodlawn Road, when I noticed there was no traffic meeting me…So I sped up to find the root of the problem. About a mile down the road, I found that a one-car accident had just occurred and that the vehicle had come to rest in the median, under the overpass of Nations Ford Road. I turned on my blue light and stopped nearby. The only occupant was still sitting under the steering wheel and appeared somewhat dazed. The car didn't have much damage, but the right side looked like it had sideswiped the guardrail, after which it had simply spun out in the median. I ran to it.

Without my hat on, I opened the driver's door, leaned into the car and placed my hand on the young man's shoulder. He was starring straight ahead, but didn't appear to be hurt…He was just sitting there. With a soft voice, I introduced myself.

"*Hey fella,*" I then asked, "*Are you OK?*"

He turned and looked at me and an expression of relief swept over his face. He gazed up at me with a look of great love in his eyes. *(It wasn't as if he was physically attracted to me or anything like that. It was like that look that a puppy gives you…When you've been gone for awhile and just come back)* Still, it did make me feel somewhat uncomfortable. Then came the shock!

"*Are you God?*" he respectfully asked.

Well, I'd seen and heard all kinds of things, but I wasn't ready for that…I'd never had an impact on anybody like that! Except for all of us being made in God's image, and having grayish hair…That's about as close as I got.

"*This is the Second Coming, isn't it?*" he continued.

"*No, I don't think so,*" I replied. "*I'm Trooper Gregory of the Highway Patrol, but I may be as close as you get to God today,*" I then said.

He would not hear of that, but kept insisting that I was God. I know what you're thinking…But there was no odor of alcohol anywhere. But he had to be high on something…I just didn't know what. He had no obvious injuries, but I checked his vital signs and soothingly coached him from his car.

"*What have you been taking,*" I asked him. "*You seem kinda rattled.*"

With that question, he changed his tune. He must've figured out that I was not who he had originally thought.

"*You're not God!*" he became belligerent now, "*Where is God? I want God back!*"

He became very nervous and he kept looking for, and asking for…God. He would not respond to any other topics at all. I advised him of his rights, told him he was under arrest for Driving while Under the Influence of an Impairing Substance, searched him and then the inside of his car, and handcuffed him.

"*What did you do that for,*" he nervously asked.

He didn't remember anything I'd just told him, and now, he was starting to hyperventilate. I figured he would be easier to handle in his previous state of mind, so I decided to go back to that. I didn't make any claims to be omnipotent…But I began to speak in a way that he understood.

"*Son,*" I slowly began, "*you're gonna see some beautiful sights, but you're on probation. You can look all you want, but you're not allowed to touch anything. That's the reason for these handcuffs.*"

That did the trick…He calmed down a lot. And here came that puppy-dog look again. God was back!

I led him back to my car and sat him down on the passenger side, seat-belted him in and then walked around to my side and got in. I wanted information.

"*Son,*" I forcefully said, "*I want to know what sins you've been committing.*"

I knew I was stooping pretty low, but I figured it was legal…So I did it anyway. With this line of questioning he really opened up. He gave me even more than I'd bargained for…He wouldn't shut up!

> "*I stole three bottles of Robitusin from a Drug Store this morning,*" he started out, "*and then I drank that.*"

He went into great detail about the what's, when's, and why's. He told me about his girlfriend leaving him because he was an alcoholic. He even told me about how the Devil had just been chasing him, down the highway.

> "*I was getting pretty high, and right before coming to Heaven, I smoked some reefer. I've still got some in my car,*" he continued. "*And then, just when the Devil was about to catch me, you rescued me! Thank you, God!*"

I told him where I was going, left, walked to his car and checked it again…It was clean! There was no marijuana in there! Then I came back and sat down.

> "*Son, I couldn't find any marijuana in there. Where did you put it?*"

> "*Oh, the rest is under the boot to the gearshift,*" he quickly replied. "*I hid it pretty good, didn't I God?*"

I went back up and checked again. Sure enough, it was right where he said.

The wrecker arrived and pulled his car away. He and I left for the Hospital and I had his blood sample drawn. Throughout all of this, he kept those puppy-dog eyes and continually called me God. He became uncomfortable and even combatant, if I was not within sight. At the Hospital, I took his handcuffs off and it got to be a joke.

They were swamped with patients in the Emergency Room and then, even more came in.

> "*Oh God,*" in desperation, one of the Doctors said.

> "*Just a minute, I'll go get him,*" one of the Nurses jokingly replied. Then she came and got me.

His blood sample indicated high levels of an intoxicating ingredient of Robitussin, and after leaving the Hospital, I took him to Jail. About a month later, the Court date came.

He was sitting in the back of the Courtroom when I walked in. As I did with most defendants, I walked back and greeted him. He was sober now and he didn't call me God, but when he first looked at me, there they were…He still had those puppy-dog eyes.

Before long, his lawyer approached me.

> *"Trooper Gregory, it doesn't look like you have much of a case here,"* he told me, *"I think you should just go ahead and let the District Attorney dismiss this case."*

I told him the story I've just told you, and told him if I got on the stand…That's what he could expect the Judge and everybody else to hear. He backed down. He and his defendant decided they didn't want the Court to hear my testimony. And since there were News Reporters in the Courtroom, maybe they decided they didn't want to be on the six o'clock News. They pled guilty and threw the towel in.

Once in a long while, someone will stop me…*"Hey, you look like a movie star,"* they'll say. Sometimes, they'll even mention someone famous, by name. Some resemblance may have been there, but I certainly wasn't mistaken for them. To be mistaken for God, I wasn't prepared for and didn't expect. But for the short time that it lasted, I must admit…It felt Great!

Snoot Full

Dispatchers don't normally joke around much…They just can't. They can't afford to make even the smallest mistake…Lives are on the line with each word that they say. The communications they deal with are formal in nature. They work in a confined area and have a Supervisor breathing down their necks all day, so their work his highly stressful. They often listen to others having fun, but seldom can they participate. Our Dispatchers heard of the pranks we Troopers pulled on each other, but they maintained a businesslike atmosphere. They rarely got many laughs of their own…But with Perry, it was different.

I'd known him for years. From his strict job he received pleasure. I watched him once when I stopped by, as he was calling a Trooper on the radio. He used all kinds of vivid profanity in a long statement…And it scared me! To me, it sounded like he was graphically chewing that Trooper out, but he'd key his mike at just the right times and all of that bad language was left out…The Trooper only heard the important parts. I was impressed…Perry always sounded so important on that Radio. He had one weakness though. He enjoyed having fun and he took pleasure in dishing it out, but when it came his turn to take it…Well, he had great difficulty with that.

He knew me! He was well aware of all the crap that I'd pulled and since he controlled my life-line, I had never even thought of messing with him. Then one day, after we'd been laughing at a prank I'd just pulled, he made a severe mistake…He threatened me.

> "Bryan! You SOB!" he laughed when he said, and then he became more serious. "*You can mess with everyone else, but you'd better lay off on me!*"

I didn't say much, but his words hurt my pride and my feelings, and I wasn't about to tolerate that. I didn't plot and I didn't scheme, but I just made sure that I had my supplies ready…Surely, judgment day would arrive soon.

Maybe a month later, that day came. I had to return a spare car and pick up my issued one, so I stopped by the Dispatchers Office to sign in on the log. What good fortune!…Three good-looking girls were working there.

That must've been part of their screening process. Females must've had to be pretty to get on, because it sure seemed to work out that way. Anyway, I was trying to impress them with some funny stories of mine…It was working too! We were all laughing and having a big time. Then, they began telling me about how dull it was around there.

> *"We hear all kinds of interesting things on the Radio,"* one of them timidly said, *"but nothing much ever happens around here."*

> *"We can't have that,"* with great confidence, I said.

I began looking around and the locker area caught my eye. Each Dispatcher was assigned a separate locker and had a key. These lockers were about head high for a short person and the doors were about 12" by 12" in size. When the Dispatchers first came to work, they'd place their personal items in there. Since I already had experience in opening locked entries, in wiring up doors with poppers of various kinds and I had an array of supplies in my car…*"Wait just a minute,"* I thought, *"Perry's locker is in a good location, he's a short person, he could stand some education and besides…He's not here!"*

After a short question and answer period, I found that he'd be off for a couple of days. So without saying much else, I went to work. The girls expressed some concern when I jimmied open his door, but that changed to nervous snickers when I wired up a party popper that shoots out ribbon everywhere. By the time that I'd finished and closed the door, they were laughing and giggling with anticipation.

> *"This is going to be fun!"* one of them said.

This little trick of mine had made their day. Before leaving, I swore them to secrecy.

> *"Don't tell a soul,"* I warned them, *"it's gonna be hard, but you'll have to keep your mouths shut! If you're here when he opens that door at shift change…You've got to play dumb!"* I went on, *"if he starts' accusing you, don't worry. I'm not going to let you get into trouble for this, and if he starts causing you grief, don't worry…I'll take the heat."*

All was said and done now. The stage was set. I left.

Several days passed and I began to worry. Not one peep had I heard and I wasn't about to call there. I was off-duty and at home, and just when I was expecting it the least...That's when the telephone rang. It was Perry. He was mad!

> *"You did it! I know you did! I saw your name on the log and I know you were here. I just want you to know that when that thing went off, a piece of plastic flew out and cut my lip!"*

He tempered this statement with a great deal of profanity and I played dumb. The less I responded the hotter he became. He kept right on going...

> *"I'm gonna turn this over to the SBI (State Bureau of Investigation) and let them get to the bottom of this. I've saved everything for them to fingerprint, too."* I know who was dispatching when you were here. They had to see! If you didn't do it...Damn it, they know who did!*

After I got off the phone with him, I called one of the girls a home and she filled me in. She said that it happened at shift change. About a dozen other Dispatchers were milling around and she had forgotten all about Perry's box being wired. He was a little late and he was in a hurry. In a mad dash, Perry came running in.

> *"When he opened the door and that thing went off,"* she said, *"one fellow fell to the floor, because he just knew we were being shot at!"* She elaborated more, *"Another girl and I where the first ones to laugh, then everybody else, except Perry, joined in. That was the most fun we've had up here in years!"*

> *"Was his lip cut bad,"* I asked.

> *"I don't think so,"* she responded, *"I didn't see any blood, but he was really mad!"*

I began to feel somewhat better now, knowing that he hadn't been hurt bad. She also told me that he was pumping them all for information, but nobody was talking.

After getting off the phone with her, I waited until the next day and then called her again. The fire was getting hotter! Perry was becoming more angry and threatening now...But still, those girls weren't talking. They were doing just as they'd promised me. They were keeping quiet and I loved them for that. When I got off the phone with her this time, I called Perry. He was working.

> *"Leave those girls alone, Perry,"* I said, *"I'm the one who wired your box up and they didn't have anything to do with it. It was all me and nobody else. So if you're going to be mad at someone, dish it out to me…I can take it."*
>
> *"I knew it! You SOB!"* he said, *"I knew it all along, and believe you me…You'll pay!"*

After that, whenever he and I were working, he'd often send me off on a wild goose chase. He'd give me instructions to go way off yonder somewhere and when I arrived, there would be nothing there. For years, he paid me back…Even until I retired. But I didn't mind…I always kept gas in my car. Without complaining, I took my medicine. If that was as bad as it got…I figured I could handle that.

Perry was always touchy about that nose full of ribbon, and when he was around, nobody mentioned it…He could be vindictive when he thought he'd been had. Even now, I'm protecting myself by not using his real name.

Maybe he'll get a laugh now and not feel so bad.

Insignificant Job

Those who work in Convenience Stores have a dangerous job. I considered it even more dangerous than mine, because at least I'd been trained to defend myself and legally carried a gun. These folks are like sitting ducks for all the weirdo's who come by, especially during the wee hours of the morning. It really wasn't part of my job description, but I made it a point to stop by these places and periodically check on these people, especially if they were working by themselves.

This particular Clerk worked the third shift in a small Convenience Store. It was off the beaten path and near a large residential section. It just so happens that she was an attractive young blond-headed girl. Now wait just a minute! I didn't have anything going on with her…I was a happily married man. But I must admit, she sure was easy to look at.

She confided to me that she wanted a better job. She didn't want to work the late shift and she didn't like working alone…But she had to do something! That's all she could find. She had bills to pay. She asked me to please come by and check on her, because she had apprehensions…Sometimes, she was afraid. You could certainly put your money on it…I'd go out of my way to come by and check on her when I was working late.

When I'd drop in, if some jerk was hanging around who she didn't feel comfortable about, she'd give me a nod, and I'd stick around until he left. Then I'd stay for a few minutes more, until she began to feel comfortable again. Sometimes, if business was slow for me, I'd come by two or three times a night. This went on for three or four months. She appreciated it, and I enjoyed seeing her too. Seeing her sure was refreshing, and she gave my eyes plenty of exercise.

I'd been off for two days and when I came back to work, I stopped by to see her again…But the store was closed! There was yellow "Crime Scene" tape everywhere! Later that night, I got up with a local Police Officer and here's what I found out.

During my days off, she'd been dragged off into the woods behind the store and then raped and murdered. I felt so devastated! If only I'd been working, maybe I could've prevented it…Maybe I would've been there.

Although her job was a small one, her life was precious too. I loved her because she was a Human Being, just like me and you.

The Trooper Bowl

Some people are just better off left alone. In a way, my relationship with Jim Klutz was like that. Since Jim was so much older and slower than I was, and I knew he wouldn't be much of a challenge, I more or less left him alone. Besides, he was not a brown-noser and I had more respect for him than I did for some other Troopers.

It was Monday. It was the first morning of another week in Hamlet. We lined up the four-wheel drive Blazers outside of the Compound and waited. Soon, the various Teams requiring Escorts would be going out.

Until we were needed, we just milled around. We stayed near our vehicles, but before our turn came up, we'd just wander around and shoot the breeze. Jim was sitting in the driver's seat of his Blazer, reading...And his partner had wandered off somewhere else. I walked back to see him, opened the passenger door and sat down.

We hadn't seen each other for awhile and we began catching up on our gossip. I don't remember exactly what we were talking about, but it was probably about the sorry Supervisors we had. Anyway, we were having a big time. In the distance, we could see a Rookie Trooper slowly heading our way. He looked like he wanted to join in on our conversation. While he was still out of earshot, Jim filled me in about him.

This young Trooper was fresh out of Patrol School and Jim confessed that he had already warned him about me.

> "Watch out for that damn Bryan Gregory," he'd said. "He'll get you!" Then he had pumped him up more with..."*The only way to handle Bryan is to get him first...Before he gets you!*"

This young buck walked up to my side of the Blazer. There were no introductions...Nothing!

> "Boy," I said, "*I'm getting kinda thirsty. Go get me a cup of coffee! Make it light and sweet,*" I added.

Jim just sat there and chuckled.

> "*Yes Sir!*" the Rookie replied, but I detected his tone of sarcasm.

He took off. Before long, he returned with the coffee.

> "*Boy,*" again, I called him, *You've done good! Just keep doing what we older Troopers tell you and you'll go far in this organization. You should be proud of yourself! You're doing exactly as a young Trooper should.*"

Right about now is when I took that first sip of coffee. Halfway suspecting something, I just slightly ran my tongue in first. Damn! It was 90% salt! It almost turned my mouth inside out! I showed surprise, but no anger...As I poured that coffee out.

> "*Boy, I've got to hand it to you,*" I calmly said. "*You sure got me with that! Since you're a Rookie, I'm gonna try to overlook it this time, cause you don't know any better...But believe me! You'll learn!*"

I got a call. I had to leave. Jim stayed behind with the Rookie. Later, I found out that Jim Klutz had scared that young fellow half to death. Bluntly and graphically, he had informed him of the terrible mistake he'd just made.

> "*Boy,*" he had said, "*you don't realize it yet, but you have just messed up!*" (I cleaned this one up...Just a little)

For the next few days, whenever somebody mentioned that salty coffee, I just laughed and shrugged if off...As if it was no big deal. Occasionally, I'd make sure that some of the other Troopers told that Rookie a story or two about some of the previous crap that I'd pulled.

He worried. I planned. He'd hear another story. He worried more. That boy was on pins and needles, and he kept a very respectable distance away from me. He became very quiet and reserved. I let him sweat...And he did!

Time was running out. Thursday came. We'd be spending just one more night at the Holiday Inn together and then Friday, after work, we'd all go our separate ways. I had to put him out of his misery. The time had come to break it off. Now was the time!

For our lodging arrangements, in most cases, two Troopers shared a room. Somehow, by the luck of the draw, Rookie had one to himself. He was all alone.

Since this young buck had shown a lack of respect for older Troopers, I enlisted the help from someone he would…A Line Sergeant. I briefly told this Sergeant what I was up to and asked him for his help.

> *"Just call Rookie on his room phone,"* I requested. *"Invite him over to watch the ball game with you and maybe have a beer or so."* I went on. *"Keeping him occupied is most important, but it would help me a great deal if you'd also watch his diet."* Now I went into more detail. *"Don't give him much to drink, but feed him well,"* I requested. *"Give him all he wants to eat and make sure he gets plenty of fruits and vegetables…You know, stuff that'll keep him regular."*

Sure enough, the good Sergeant obliged. The Sergeant called Rookie and invited him over. In about thirty minutes the ball game would start. Under his instruction, Rookie took off for the store and came back with a load of groceries. The game started. The plan was coming together.

I grabbed the empty ice bucket from my room…Then walked down to the ice machine and filled it with ice. After which, I walked up to the Front Desk.

> *"I've made a stupid mistake,"* I told the Clerk at the desk. *"I've locked myself out of my room." "Will you be kind enough to let me back in?"*

> *"Certainly,"* he responded. *"No problem at all. This kind of thing happens all the time."*

I led him to Rookie's room and without hesitation, the Clerk let me in. I opened the door, took a deep breath and walked in.

No, I didn't tear up his room! The first thing I did was reset his alarm clock. I set it so he'd wake up three hours early the next morning. Now, on to the only other mission at hand.

Have you ever heard of wrapping a toilet bowl with Saran Wrap? I had, but I'd never tried it before. It works! When the bowl is wrapped tight, it's damn near impossible to see…Even with a bright light. After accomplishing that, I left. I can't be sure about Rookie, but that night…I slept well.

As usual, the next morning, we all met at Bojangles for breakfast before going to work. We were all there, except…Where was Rookie? Nobody had seen him, anywhere. The clock was ticking. If he didn't show up soon…He'd be late for work! Finally, after we'd all just about finished eating, he showed up. By now, I'd told everybody about that caper last night.

He looked mighty dragged out. He didn't have much to say and he looked like he'd stayed up all night. He grabbed a table off to himself and just sat there. The rest of us were all joking and laughing. Still, he just sat there. The subject of last night was never mentioned.

Maybe it was my imagination, but to me, his jumpsuit looked wet. Was it possible that he'd had an emergency situation? Had he somehow messed it up? Had he hurriedly hand-washed it and blotted it dry with a towel? That was my impression, but there are some things that I'll never know. Regardless, after about five minutes of his awkward silence, he finally spoke.

> *"All right!"* he blurted out. *"I know ya'll are all wondering if that Saran Wrap worked…Well it didn't! I found out that commode was wrapped when I tried to throw in a Kleenex, and it bounced out."*

Right!

Excepting for him, we all laughed. The Trooper Bowl was over now…And that's the end of this tale.

Free Firewood

Although this story is true, to protect myself and his identity, I'm going to flat out lie. I'll just call the star of this performance "Rooster." That should do.

He knew what he wanted and he knew what he must do. He was ambitious. He was an achiever. He was one of my heroes, too. I never had what it took, but I loved to watch him in action. He was a full-blown, dyed-in-the-wool brown-noser, without any distraction. If you asked him, he'll tell you…That's what he was and he was proud of it! In private or before a large crowd, he would kiss anybody's rear end who could help him move up. I've never known one as flamboyant as him…And it all paid off! He moved right on up in rank and I was glad to see it. I sure hated that he chose that way, but he was sharp and motivated…And I understood.

When he came to Charlotte, he was already reaping the rewards from his industrious butt-sucking. He had just been promoted to Line Sergeant, was single and had numerous political contacts. He never used his answering machine. Not wanting to miss any golden opportunities, he personally answered his phone.

The elections had just ended and campaign signs were still everywhere. We were getting our first cold snap of the Winter. I decided to make use of some of those trashy-looking signs, so I collected a few. I reversed them so that the blank sides were facing out, then stapled them together again and wrote on them…

> **Free Firewood**
> call Rooster at…
> *(His home phone #)*

I threw them in the trunk of my Patrol Car and waited until the night before he was scheduled to be off. Then, in the wee hours of the morning, I placed these signs in several strategic areas around Charlotte. I was off the next day also and I got up early…I was so excited! Just knowing that he was going to be busy answering his phone this morning excited me…So I had slept very little the previous night. Along about 10am, I received a phone call from an unfamiliar source. I was surprised!

"I'm calling about your free firewood," he said. "I just called Mister Rooster about his and he said that he'd run slap out, but that you were his brother and that you had plenty of free wood."

"That damn Rooster!" I thought. He nailed me pretty good with that. He turned out to be much smarter than I'd given him credit for. He had sure turned that practical joke back in my direction. My phone rang almost continually for several hours after that, but I would just laugh to myself...I started letting my answering machine pick them up and I knew that Sgt Rooster was answering his in person. Needless to say, I didn't waste any time going out and gathering up those signs. Damn, I loved Sgt Rooster. During the short time he was in Charlotte, he made many of my days.

Maybe it's the nature of the beast, or maybe, I just never had the "Need to Know." From the sidelines I watched in astonishment, at the magical nature of our promotion process. I never expected perfection and I could see a few signs of improvement before I retired.

Hopefully more of the mystery has vanished now...I sure hope so.

Bullethead

From the moment I got behind the wheel of that first Patrol Car and felt the power of that engine, it became a part of me, and I've loved to drive aggressively. And it wasn't just me!...I really believe that car enjoyed going fast too. If the offender refused to pull over when I turned on that blue light...Chances were pretty good that there was going to be a wreck.

In one ten day period of working the third shift, I tore up three Patrol Cars...All from high-speed chases. My wrecking Patrol Cars had become so commonplace that whenever I called in that I was involved in a chase, my Supervisor knew what to expect...And he would just start heading that way. One of my Line Sergeants got so tired of investigating my wrecks that he would sometimes take off in the opposite direction. I can visualize him now...Shaking his head while saying, *"That damn Bryan!"* and *"Here we go again."* It got so bad that when he did see me, he would just throw me the forms and make me investigate my own. That's probably one reason I didn't write more tickets than I did...I was doing HIS paperwork for all the wrecks that I'd been involved in! And it's probably also a reason that he looks as badly as he does today.

Oh yes, "Bullethead." If you saw his closely-cropped head, you'd know why we called him that. For those ten days in a row that I was telling you about, Bullethead and I worked the late shift together. We didn't ride together. We just listened out for each other and worked the same general area...The interstate highways in Mecklenburg County. I couldn't have asked for a better working partner than he was.

I don't see how he got any other work done during that time...Because I was constantly getting into trouble and he was always coming to bail me out. He was a big fellow and easy-going, but whenever I got into a tight spot, he would always take up where I left off. It always made me feel a lot better to see him come driving up.

I have no intention of detailing each one of those three wrecks here. Damn, I could write another entire book on just the wrecks that I've had. The last wreck of these three is the one that I will relate now. It was very colorful and more importantly, it also involved my good friend...Bullethead.

Just the day before, I had wrecked my Patrol Car and it had been pulled to our Salisbury Patrol Garage Body Shop for repair. But there was one small problem now. Here I sat at home and it was time to go to work…And I had no car. So, shortly before midnight, Bullethead came to my home and picked me up. Tonight, we would be working the third shift together again. I rode with him the thirty-five miles or so to Salisbury. At our Patrol Garage, I would pick up a spare car.

Bullethead had an unmarked car and he loved it! He took good care of it, and unless he absolutely had to…He drove it like a little ole lady. By the time we reached Salisbury, I'd had just about all I could stand of his slow driving…I was about to explode! After he dropped me off, he turned around and headed back to Charlotte. He was going back to work now. His plan was not the same as mine.

I walked into the Dispatcher's Office to sign the log and shoot the breeze for awhile. As a matter of fact, I believe the pretty girl that he's now married to was dispatching there. Regardless, I did shoot the bull with the Dispatchers for a few minutes. Then, I also left.

I fired up that Chevrolet spare car and took off. After I got onto I85 heading south, there was no traffic out…So I opened her up. Somewhere around the Kannapolis exit is where I came up behind him. Without even speaking to him on the radio, I blew his doors off. He looked like he was sitting still when I flew by him, but I could see him shaking his head. *"There goes that damn Bryan Gregory,"* I can almost hear him say.

About five minutes passed and I still had her on the floor. There was still no traffic out and the radio was dead.

> "H-551," I could hear him call me. *"Something is going on with the Kannapolis Police Department. I'm listening to them on my scanner, and it sounds like they're involved in a chase."*

I acknowledged him, but I didn't talk much…I slowed down some now and just listened. Shortly thereafter, he broke the silence again.

> *"It sounds like they're getting onto I85 now and they're heading south,"* he said. *"There they go!"* *"They didn't recognize my unmarked car and they just blew by me."*

"Bring him on down here to me," I said. *"I'll get in front of him and we'll block him in."*

I was on a long straight stretch now…So I just pulled over onto the emergency lane and waited.

In just a few minutes, in my rearview mirror, I could see them coming. With blue lights going, I pulled out onto the highway, gained speed and positioned myself in front of the car they were chasing.

He'd swerve to the left and try to pass me. But I'd jump back in front of him and hit my brakes…He'd bump the back of my car and then he'd try to go around me again. From the headlights of the other Patrol Cars behind him, I could see that there were two occupants inside the vehicle, and their heads were bobbing around. I could tell that my car was faster and better than his, because he was obviously maxxing his out…And I still had much more gas pedal left. Damn, I loved those Mechanics we had and these Patrol Cars!

But somehow, I did not like this picture. I knew I could take him…But not from the position I was in. I needed to be behind him. Yes, for me, that was the best place to be. So I backed off and let him come around me. That's when the show really started. That's when it all began.

I got up on his bumper and played with him…I'd wiggle mine a little from side to side while I was still in contact with him. Then, I'd back off a little and he'd start fish-tailing some. I pulled up beside his left quarter panel and was ready to take him out. But I decided not too. *"What about that poor passenger?"* I thought, and *"This chase may not be his fault."* So I backed off a little…About two feet.

We were coming up on Harris Blvd now and we had a nice parade. In my rearview mirror, I could see Bullethead behind me…Then, behind him were two other Police Cars. There was an extra lane to the right now for the Harris Blvd exit. The car I was chasing got into it and slowed some. Then, at the last second…He didn't take the exit! He swerved back onto I85 and we kept going south. We had a long straight stretch ahead of us now, so I just lay back there behind him and waited. Then, our Patrol Dispatcher spoke, because by now, they had taken over the communications for the chase.

"*H-551,*" she called me, "*the subjects you are chasing have both been involved in an armed robbery.*"

Well, that made me feel somewhat better about the passenger in the car...He was a criminal too. Now, I knew what to do! If they didn't pull over for me now, it was partially his fault too.

I pulled up beside them again. This time I turned on my interior light so they could see me. As I spoke to them on my loudspeaker and commanded them to pull over...With my right hand, I pointed in that direction too. They both ignored me. Still, they refused to back off. They had no idea what they were in for! They didn't know it yet, but they had just bitten off more than they could chew.

I backed off again and fell back in behind them. By now, we were approaching Sugar Creek Road and we had just rounded the minor right curve to it. On the ramp, and even the overpass itself, there were blue lights everywhere...It looked like a Christmas show!

By now, I was up on his bumper again...Pushing him, nudging him, playing with him...Then I backed off again. *"He's had enough of this,"* I thought. *"He'll probably jump off at this exit."* Right before he had to make his decision, I got back up on his bumper again. This time I pushed him. As I did, he decided to go to the right and take the exit. When I felt that right movement of his, that's when I jerked my car to the left...Then instantly, I backed off. He lost it!

That car fish-tailed around in all directions. Since my speed was up, I shot right on by him. As I locked my brakes down and looked to the right, he was colliding with the concrete wall of the exit ramp. Damn, I hoped nobody was dead.

Bullethead sped up the ramp to him. As I slid my car to a stop in the grassy area between us, the driver jumped out of his car, leaped over the hood of it, and climbed the concrete exit wall. He didn't have a chance...Bullethead was all over him! The chase had ended now. Police were everywhere.

As I walked up to the scene, a City Police Officer approached me.

> "Damn, Bryan," he said. "*I was standing up on the overpass watching all of this, and I've never seen anything this good on 'The Dukes of Hazzard's show.*"

Sure, I may have been the star of this show. But there is so much more to life than just glamour.

I wish that all big businesses took more pride in their employees…like Bullethead.

The Kidnapped Wife

Barbara and I, and our two young sons, were building a large log house in a suburb of Charlotte. My Husband-in-Law *(You've already met him)* had without pay, come over and helped us on many a day. If I was digging a ditch, he was right there beside me…Digging away. He was my friend in fact and in deed.

After Church one Sunday afternoon, we rode by the apartment that Husband-in-Law and Sweet Thing were renting. He'd been telling me about an old truck he had and I was under the impression that he would possibly sell it, and I needed one. His Patrol Car was nowhere in sight, but there was Sweet Thing sitting on the front steps. We pulled in.

Sweet Thing said she didn't know anything about him selling the truck and that he was still at work. Although he'd been over numerous times to help us, she'd never even seen our log house…So we invited her to ride over there with us and piddle around for awhile. It didn't take much persuading…She was bored and excited to go!

> "Wait just a minute," I said. "Let me leave a note on the door for him so he'll know where you are."

Here's what the note said…

> "Dear Husband-in-Law,
> I came by to see you about the truck, but Sweet Thing kidnapped me and made me take her to the log house. When you get off, please come over and rescue me…Because I'm not sure what she has in mind. Bryan"

We made the five-mile trip to our new house that was still under construction. It was a nice day and we all had a good time. We worked together, talked, worked some more, messed around and time kept passing. Eventually, it started to get dark…Still, no sign of Husband-in-Law. We decided we'd better get Sweet Thing back home so we did.

When we drove up into their yard, we noticed his Patrol Car was there, but the apartment door was locked…Husband-in-Law was nowhere to be found!

Where was he? Before long, he came stumbling out of a neighbor's apartment...Drunk as could be. *(This was highly unusual, because I'd never even known him to drink)*

"Boy, what's wrong with you," I asked. "Why didn't you come on over and get Sweet Thing?"

"*You SOB,*" he mumbled back, "*I knew that if I came over there, you'd start hugging up on her and I couldn't stand it. So I've been over at the neighbor's place, watching football, eating pizza and getting drunk.*"

I realized then that I was a low-down scoundrel...But I got over it.

The Wildcat

Learning how to drive a Big Rig was not a part of our Patrol training, but having that knowledge was something I had always wanted. Since I constantly dealt with Truckers, I felt that I should know more about their world up there. The road looks and feels a lot different, when you're that high off the ground. So that's what I did. Long before CDL licenses were required, I drove Tractor-Trailers for a friend of mine. He bought and sold used Trucks and Trailers, and he hired off-duty Troopers to move them around. I got lots of experience in driving and the necessary endorsements on my license. Surely, that knowledge would come in handy at some point in time. I'm glad I did it, because sure enough, that time came.

Late one night, I was working up on Old Statesville Road. The local beer joint had just closed down. There was a large open area across the road from it, which the Truckers used to park, sleep and hang out. Not much other traffic was out, and I decided to keep an eye on this area…So I'd drive by the place, go down the road a piece, turn around and come back by. I just kept making long sweeps back and forth.

As I approached this area one more time, a Big Rig was slowly entering the road ahead of me. I came up from behind it. Something was wrong!

It was just idling along. It didn't make any sudden movements…But now, it began drifting towards the center of the road. I turned on my blue light and siren and then pulled up alongside. When I got parallel to the driver's side, I looked up and saw a small female behind the steering wheel, with a frightened expression, staring back at me. From the frightened look on her face, it was obvious…She had not mistaken me for Santa Claus. *(State Troopers with blue lights going, are not notorious for bearing gifts or delivering good news to Publishers House Sweepstakes Winners)* I briefly glanced at the road ahead of me, and when I looked back up at her again, she was scrambling back into the sleeper behind her…In an instant, she had disappeared. That Truck had no driver, and now it was moving more briskly down the highway! *"Damn!"*

I had two choices. I could catch up to and climb up in that Truck, not knowing what was going on behind me in the sleeper, and pull it off the roadway and stop it…Or I could just stand by and watch it keep going. Whether I acted or not, something was going to happen! Either I could jump into unknown territory, or I could do nothing and watch a wreck, possibly a bad one. That was one Big Truck, but I chose the first.

I stopped my Patrol Car in the road, jumped out, ran up beside the cab, climbed up to the door and got in. I pulled it off the road to the right and shut it down. Only then, did I open the curtain behind the seat and look into the sleeper. Before that, I just didn't have time.

Stretched out on the bed was a large male. His head was leaned back, his mouth was wide open and his eyes where slightly closed. He was breathing deeply and snoring loudly. The odor of stale beer was strong in the air and empty beer cans were scattered everywhere. When I shook him and hollered at him, he didn't respond...He was obviously passed out. At the foot of the bed was a lump in the covers. I pulled them back. That's when I first came in contact with...The Wildcat!

Scratching, screaming and cussing, she came up. She's the one I'd just seen, driving that Truck. She was beyond scared now. She was tough! I'm the one who felt cornered now. She was swinging, crying and clawing the air! Although I hadn't really touched her yet, I felt like I'd just hit a hornet's nest. I reached into the middle of this commotion and grabbed a fistful of hair. Somehow, I got the handcuffs on, arrested her for *"Driving Impaired"* and drug her out of there. My uniform was torn up pretty badly, but I came out with only a few scratches. When I got her tied down and in my car, she calmed down some, but not much. I didn't have to ask her any questions...She knew how to talk.

She had come down from Alaska and she would hook up with various Truck Drivers at the Truck Stops. She'd party with them and they'd pay her. She was a Working Girl and made no bones about it. Truck Drivers would call her a Lot Lizard...This was a paid date. She and the Driver had been drinking all day in that sleeper and between the two of them...They'd consumed more than a case of beer. He'd been passed out for more than an hour and she was still up. Since she wanted to learn how to drive and he was too drunk to help, she had just decided to try it herself. Then I showed up and ruined everything...Yes, this was all my fault. She hadn't forgiven me yet and I didn't apologize. She was still mad.

I went back to the Truck to check on her mate. When I left my car, she was still talking with occasional bouts of screaming. When I checked on him, he was still in the same position. I still couldn't wake him, so I just left him a note…Telling him that a State Trooper had taken off with his Date.

The trip to the Jail was not too bad. She talked a lot and she let out an occasional yell, but with the help of those handcuffs, she behaved herself pretty well. She had no Driver's License, and the breathalyzer indicated she'd consumed more than twice the legal limit of alcohol. I stayed with her for several hours, until the legal process was through. She ended up staying in Jail for a couple of months after that.

As soon as I left her, I went back to the Truck. That fellow was still passed out in the sleeper…But this time, I woke him up. I told him all that had happened. He was still drunk when I left him and most likely, he didn't remember anything and went back to sleep.

When I think back on this incident, several visions come to mind…The fear that I felt seeing that Big Truck with no driver. That drunk passed out and sleeping through the whole thing. And coming in contact with, an active Wildcat.

Brown-Nosing Doesn't Pay

If you met Ted Painus, you'd like him right off. He has that kind of bubbling personality that just makes you feel better. He's always running around like a beaver…Talking and laughing with everybody. Ted's a lot of fun to be around.

Ted, Frank and I were the Troopers from our area who had been assigned to work a football game in Raleigh. On these types of duties, we would normally meet at the Patrol Office, gas up our vehicles and then drive our individual cars *(together)* to the assignment. The three of us had agreed beforehand to do that.

Early in the morning, Ted and I met at the gas pumps. Where was Frank? As we were gassing up, Ted noticed that Frank had signed the gas log about an hour earlier and had then taken off without waiting for us. Ted got mad…And his face turned red.

> *"That SOB has taken off and left us and I know what he's doing. He thinks that if he gets up there first, he'll get the best assignment…But don't worry Bryan, I was in Raleigh last week as an Instructor at our Patrol School and I've got a lot of contacts. Frank's not gonna screw over us!…I'll make sure we both get a good post."*

He and I took off for Raleigh. When we arrived at our staging area, a large parking lot, I didn't recognize anybody. They were mostly newer Troopers and Supervisors from other parts of the state…I didn't know a soul! Ted went his way and I went mine. I just assumed he was sucking up to somebody to get us good assignments. Before long, the First Sergeant who was in charge formed us all up and read out our duties…I was assigned a pedestrian crosswalk and a major intersection, and Ted's assignment wasn't much better. We were both going to be working our tails off. After he'd read out all the assignments, the First Sergeant loudly asked…

> *"Any questions?"*

> *"Yes First Sergeant, I've got one,"* immediately, I responded. *"I came up here with Trooper Painus, and he told me that he was gonna make a contact and get me a good post. I was just wondering where that good post is."*

It got really quiet. In the stillness, I glanced over at Ted. Nobody knew how to take it, except Ted. His head turned as red as a beet. Then he made a move I'd never seen anyone make before…He slowly bent over forward and placed his face between his knees. What was he doing down there? I've seen and caused all kinds of reactions, but never anything like that. Finally, the silence was broken by laughter.

Since then, Ted has concentrated more on sharpening his brown-nosing skills.

Chitlins

Up until now, I'd never tried them...And just thinking about them now, almost makes my stomach turn inside out. I've always associated eating chitlins with long periods of heavy alcohol consumption, because the only way I can imagine getting them down, is if generous portions of alcohol were consumed beforehand and if it was also used to wash them down...And I've just never been that much of a drinker. Do you know what they are and where they come from?

Well, let me put you on the right path. They're hog intestines...Hopefully cleaned extremely well first and then cooked up in one of several different ways. Their name almost gives them away.

To be honest, I'd trust someone with my life before I'd trust them to clean chitlins...I just think it's impossible to get all the filth out of there. Surely, unpleasant surprises lurk in hidden nooks and crannies everywhere. In my humble opinion, regardless of whether they're baked, boiled or fried...They're not meant for human consumption, unless camouflaged as "meat" or "pork" on an ingredients label somewhere. I don't mean to turn you into a vegetarian, but just think about it for awhile. Words like "meat" or "pork" cover damn near all parts of the animal...There might even be some hair, and lord only knows what else is thrown in there. I have no problem with chitlins being ground up and hidden in hot dogs, sausage and bologna, or even potted meat. But straight-up chitlins...No, Thank You, Sir! I've never been quite ready for that. It takes a much stronger person than I am, because I never could get past the smell. Oh well, enough of that. On with the show.

Our home was at the end of a cul-de-sac. There was only one way in and one way out. Then he moved in up the street from us. Whenever I went anywhere, I had to go by his house. He was a good neighbor...We'd holler at each other when I passed by and I'd stop by to visit him every once in awhile.

The Winter months had just set in and almost every morning, frost was in the air. Old southern folks would call it, "hog-killing time." Some people began preparing their favorite seasonal foods. Not to be outdone, he decided he'd whip up a nice batch of chitlins and share them with his new neighbors and friends. Since his wife wouldn't let him cook them inside of the house, in a large pot, he cooked them outside. Oh, he let us all know what he was up to, but he didn't have to advertise much…We could all smell them! He stunk up the whole neighborhood!

What was I going to do? It was time for me to go to work and he knew it, and I had to go by his house. I was cautious, but that didn't help. As I eased up the street in broad daylight, there was no way I could hide that marked Patrol Car. Just when I thought I had escaped, he saw me and it was too late. He came running out to greet me.

> "Wait just a minute, Bryan," he called out. *"I want you to try some of my chitlins. You've never had any good chitlins until you've tried mine. Mine are the best around."*

I tried every way I could think of to be diplomatic and decline, but my lines weren't working, because…Well, I wasn't going to mention it before, but I guess I might as well now…He was one of our new Line Sergeants, and he was off-duty at the time. There, I said it.

In a flash, he produced a teacup saucer of that steaming, stinking and slimy mess. They had a pale, sickish color and to get right to the point…They looked like warmed over death.

> *"Just try these,"* he insisted. *"You'll like em…I guarantee!"*

If there ever was a time for me to enjoy chitlins, except for me being sober…This was it. Matter of fact, I felt I was forced into it. *"Oh what the heck,"* I thought, *"I've lived a good life and I've got two young boys who may make it to adulthood. If worse comes to worse, maybe they'll take up where I've left off."*

The next few moments dragged on forever. Instead of thirty seconds, it seemed like many years. My right hand, with the spoon in it, didn't help me any. Instead of protecting me as it was supposed to…It brought that crap up to my lips! And before my mouth could spit them out, my brain kicked in and reminded me…

> *"No matter what, keep them down! They will probably be unpleasant, but they won't kill you. This will all be over in a few seconds and he'll think of you as a much better friend."* It assured me more with, *"this is very important to him. Just go along. Now put a smile on your face and just do it. I won't leave you! I'll be right here with you until the end."*

I swallowed real fast and got a small amount down, and I even managed a weak smile. But although it wasn't even a teaspoon full, it seemed like a shovel full. When he asked me, *"What did you think of them?"*...I don't remember my exact response, but I'm pretty sure that I lied. I also know that within a very short time after that, I had made my way out of there.

They stayed down and I didn't throw up. But for the rest of my shift, it felt like they were hung in the back of my throat and that grease sweated out of my skin. Even the next day I could feel them, in my stomach sloshing around. Thank goodness for diarrhea...In two or three days they were gone.

Upset Stomach

Jim, Morgan and Siler, all worked at our Highway Patrol Radio Repair. Since the Patrol Garage was in the same compound and I was constantly going there, I would always make it a point to drop by their shop and shoot the breeze. They were an unusual mix.

Jim was the most normal of the group. He could always come up with a solution. He was quiet and even-tempered. Jim knew his stuff and always enjoyed a good laugh. He didn't need any of my special therapy and besides, it's always been hard for me to mess with this type of person.

Morgan was one of the most physically sick people I've ever met. He was always suffering from something. Well…He was! I've don't ever recall seeing him in good health. I don't know whether I had anything to do with his health problems or not. You'll have to figure that one out for yourself.

Siler was the crazy one. Sometimes, he used some awfully unorthodox methods of repairing equipment. I actually looked on as he repaired my speed-timing computer *(it was a TDS unit then)* by using a garden hose, dishwashing soap and a scrub brush on the motherboard…Then blew it dry with a hair blower. Believe it or not, that fixed it! He was one of the wildest human beings I've ever run across. Like me, he loved to pull pranks. The main difference between him and myself was that I did try to set a boundary to my mischief…I would try to break it off before endangering life or valuable property. I don't really think Siler had a limit…I believe he was running without any brakes. He's one of few who really scared me! I once watched in awe as he poured a bottle of bourbon onto the convertible top of Morgan's prized VW convertible…Then laughed as we watched it leak down into the interior, and that's nothing. One day, he opened the trunk of my Patrol Car and pulled out a skyrocket that I'd forgotten was even there. He laid it on the shop floor and fired it off…Towards Morgan! Poor ole Morgan…I didn't know he could dance.

Just a minute Levi.

OK! OK!…Show us what you've got, Levi.

Thank you, Sir.

There's no wonder that Morgan suffered from so many ailments and was so nervous all the time. That damn Siler probably drove him to it. Well, I didn't help any either. Among many other things, I was constantly stealing his tools and hiding them. Morgan just didn't trust me. His skepticism of me got so bad that he would keep checking the appointment log to see when I was scheduled to come in…So he could be gone.

One day I popped in unannounced. Siler and Morgan were there. Morgan was sitting on a swivel chair and wasn't talking much. When I moved from one side of the shop to another, Morgan would swivel his chair around to where he was always watching me. It's like we were both magnets…He was always facing me. Before long, Siler got me to the side and told me a secret. Right before I came in, Morgan had taken a large dose of Milk of Magnesia…This time, he was suffering from constipation.

With this valuable piece of information, I decided to hang around for awhile. I became one of the friendliest people you could ever meet. I rattled on about everything. I sensed that Morgan was getting a bit antsy…His conversation was getting short with me and he just wasn't being polite with his guest anymore. He was waiting for me to leave, but I wasn't ready to go…Not yet!

After he'd held it for as long as he possibly could…Morgan made a mad dash for the toilet. *(This toilet was surrounded by a wall and had a lockable door, but there was one problem…It was a free-standing wall and it had no ceiling)* I had been preparing for this moment. I waited until some of the shameful sounds from the toilet died down. That's when I lit up a smoking stink bomb and tossed it over the wall. A commotion you wouldn't believe took place…It sounded like a herd of elephants was in there! Directly, the door flew open and out came Morgan, surrounded by a cloud of stinking smoke…With his pants down around his ankles.

Damn, you're good, Levi.

I understand that Morgan's health has improved dramatically…Since both he and I have retired.

Bad News for the Doctor

It takes determination. It takes lots of money. It takes years and years of difficult training and only then does the long and hectic schedule really begin. Those truly dedicated to the medical profession are very special…And if anyone on earth ever makes it there, surely, they'll have a special place in Heaven.

As a matter of courtesy to affected family members, when a person is killed on the highways of North Carolina, the State Highway Patrol makes every effort to immediately and personally notify the next of kin…Not by phone, but in person. This information is not broadcast over our airways and until we have completed our mission, the news media is discouraged from making it known to the public. It has always brought me great pride that the Highway Patrol has taken this responsibility. It shows compassion. It shows caring. This task was never easy. I performed this duty numerous times during my career and this was but one of those times.

My Line Sergeant called me to the Patrol Office, told me about it and then gave me the assignment. A little old lady had just been killed in a traffic accident about three hundred miles away…Way up in the mountain area. Her only son was now far away from her, working at the Charlotte Memorial Hospital. He was a Surgeon there.

When I arrived at the Hospital, I headed straight for the Hospital Administrator's Office and told her what I had to do…I was the messenger of bad news. She told me that the Doctor I was looking for was right in the middle of surgery, but she agreed with me that just as soon as possible, he had to be told. In a very professional manner, she set the stage.

Using some lame excuse, she had another Surgeon go in and replace him in the operating room. He was then directed to a private room in which some of his Hospital friends were now gathered, and there in the midst of these highly skilled Doctors and Nurses, I also sat. As soon as he walked in, I stood up, and immediately he sensed it…Something bad was up.

This was not a meeting of casual greetings and small talk. He knew something was wrong and he wanted information, fast. I introduced myself quickly and without further ado, I gave him the information I had. Of course he was heartbroken...His Mother was dead! The few questions that he asked me, I answered the best that I could.

This was a very humbling experience for me, because this was a chore that I just occasionally did, whereas he had to do it quite frequently...Sometimes many times a day. Although this was not a part of my job that I looked forward to, without reservations, I did it...Because it was the right thing to do.

Death is always around us. I'd see it wherever I'd go. We have no control of the future...And thinking we do won't make it so.

Dial a Page

For several weeks, our communications system had been rotten. There was a constant interference from some unknown source. For long periods of time, we could not hear or talk to anyone. If we needed help or got into trouble, we had no back-up…Nobody would know! This was a life-threatening situation! Somewhere, there was an illegal, beefed-up transmitter that was knocking out our lifeline…Our radio.

One morning, a Radio Engineer and a Telecommunications Center Supervisor showed up at our Office. They were both friends of mine…Siler and Frank Fowler. The general source of the predicament had been located. It appeared that Dial a Page, a major paging company, was the culprit and it was transmitting from the crest of one of the high-rise buildings in downtown Charlotte. They had some dirty work to do and they wanted a Highway Patrol escort. Our First Sergeant wanted to have a Line Sergeant guide the party. Siler was persistent.

> *"We don't need a damn Line Sergeant,"* he said. *"All we want is Bryan Gregory. We know he can get handle it!"*

So, I was called to the Charlotte Office. Siler had made this one of my proudest moments.

The three of us took off in my Patrol Car. The source had to be on top of one of four buildings. We checked three with no luck…It had to be on this last one. Knowing that it would be a secured area…I proceeded as I had on the previous searches. I located the Security Office for that building and spoke with the Security Manager.

> *"We must get to the top of this building,"* I said. *"We believe there is an illegal transmitter up there that is wiping out our communications system."*

He called a Guard who was already up there and told him we were coming. We met him and I kept him busy. Frank and Siler wandered off. In no time, Siler returned.

"We've found it," he whispered to me. "You keep that Guard busy and I'll solve the problem."

I began engaging the Security Guard in more conversation. Then I guided him to an area out of sight of the transmitter. We had just begun observing the beauties of nature when we heard a loud thump. I looked around the corner and there was Siler...With steel pipe in hand, preparing to take yet another swing at the offending transmitter.

"What was that?" the Guard asked.

"Believe me, its better that you didn't know," I replied, "now isn't that a beautiful sight over there?"

After hearing a couple more whacks and crashes, Siler gave me the sign that all was OK. Shortly thereafter, we left the Guard up there by himself...We got out of there.

Even before we got back to the Office, the phones had begun ringing. The Highway Patrol was receiving heated complaints from Dial a Page...Threatening lawsuits for destruction of property.

The basic Highway Patrol response was this..."*Let them go ahead and sue us for damages, and we'll see what Uncle Charlie (the FCC) has to say about their ille-*

gal transmitter and other activities." Immediately thereafter, our communications became much better, and no lawsuits were ever filed.

There's one thing that has kept us like family…The understanding and support from those in Command…Even when we might be a little wrong.

Stolen

This was one of those boring, middle of the week, evenings. It was foggy and a light drizzling rain was falling. Nobody was on the road much, unless they really had to be. It was just now turning dark and we had a long way to go before our shift would be ending.

Charles and I were at the Charlotte Office piddling around with our paperwork and reorganizing our filing cabinets. No doubt about it, Ted Painus was way down in the southern part of the county, in the Pineville area…That's where he always was. There was also a fourth Trooper working, but for the life of me, I can't remember who it was. The new Sergeant Rooster was also working. Lord only knows where he was. But you could put your money on it, he was out politicking somewhere.

It was so dull that I was having trouble staying awake. We had to do something…Anything! Slowly but surely, my brain started churning. I began formulating a plan. We were going to steal Ted's Patrol Car…Right from under his nose!

Charles and I sat down at a table and worked out the details. Then we drove to the chosen location and got into position. Here's how it all came together.

I77 and I85 intersected at the center of our county. We knew that Ted was probably about ten miles south of there, somewhere near I77 South. Charles made up some cock and bull reason to have Ted meet him, then called him on the radio and asked to meet him on I77 North, just north of LaSalle Street. Ted said OK.

Charles parked his Patrol Car on the left side of I77 North, in the median emergency lane. *(There were emergency lanes on both sides of the northbound lanes there)* The median was about three 300 feet wide in this area and very large bushes were growing there. I parked my Patrol Car on the southbound side of I77 and turned off all my lights. I was directly parallel to Charles but was completely out of sight.

Ted came whizzing up I77 North and as he rounded the slight curve to the left at LaSalle Street, ahead of him in the left emergency lane sat Charles…With his emergency flashers on. This was a rather unusual location, but Ted pulled in behind Charles' car anyway. Ted got out of his car and walked up to Charles' passenger side, opened the door and got in.

As soon as Ted was comfortably inside of Charles' Patrol Car, Charles gave his radio microphone a few clicks…That was my signal to go to work.

I ran through the median towards Ted's unattended, unlocked and running Patrol Car. I got in and slowly backed it down the emergency lane about 100 feet, then eased it into the median behind some bushes and left it just sitting there…Running, but with the lights off. *(Ted had no way of seeing all this. Besides, he was busy shooting the bull with Charles)* I made my way back to my Patrol Car and gave a few clicks on my mike…Just to let Charles know I had completed my job. My part of the scheme was complete. Now it was all up to Charles.

Charles was awesome! He carried out his end of the job beautifully. He soon terminated his conversation with Ted. Ted got out and turned to walk back to his car…But it wasn't there! Where was it? He turned back to Charles' car but he was too late! Charles had already hit his automatic door locks and was leaving town. *(I can almost hear his four-barrel kicking in right now)* By now, I'd made my way to LaSalle Street and had positioned myself up on the northbound ramp to I77.

In the heavy fog and drizzling rain, I sat there with my lights off, watching Ted through my binoculars. *(Ted got excited easily anyway. I wanted to make sure nothing bad happened to him, he didn't stroke out on us and his car was OK)* It took him quite awhile, but finally…He found his car, got in it and drove away.

This was just the beginning. A snowball was forming. An otherwise boring evening was turning into a very exciting and memorable night.

Payback

Every once in awhile, I'd have to pay for the crap I pulled on everybody else. This was one of those times…And it was a good one! I had it coming.

Shortly after Ted found his Patrol Car, Charles and I met at a predetermined location nearby. We were having a big time, slapping each other on the back and hee-hawing. Boy, Ted had sure made our day…Up until now.

Meanwhile, without uttering a word on the radio, Ted limped off to lick his wounds. Before long though, we could hear him call Sergeant Rooster on the radio and request to meet him at the Charlotte Office. Surely, Charles's butt was as tight as mine when we heard that. There was no doubt about it…That damn Ted was going to squeal his guts out. Like thieves in the night, we split up and slipped away.

I guess it was about ½ hour later when I heard Sgt Rooster call Charles on the radio. With a stern voice, he ordered Charles to meet him at the Charlotte Office. That about did it for me…The fit had obviously hit the shan!

For about an hour, I fretfully wandered around…Waiting, wondering and worrying. I think that's where all of my gray hair came from. Finally, Charles meekly called me on the radio, wanting to meet me on the road. We met. Charles was perspiring. I'd never seen him scared like that!

> "Bryan!…You're not gonna believe it," he nervously said, *"Ted fell in the mud while he was looking for his car and twisted his ankle. Sgt Rooster is mad! He said Ted's gonna go to the Hospital to have his ankle x-rayed. And I've got to make a statement as to what happened, for Workman's Comp purposes."*

Somehow, I smelled a rat…Because I'd been watching Ted through my binoculars the whole time, and I hadn't seen anything that looked like he fell.

> "Charles," I said, *"that sounds like a bunch of crap to me, because I was right there watching the whole thing, and he didn't fall."*

> "Bryan!…*I saw Ted!*" He wasn't persuaded much by what I'd said. *"He was at the Office too! His ankle was all swollen up and he was obviously*

in pain. I could see tears in his eyes and him sweating all over. We're in deep trouble now, Bryan. I've got to make a statement! Damn!…What are we gonna do?"

Now, I was beginning to have doubts as to what I'd seen or hadn't seen.

"I'm gonna go check it out," I said. "I'm gonna go find Ted and find out how he's doing."

I drove straight to the Charlotte Office. Ted's car was there beside Sgt Rooster's. I went inside and there was Ted, alone. The Sarge had already taken off to ride with another Trooper.

"Ted, how's your ankle," I nervously asked.

"You SOB! I gotcha, didn't I?" He laughed when he said, "it's about time somebody paid you back! Ha! Ha! Ha! Me and Sgt Rooster decided to get you back. He was in on it too. I took a piece of paper and shoved it into my sock to make my ankle look swollen. Then, I took a paper towel full of water and wet my face down so I'd look like I'd been crying…for Charles to see. Payback's hell!!…Ain't it, Bryan?"

The night was still young. It was not over yet.

Overloaded Vehicle

I can't remember if it was right then or shortly thereafter, but it was that same night…When we loaded up Sgt Rooster's Patrol Car.

The Sarge had left his Patrol Car at the Office and locked it up tight, while he was out riding with another Trooper. He shouldn't have done that, because he'd just scared me half to death with that deal on Ted's ankle. He'd gone too far this time by backing up Ted in that lie, and besides, he was a Supervisor…He was supposed to be above all of that! Now it was payback for him.

Soon, Sgt Rooster would be returning to his car, because it was about time for him to go home. It was close to shift change and several Troopers had arrived at the Office…To gas up their cars and to check their boxes for messages. I had no trouble soliciting their help. It went without saying…We all just supported each other in our endeavors.

The rain had picked up a little. I'd say it was about moderate now, but I didn't care…I slim-jimed my way into his car anyhow. Without talking much, we all went to work. We knew what had to be done. Everybody just started taking objects from the Office and putting them into his car.

While the others were filling up his car, I went to work on his radio microphone. *(The mike we used was a black telephone receiver that was attached by cord to the radio head on the floorboard)* All I did was slide his real mike under the seat, then took the receiver from an office phone *(they looked exactly alike)* and placed it into his mike holder…With it being connected to absolutely nothing. I could just visualize him trying to talk on that.

Trashcans, paper clips, traffic cones, boxes, paperwork and even chairs…Anything that wasn't tied down and would fit inside went in there. Somebody even took a framed picture of our beloved Governor and propped it up on his steering wheel. In short order, that car was crammed! Of course, we turned his siren on, so that when he turned the key to his ignition it would go off. Then, like a flash, we were all gone.

It began raining much harder now. For most of us, our shift was ending. Each of us began to make his way to his individual place of residence. It took me about fifteen minutes to arrive at my home. It was after midnight now and our radio remained quiet. Sgt Rooster never uttered a word and we didn't expect him to…Neither did we. As I sat there in my driveway doing my paperwork, I reflected.

This had been a long day and as far as work was concerned, I had accomplished little or nothing. In spite of that, somehow, I felt very good about myself. I was happy. It was days like this that made life more worth living. It was days like this that balanced out the others.

These last three episodes all occurred within an eight-hour period.

Blood Run

Surely, you've seen them, I know I have. A State Trooper will come flying by you and you wonder *"Does he really have a reason for driving that fast?"* Sometimes his blue light will be on and sometimes it won't. *"He's just heading for a coffee break,"* we say, as he goes out of sight. Yes, sometimes that's true, but it's not always so. Quite often I'd be called upon to make a blood run, sometimes several times a day. If you needed blood and I was taking it to you...Well, you'd want me to be in a hurry too.

We have a large Blood Bank in Charlotte and its run by the Red Cross. When blood or an organ transplant was needed at that distant Hospital somewhere, it would be packed with dry ice and we would be called. It was the Highway Patrol's job to get it there...We did it and we still do it well. Wouldn't you want it that way, just as quickly as possible? Now, do you feel somewhat better about speeding Patrol Cars?

Many times I didn't turn on my blue light, because when I did, traffic ahead of me would lock up. For me, I had much better luck at slipping around traffic, if sometimes I just left that blue light off. Normally I'd make the transport to a county line and another Trooper would either be waiting, or he would soon be there. That's the way it happened on this particular night...Well, almost.

Traffic was light and I upheld my end of the bargain, I got to the Mecklenburg and Iredell County line pretty fast. The Interstate there was long and straight. Since I had just talked to the Iredell Trooper on my radio, I knew he was running late. To make it easier for him, I jumped the median and got on his side of the road. Then, with a large box of blood there beside me, I sat there and waited.

That Iredell County Trooper would arrive from my rear. There was no other traffic now, so I aimed my Radar in the direction he would be coming from, and continued waiting. This could be interesting. How fast would he be driving his Patrol Car, I wondered.

After a couple of minutes, in my rearview mirror, I could see his headlights coming. He was about a mile off and my Radar didn't give a reading yet, but with a pretty high pitch, it began humming. Then that screen came alive..."119," "120" and then "121" the display screen read. He was getting on it, but there was one small problem. As he drew closer, he wasn't slowing down any…He was going faster! By now the Radar was showing "124" and he was almost on top of me. There's no way he could stop now and pick up that blood I was carrying. What was his problem? He knew exactly where I was, because I had just told him!

My headlights were already on, but I turned on my blue lights also and accelerated on the emergency lane. Without slowing any at all, he breezed right on by me. But wait just a minute! That wasn't his speeding Patrol Car…That was a Mustang!

As he went by the Davidson exit, I was lagging behind. But as we approached the Cornelius exit I began gaining ground. He got off at that long ramp and when he reached the top of it, he made a right turn. I broadsided through the intersection and came right up behind him. Two young fellows were in there and the passenger was nervously looking around. By now, all other Officers in the area knew what was happening, because with my Dispatcher, I had constantly been talking.

To the right, a new Bank had just been built and the whole Bank area was pretty well lit. The Mustang made a right turn there and in a clockwise motion, we began circling it. After chasing him for a few laps around, I could see I wasn't making progress, and besides, I was getting dizzy and needed to calm down. So I stopped. After a few seconds, he didn't show, so I drove around to the back of the Bank…And there that Mustang sat.

The driver's door was wide open and the driver was running down a slight hill…Towards the undergrowth, about two hundred feet away. The passenger still sat in the car with his hands in the air. I went to him first.

> "Officer, my friend took a pistol with him," he said, "but don't worry about me, I'm not going anywhere."

Now, with sirens blaring, other Officers arrived. A young Trooper, who was working the third shift with me that night, was followed by several local Officers, all in their individual Patrol Cars. He already knew the details, because I had been telling him all about it. Local Officers watched the passenger.

(The other Trooper, who was supposed to pick up the blood I was carrying, at some point, came and took it from my Patrol Car and continued on his way with that. Now you can forget all about him. Poof! In and out of here…He's gone)

The driver had a pretty good jump on me. He was disappearing now into the distant undergrowth. Some of this thicket was pretty well lit. As I took off after him, the young Trooper who had come to help me called out.

"*I'm coming,*" he stated. "*Just let me get my AK 47 out of my trunk first.*"

"*What in the hell for?*" I shouted back. "*How many weapons do we need?*"

As I ran more, I thought more. "*Let's see…We're wearing bullet-proof vests. We carry a 9mm automatic pistol, a nightstick, pepper spray, handcuffs, a steel flashlight and probably a back-up weapon. We've not only been highly-trained in all these, but we are also highly-skilled fighting machines. Now where would an AK 47 assault rifle fit in? And what,*" I wondered, "*do we really need here? I've got it! I've got it,*" I thought. "*More guts! Yes, that would be good, indeed.*"

Maybe I'm coming down on him too hard, but I got the feeling that at a very critical time, he was backing out on me. Maybe he was afraid of the unknown, or it might have been…He just simply didn't want to mess up his nice uniform. Regardless, for the moment, I found myself out there alone…Except for the fellow who I was chasing and may soon come upon, and he was carrying a gun.

As I came to the edge of the thicket, I noticed all movement ahead of me had stopped. Most likely, he had lain down somewhere. I moved on, and about thirty feet inwards, I found him.

There he lay…Face down in the tall grass with his hands underneath him and out of sight. When I commanded him to show his empty hands, he didn't move. So I stepped on the small of his back and pulled one of his arms back. As I started handcuffing him, a local Officer came up and helped me. Then, we rolled him over and there on the ground, lay the pistol that he had tried to hide from me.

We walked him back to my car and I took him to Jail. I didn't have to question him much either, he gave me all the details. He said he had a drug problem and had just come out of a Rehab program. He had talked his friend into celebrating one last time and then he planned to go straight. They had both consumed a fair amount of alcohol beforehand, and were trying to see how fast they could get to Charlotte. He said he was scared and had no excuse for carrying that gun. When the Court day came, his Father hired a high-priced Lawyer, but this young man ended up paying very dearly anyway. Although he was wrong and I didn't believe all that he said, after listening to him, I came to understand him better.

On the other hand, there's one who I've never understood at all. And when I think of this story, the first vision I see is of him. I can see him now. After we had that young man safely in custody and were walking him back to my car…There he stood on the crest of the ridge. He was so competent-looking and he struck such a good pose. He was one of the largest and strongest Troopers, and with him, he carried one of the largest guns. But unlike most other Troopers would do, he had been of little service at all. He had just looked good.

There are many of us like that. We may have good intentions, but some of us will jump right in there, and some just leave the impression that they will.

That's just the way blood runs.

The Padlock

The Mecklenburg County Sheriff's Department had the responsibility of closing down businesses that were considered a nuisance, such as massage parlors used as fronts for prostitution and other questionable establishments. By court order, a Deputy would place a large yellow sign with large bold red letters exclaiming "Padlocked" on the front door of a condemned property and then chain and lock the front door with a padlock. I managed to get one of these signs from one such Deputy. Although I had no immediate plans for using it, I stuck it in the trunk of my Patrol Car and there it stayed for months, before I could find a use for it. The sign looked something like this…

Mecklenburg County Sheriff's Department

Contact person _____

Phone Number _____

Padlocked
by Court Order

What follows next will appear to be rambling paragraphs. But believe me…They will all come together in the end.

Joe and Dot Manus were like family to anyone who darkened their door. I met them when I first moved to Mecklenburg County in 1975. They operated a Gulf station and small restaurant on Hickory Grove Road at the intersection of Harris Blvd. It was a hub of activity. If you needed tires, Joe would get them for you at the best prices anywhere. If you were hungry, they'd feed you for little or nothing. Even if you needed a place to stay, Joe and Dot would probably invite you into their home. This world could really use more people like them.

Joe kept the snow tires for my Patrol Car at his station. At the onset of snow or icy road conditions, Joe would come to the station and install them for me. He did the same for other Troopers also. Joe had a special fondness for the Highway Patrol. Many times, when I was working the night shift, I would stop by Joe and Dot's place long before daybreak. Joe was always the first one there. He'd get there about 3:30am to start preparing for the breakfast crowd. We'd shoot the bull, smoke cigarettes and drink coffee, while I listened to my Patrol walkie-talkie. He'd make me breakfast to take home for my family. Joe started a catering business and catered many races and functions for the Highway Patrol. He catered my retirement dinner. Joe's dead now and I miss him...And I'm sure anyone else who knew him does too.

Well, back to the story. As time passed, I started to notice unusual activity going on in Joe's service station and specifically around his bubble gum machine. It seemed to be getting a lot of action...Joe's ole cronies seemed to be consuming an awful lot of bubble gum. Upon closer inspection, I observed that this machine had various colors of gum balls and if you dropped in a quarter, it would spit out five small gum balls. Before long, I discovered that this machine was used for gambling and that the gum balls were used as a poker hand. Two balls of the same color were considered a pair. Three of the same color was three of a kind, etc. Joe kept a lot of cash on him and would willingly bet any amount to anyone wanting to play with him. No real effort was made to conceal this "illegal" activity.

Joe loved his two little Chihuahuas. They had free run of the Gulf station and anyone entering Joe's establishment had to first meet their approval. If his dogs liked you, Joe figured you were probably OK. Buster was the male and the more cantankerous of the two...He thought he owned the place. If he took the notion, he'd sneak up behind you and bite your ankle. Lucky for the both of us, he never bit me. One day a female customer came by. She told Joe that she had a female Chihuahua that was in heat, and asked Joe if he would let her dog get together with Buster, so they could make puppies.

> "Sure, no problem." was Joe's reply. *"I'll just put em in the back room and they can do their thing."*

So that's what happened. Without being legally married, the two happy dogs took off on their honeymoon. Before long, in came one of Joe's everyday cronies, Tommy Smeth. Joe was telling Tommy about the two dogs who had fallen in love and were now in the back room.

"*Can I go back there and watch em?*" Tommy interrupted and said.

Joe was a shrewd businessman.

"*Sure, that'll be five dollars.*" he said.

Well, the five dollars passed hands and Tommy went back to watch the show. *(Joe had no idea that I knew about this incident. One of my spies filled me in)*

During the previous Christmas season, a local TV station sent a reporter out…To get stories on how different people celebrated the holidays. Somehow, this reporter got into Joe's house and a blurb was shown on the 6 o'clock news. Anyone who knew Joe and saw this segment on TV really got a big laugh. Joe and a bunch of his buddies were sitting around the dining room table, drinking Crown Royal, playing poker and money was changing hands in all directions. *(Technically, he should've been arrested by the first law enforcement officer who saw that)*

The lease on Joe's Gulf station would run out in a couple of months, and since the value of the property had gone up so much, it didn't look like Joe and Dot were going to renew it. A new shopping center was likely coming in. Joe and Dot were making plans to relocate with a new restaurant a couple of blocks away, so they didn't waste their time crying the blues.

Ah Ha! A plan was coming together for the use of that sign. Now I carefully filled in the blanks on the Padlock sign with fictitious info...

Contact Person—<u>Lieutenant Seymour Cox</u>
Phone Number—<u>800 Dial-a-Prayer</u>.

Patience had paid off. Sure enough, Joe and Dot closed the station down one Friday evening. They drove their Cadillac to Myrtle Beach for the weekend to play Bingo and just to get away. They'd take off like this quite often, so I knew that they would most likely return late Sunday evening.

Getter done, Levi.

Their station was right across the road from Hickory Grove Baptist, one of the largest churches in Mecklenburg County. The station was always closed on Sundays and the Church parking lot would always overflow into the Gulf station lot, and even fill it. With this knowledge, I waited until Saturday evening so the Sunday crowds could get the full benefit of the sign. Churchgoers would certainly see the obvious padlock notice on his front door. Under the cover of darkness, I waited for traffic to die down a bit. Then, like a bolt of lightning, I stapled the sign to the door of his station and split.

Sunday passed and the sign stayed up all day long. Surely, many unanswered questions and eyebrows were raised.

Bright and early Monday morning, the station reopened…The sign came down. Shortly thereafter, the intensive investigation began.

I waited a couple of days before I stopped in again. Sure enough, when I made my appearance…I was a prime suspect. Joe approached me the same way, I'm sure, that he had many others. A few vulgarities were exchanged between us and he flew into a tirade.

> "*You might as well go ahead and confess,*" he threatened. "*I know you did it, you SOB!*"… "*You did it, now didn't you?*"

Calmly, but with a smirk on my face, I then asked him to go into the details. That really set him on fire! He became even madder than ever and he demanded an answer to his question.

> "*No, I didn't put that sign up!*" I then said, with that same smirk on my face. "*But if I did, I'd lie to you.*"

That made him hotter, and his language along with his good manners began quickly deteriorating. I hung around for awhile and tried to change the subject to more pleasant topics, then left. I was on his short list of suspects, but his investigation continued for a few more weeks, until…

I made a tape. I worked hard on it. I held my nose and tried to disguise my voice. I recorded, re-recorded and re-re-recorded until I was finally satisfied with the results. The tape was made to be played over the telephone to Joe, from that fictitious character whose name appeared on the padlock notice…Lieutenant Seymour Cox. After making the tape, I solicited help from another Trooper…Ralph Smeth. Ralph carried it out beautifully. Here's what happened.

We picked a time right before Joe closed the station, when there was no one there but himself. I walked in and shot the breeze with him for a few minutes. When I felt the time was right, I clicked my walkie-talkie mike a couple of times. *(Ralph could hear these clicks on his radio)* That was Ralph's signal to call Joe's phone number and play the tape as soon as Joe answered. *(The tape was made in such a way that there was no time allowed for Joe to respond. It was strictly ranting and raving from Lt Seymour Cox)* The phone rang. Joe answered. Here's what Joe heard on his telephone. *(Meanwhile, I was standing right next to him, looking innocent)*

> "*Mister Manus…Anus…Whatever!…This is Lt Seymour Cox of the Mecklenburg County Sheriff's Dept and I'm calling you in regards to that Padlock notice I placed upon your door on the 23rd of March. I understand that you have completely disregarded that notice and have, in fact, reopened your place of business to the public. (The tone becomes more heated) Mister Manus, this county will not tolerate the types of activities that you have been carrying on in your establishment!*"

Without much of a break for breath, it goes on.

> "The reason I padlocked your place to begin with was because I saw you on the six o'clock news drinking liquor, playing poker...And money was changing hands every which away. Damn, Mister Manus, how could I ignore that...The whole world saw you making a fool outta yourself. Now Mister Manus, that was such a shock to me, I just about fell out of my chair! I couldn't believe my eyes!...So I sent an investigator, in uniform, over to your Gulf station. I have you know he lost twenty dollars on your damn bubblegum machine! Mister Manus...I had to pay that $20 outta my own pocket. (louder and hotter now) *While he was over there, my investigator was told by one of your patrons, Tommy Smeth, that you're also running a house of prostitution...You're charging admission for people to come over there and watch dogs having sex.* (That wasn't the exact word, but it's close enough) *Now Mister Manus, I've had just about all I can stand outta you. My doctor told me that the stress of this job is surely gonna kill me...So here's what I'm gonna do...*(a little calmer now)*...Being the kind person that I am...I'm gonna give you two weeks to close that place down, on your own.* (hotter now) *If you don't...We're gonna take a bulldozer to your ass, and we'll push that place down. Mister Manus...Goodbye!*"

Joe was so confused when he got off the phone. When confronted by his further accusations, I used my standard replies.

> "*No, I didn't do it...But if I did, I'd lie to you.*" and "*Yes, I did it! Now what are you gonna do about it?*"

By using responses like this, over the years I received credit for even things that I didn't do. But I didn't mind.

I'm sure that pulling pranks was just one way of my dealing with stress. And surely, a grain of truth flows in what I've heard said..."*Even if you do it wrong...Do it well.*"

Two of a Kind

Right before dark, I was patrolling on US 74 East *(Independence Blvd)*, in the Matthews area and near the Union County line. Our Dispatcher was advising us of an ongoing chase. Union County Public Safety Officers were in pursuit of a blue Ford pickup truck. At first, I didn't pay much attention, because I was not assigned to work in Union County and the chase was about fifteen miles away. I listened as Union County Troopers tried to get into position to intercept the vehicle, without any luck.

It sounded like the driver of the pickup truck was doing some fancy driving, with frequent turns and changes in direction and then accelerating to speeds well above 100mph. The train behind him was growing in length, with ever-increasing numbers of Police Officers in hot pursuit. Slowly but surely, it sounded to me like they were making headway in my direction. I eased just inside Union County to the intersection of Stallings Road and pulled off onto the grass median at the traffic light. US 74 was straight and flat in this area, and I could see down the road for a couple of miles.

Sure enough, in the distance I could see lots of blue lights approaching and then abruptly turn off to the right and go out of sight. That had to be the chase! I decided to just sit right where I was and wait…Maybe it would come to me. From the descriptions I was hearing on the radio, it sounded like they were right on his tail. I waited.

The light on US74 was red for me and I watched as traffic on Stallings Road crossed. There was a slight break in traffic and then a blue pickup came through rather quickly. Could that be him? I pulled out and fell in behind him. If that was him, where were all those Officers who were supposedly chasing him? Oh, what the heck!…I'll just go stop him and check him out.

When I turned on my blue light and siren, he didn't stop…He floored it! Stallings Road was narrow and curvy and we drove it hard. He couldn't leave me and I couldn't catch him. Mostly, I stayed about three car lengths back. A couple of times, I tried to pull up beside him, but he'd swerve over, blocking me off. Finally, I fell back in behind him and became focused on maintaining the pressure on him, by keeping the nose of my car up his rear end.

I kept the Dispatcher and other Troopers informed as to our whereabouts, and could hear that welcoming committees, in his honor, were being prepared at various locations…But we'd breeze right on by them before they could get set up. As we twisted and turned on the narrow roads, the Police population was increasing, but none were within sight behind me. We crisscrossed our way back across US74 and then into beautiful downtown Indian Trail, and at the railroad tracks, we became airborne for about 30 feet. He led and I followed.

It was getting dark now as we made a right turn towards the Elementary School and then did a few donuts in the schoolyard. Then, we pulled back onto Indian Trail Road heading back toward US74. *(The hornets were really mad now, and were swarming everywhere)* Once again, we approached the railroad tracks with me right on his bumper. Two Patrol Cars were now meeting us head-on with all their resources turned on, and were obviously trying to force him off the road. We took to the shoulder and went around them, and US74 was coming up fast. By now, I knew that both our engines were about equal. Boy! He could drive that truck!

He hit his brakes and slowed some as we came up to the intersection. As we made a right turn onto US74, I kept mine in low gear. *(This roadway had two lanes in each direction, and was divided by a grass median)* He got into the right lane and I wound mine up pretty tight in low gear, and was still on his bumper. When I shifted to second, that gave me a short burst of energy, just enough to where I was able to get into the left lane and get my front bumper parallel to his left rear wheel. We were running about 80mph now and he swerved to the left to block me off, but it was too late…I was already there. I let him come over into my lane and make contact with my car. I was ready for him. Without leaving that left lane, I swerved to the right and into him as I hit my brakes. My front bumper hooked his rear bumper and he lost it.

That truck fishtailed from the median to the shoulder several times and then overturned on the shoulder, right in front of The Crystal Shoppe. I pulled over onto the emergency lane and that's when all the other Police Officers arrived. The Public Safety Officers, who had initiated the chase, drove directly up to the truck and pulled out the driver…They got to him before I did! He didn't appear to be injured, and they had cuffed him and were preparing to put him in one of their vehicles when I walked up.

I smiled at him. He smiled back. I introduced myself and he told me his name was Karl Strickland.

"Karl," I said, "You sure were doing some fancy driving."

He returned the compliment and I told him…

"Karl, they're gonna take you to Jail now and I'll be along in a little while."

They hauled him off to the Union County Jail and I stayed around the scene, for about ½ hour, while the local Highway Patrol Supervisor collected my information *(He was investigating the collision that I'd just been involved in)*…Then I also headed for the Jailhouse.

I arrived at the Jail about 45 minutes later and the Public Safety Officers were just winding up their paperwork. Karl had a stack of driving charges, about an inch thick, that they'd made against him. That upset me some, because I'd done the hard work and they were grabbing the glory. I was also angered to see a few bruises on him that I hadn't seen before.

"Karl," I asked him, "what happened?"

"Oh, on the way here, they roughed me up a little bit," he said, "but I probably deserved it. I didn't stop for em when they wanted me to."

Although he'd been drinking some, I was impressed by his honesty and humility. I made three significant charges against him and set my court date for the same day as the other officers.

When that day came, I located Karl in the courtroom and walked over to him.

"Karl, where's your Lawyer?" I asked him.

"Mr. Gregory, I can't afford a Lawyer," he replied, "and besides, I don't need one, because I'm gonna plead guilty to it all anyway."

All in all, Karl had about 15 charges against him, probably even "Spitting on the Sidewalk." Immediately, I walked out into the hallway and grabbed the first friendly looking Lawyer I could find, told him Karl's story and then asked him to help Karl. Without hesitation…He did! I know it's hard to believe, but there are a few good ones out there.

It took about a month for all the cases to be finalized in Court, and after his Lawyer had a lot of them dismissed and consolidated as many of the rest as he could, my charges were about the only ones that stuck. When I testified, I stated the facts and made it short and sweet. Karl's fines totaled about $1000 and the Department of Motor Vehicles *(DMV)* was notified to revoke his driver's license.

From time to time, I'd stop by Karl's house to see how he was doing. I learned that he was a Racecar Mechanic who built motors for some pretty big-name Drivers. About six months passed and one day he told me…

> *"Mr. Gregory, the DMV was supposed to revoke my driver's license but I've never heard anything from them. What should I do?"*

For several days, I did some careful checking and found that, somehow, Karl had slipped through the cracks…His license was still valid! The DMV must've slipped up!

Sure, I could've squealed on him, but instead, I sought him out.

> *"Unless you hear otherwise,"* I told him, *"keep on driving, my friend."*

I think I would've loved racing, but couldn't take that chance. If injured or disabled, I'd be out of a job, and a livelihood that I really enjoyed.

Blood Pressure Problem

As I've mentioned before, Husband-in-Law and Sweet Thing had moved to an area closer to their farm, and not too far from our Highway Patrol Training Center. Whenever I was up that way, I'd give them a call. If he knew I was there, Husband-in-Law would come to the Training Center, pick me up and take me to their home to eat supper and sometimes, even spend the night. Afterwards, he'd return me safe and sound to the Training Center. Throughout all of this, I constantly harassed him about his wife…That pretty little Sweet Thing.

About a year had passed and I hadn't seen them. The time came for me to once again go to the Training Center for the weeklong re-certification. We'd be updated on new laws, re-certified in the use of breath testing instruments and speed timing devices and our driving skills would be fine-tuned. We never knew who'd be attending that particular class or who wouldn't. The classes varied constantly. Since we all worked different schedules and areas, there was always a different crowd.

The process always began with physical activity. As soon as we arrived, we'd go to the gym and have our blood pressure checked. If it was OK, we'd do warm-up exercises and then take off of on a 1½-mile run. Those with blood pressure problems were not allowed to participate in the physical exercises. They'd be examined by our Doctor, placed on restrictive diets by our Dietician and medication would be recommended.

Upon arrival I went to my room, changed into my sweat suit and headed for the gym. As I stood in line to have my blood pressure checked, I thought about calling Husband-in-Law and planned to do so as soon as I got a break. As my thoughts wandered towards my friend, I looked up and there he stood…In line and right in front of me! What a pleasant shock! We stood there, slapping each other on the back and reminiscing. The line grew shorter now and there was but one Trooper ahead of him.

> "Boy," I said, "*we sure do miss you in Charlotte.*"

> "Well, *I miss you too*," he replied…He was always polite like that. "*But you know how it is. I've got this farm up here and I wanted to be closer to home and everything.*"

"Yeah, I understand," I went on, *"but we really do miss you…You and Sweet Thing too."* Then I broke it off with, *"You know, that girl has got one mighty fine rear end!"*

His head instantly turned purple. I'd never seen him look quite like that, and had he not been on the verge of a heart attack, he may have knocked me flat!

It was now his turn to have his blood pressure checked. They slapped the cuff on his arm and the reading was about 180/110 *(diastolic was well over 100)*. The Instructors gently laid him down, stretched him out, raised his lower extremities and treated him for shock. After letting him rest for a few minutes, they tried it again. Damn, his blood pressure was rising! By now, his blood must've been boiling! Not wanting to kill him, I left the area.

I came back later and had my pressure read. He was still lying on his back with his feet propped up when I left for the 1½ mile run. I don't remember if he was ever able to run that day or not, but I do remember this. When that day was over, he took me to his home for supper. I spent the night, too!

Yes, so far as I'm concerned…He's a mighty Big Man! Even after all the stress I've caused him, he still calls me his friend.

Early Retirement

For a good fifteen years he tried to lead me to water, but I wouldn't drink. He tried so hard to guide and direct me, but mostly, I stayed on the brink. He wanted so badly to climb further up the ladder, but I'm so glad he didn't. I would've a lost a good friend and Supervisor...Line Sergeant Klink.

All Supervisors need at least some of it and he never did have very much, but by the time our careers were winding down...He was completely lacking of any Hard Assness at all. Oh, he had a tremendous bark and he could really scare the Rookies, and let there be no doubt about it...He would even scare you! But we older Troopers knew how soft he was inside, and we weren't afraid of his little threats.

For years, it would happen on an annual basis. With a hopeful attitude, he'd go through the promotion process. Sometimes I got the feeling that he might be riding the right political horse, but then he'd come back home with that same frown on his face. That damn horse he was riding just wasn't strong enough. Just when he thought he had it in the bag...Every year, he'd get passed over and he'd lose the race. Then we all suffered! We had to put up with all of his farting and snorting for another whole year...Until the next race started.

For the last few years now, he'd been threatening to retire early...He just kept whining about how he'd had enough. Then the next year would roll around and he'd climb right back on that weak horse again. His threats to retire were becoming more frequent now. And since I didn't think he'd really do it, and I was afraid he'd ride that poor horse to death...I decided to help him, his horse and everybody else.

On my days off, I went to work on my word processor and composed a fake "Request for Retirement" letter for him. Then I sent it to the Troop Commander *(The Captain)*, who was a good-natured fellow...I just didn't bother to tell Sergeant Klink, the apparent sender. I showed it to everyone else and placed a copy in his message box though, for him to later view and remember.

I must warn you! There are some bad words in it, but I tried to tone it down in a manner that Football Coaches and Drill Sergeants could handle. If you're ready to go now, we'll fire it up.

Troop Commander
Headquarters, Troop H
Monroe, NC

Dear Sir;

With your permission, I intend to retire effective 14Dec87. I set a goal when I was in our Basic Training School to be a Major by the time I had twenty years service and have tried everything from intensive brown-nosing to putting up campaign signs to achieve this unattainable dream, to no avail. There are many other reasons for my decision to seek retirement now.

Unless someone corrected my promotion test for me, I know I failed it. One of my "contacts" gave me the answers to all the questions that were supposed to be on that exam. I stayed up all night before the test making cheating notes and when they passed out a different one, I just about shit. I only answered about half the questions and on the rest, I guessed. I was so tired, I don't even think I spelled my name right. My politician told me I had to pass this step before he could get me promoted and send me to Concord and I know my chances have just been flushed.

Over the years, my family has really suffered economically because of my driving ambition for promotion. As you know, I have faithfully had $500.00 per month deducted from my paycheck for my favorite politician. The problem is that my choices have been bad and my political friends have never gained enough clout to really help me. I am now financially drained. After careful consideration, I have decided that it would be more economically sound for me to retire now and go to work for Steve Dredge. He has been gracious enough to offer me a steady job and although I'll be starting at less than minimum wage, he promised me that if I do as good of a job for him as I have the Patrol; he will give me a $.25 raise after two years.

Over the years, I have learned that running relieves some of my frustrations. This all started out nicely. For awhile, I found that running really helped me...I was happy and in good shape. But for the past several years, my frustrations have increased and to compensate, my running has increased to the point of being ridiculous. I run practically all the time that I'm not working or sleeping and I only sleep about four hours per day. I am now running more than 120 miles per week and my body just can't take it anymore. It's about to kill me! Don't I look like I'm 90 years old? Well, that's how I feel.

And something else. Everybody is always pulling pranks on me and making fun of me. I get no respect at all. It's gotten so bad that when I give any of my Troopers an order, they just laugh at me...To my face! Maybe I should just go ahead and charge all Troopers with insubordination, because if they haven't already disobeyed my commands, they eventually will. My doctor tells me that if I don't soon get out of these stressful situations, I'll have a heart attack. Could you promote me to Lieutenant and let me pump gas at or West Weight Station pump? I know you won't.

You have probably just received a complaint about my giving too many unauthorized breathalyzer tests at the I77 South Rest Area men's room. Some turkey wasn't aware that I am qualified to give these tests without the use of an instrument. I've been doing it for years.

Please allow me to retire with dignity before Internal Affairs gets a hold of me.

Very Sincerely,

(Forged signature)

Line Sergeant Klink

When he looked in his box and found his copy, I made it a point to be close by. He didn't say much, but from the color of his head, I knew his blood pressure was up. He didn't retire then and I didn't get fired...But from then on, he didn't ride his horse quite as hard.

If you were to check on him now, you'd find that compared to those above him who tried so hard to hold him down...Well, let's just say that since he's retired, he's amounted to much more than they ever have.

Guardrail

Do you remember your first ticket? Of course you do. That experience is almost up there with the first time you rode a bicycle, or your first date. For the young man who I stopped on this night and myself, this was an incident like that.

On I 77 North, just north of Wilkinson Blvd and where the Interstate bends slightly to the left...That's where I stopped him. I had pulled him over on the right emergency lane. He and I were back in my Patrol Car, blue lights and flashers were going. I had just begun writing him his very first ticket, for following too closely. I had just written his name on it when within seconds, it was splattered with blood!

Blam!! Something hit us very hard from the rear...So hard that I blacked out for a few seconds. When I opened my eyes, the front seat back had been broken and we were both lying flat on our backs...Our heads were in the back seat. He was still out like a light, but his pulse and breathing appeared to be OK. My left knee had a gash on it where it had come up and hit the steering wheel. That was strange...Somewhere I could hear an engine running at full speed! My head was still spinning as I opened the door and stumbled out.

The first thing I noticed was that the front of my car had a lot of damage...So much so that my engine had stopped running. I managed to use my radio to call for help just one time. After that, all my lights faded and nothing worked anymore...My battery had been knocked loose and was totally dead.

My car had been forced into the car that I had stopped...But on it, the damage was slight. As I made my way to the rear of my car, I found the cause of the problem. My Patrol Car had been hit in the back right by a small compact car. It was now wedged there, between my car and the guardrail. The driver was still in it, because I could see him and hear him revving his engine, trying to get his car out of there. The rear wheels of it were up in the air, spinning away. Before I ever laid eyes on him, I was mad at driver...I had to restrain myself from wringing his neck!

As I pulled him from his car, I could tell he was slobbering drunk. As I expected, he wasn't hurt at all. Unlike the victims they run into, drunks seldom are. I was still feeling somewhat frail and had other issues to deal with, so, not knowing what else to do with him…I just handcuffed him to the guardrail.

I staggered back up to my car and checked my passenger again. He was trying to set up now and was coming around. Right about now is when my comrades arrived. What a relief it was…I had seen all the action I wanted to. They were here now, so they took over the show.

The young man I stopped was taken to the Hospital. He suffered some from whip-lash, but that was about it. I didn't finish writing his ticket that I'd started writing until the next day, and unless I'm mistaken, he just paid it off.

My knee required about a dozen stitches. But it couldn't have been hurt too badly…Because that sorry Line Sergeant that I had, talked me into continuing to work, without taking any sick leave or using my Workman's Compensation.

And the drunk on the guardrail? Well, for the life of me, I can't remember whatever happened to him. I just hope I didn't leave him out there cuffed to that rail.

So if you're somewhere down in that direction today, how about checking on him for me…While you're on the way.

Hello Henry

Ted Painus was one of those rare Troopers who not only had a sparkling personality, but also had the ability to back it up with his words. I believe he had a background as a Disc Jockey...Crowds didn't bother him much. He could make vibrant speeches before large gatherings, no problem. Ted was a one-man show! Among many other similar functions, Ted was Master of Ceremonies for my retirement dinner...He made it happen! Ted was constantly in demand for his colorful speaking abilities.

Ted kept it a secret. He didn't let any of us know. Tonight he would make his appearance on a local radio station talk show..."Hello Henry." The show had just started and it didn't take long...One of my Trooper buddies heard him and the word spread like wildfire. Ted was answering questions from the public on points of traffic law. He would be on the air for one hour, and no more.

With great haste, all of us who were available made our way to the Charlotte Office. Something had to be done! We could not let this event pass lightly. About half a dozen of us gathered there and immediately began scheming. Jim Klutz was the most seasoned, and knew the traffic laws inside and out. I believe I was next in seniority, and was training the Rookie...Steve Bullock.

Since Ted would most likely recognize other voices, I asked my Rookie to make the delivery. I promised to cut him loose from his training two weeks early if he could pull it off. He agreed. Jim immediately began compiling questions of interest. I began throwing my two cents worth in and putting it all to paper. Steve did some relaxation exercises and prepared to read. Upon achieving constitution of defecation *(look it up in your dictionary)*...The call was made. This is what Ted and the multitudes of others who were listening, heard...

"Trooper Anus," Steve calmly began. (The radio technician almost cut him off the air with that one) *"I drive a truck for a living and I was just wondering what the law is...Are breakaway switches required for tandem axle trailers?"*

>>>> Brief silence <<<<

"I'm not sure," Ted stammered back, *"you'll have to check with the Department of Transportation on that one."*

They were about to go on to the next caller, when…

> "Wait please. I've got just one more question," Steve continued. "I also do a little farming on the side and I need to get my 24ft wide combine from Huntersville to my farm in Matthews. When would be the best time for me to drive it down Independence Blvd?" (A main thoroughfare in Charlotte that was only two lanes wide at the time. This was impossible, because the road was too narrow and traffic was always heavy on this road)

Ted was completely flabbergasted on this one and his response was not understandable. He could smell a rat somewhere…But couldn't be for sure where the odor was coming from. Somewhere in his reply, he mentioned "Bryan Gregory" and "Jim Klutz," but other than that…He was floored!

Lucky for him, his time on the air expired shortly thereafter…And we were all the stars of his show.

The Paper Trail

By now, Ralph and I had been around a long time. Except for that ancient Jim Klutz, we were about the oldest Troopers left. The rest of our older buddies had either retired or brown-nosed their way on up in rank. Ralph knew me. We got along like bandits, but he didn't trust me any further than he could throw me. He was nervous…Today was his "over-the-hill" birthday. It was also a big Race Day at the Charlotte Motor Speedway.

For the major races, our District worked a good bit of the traffic for the Charlotte Motor Speedway *(It changes names quite often now, but you probably know what I mean anyway)*. Anyway, Troopers had converged on our District Office from everywhere to direct traffic, deal with the drunk drivers and look pretty for the motoring public. After all, we were "*The Showcase of North Carolina*" and still are, even to this very day.

It was hot! The Race would start in a few hours. Traffic was backing up. While the Supervisors and out-of-town Troopers left to go out and work and sweat in the Race traffic, we older, local Troopers hung around the Charlotte Office, tidied up the place, drank iced tea and stayed in the shade. *(You don't get to be old by being stupid)*

Just outside the Office and near the back door, Joe Manus was catering steak dinners for us and had his grills all fired up. After all the traffic had been taken care of and the Race had started, those hard-working Troopers would return to our Office and pig out. Yes, a lot was going to happen today.

Ralph had a good friend who owned a printing business about five miles from our Office. Like me, he loved to pull pranks and he wanted to make a big production of Ralph's birthday. He had a plan. He needed help. He came to me. He wanted me to steal Ralph's Patrol Car and drive it to his place of business. He and some of his workers would be waiting with large bins of shredded paper there. They would load Ralph's car up. I would then drive his car back to the Office. All of this would be done in broad daylight and right under Ralph's nose. It should take less than fifteen minutes. Could we pull it off?

Ralph had parked his Patrol Car at the backside of our large parking lot. There were numerous others parked there too, but his was in a position where all he had to do was look out an Office window to see if it was OK. He was antsy! He kept nervously walking around and eyeballing his car. The subject of his birthday was never mentioned, but surely, he felt something was going to happen, but what?...And when?

By now, traffic had died down and the Race had started. Although many Troopers went in to watch it, many others came back to the Office to relieve themselves, to get liquid refreshment and to get one of Joe's juicy steaks.

I recruited several loafers to keep Ralph busy in the Office for a while. Under no circumstances was he to be allowed around any windows and he must remain inside...Even if he had to be hog-tied. The stage was set. I went to work.

For insurance purposes, I left my car a good distance away from the Office and then had another Trooper drive me back from there...Just to make sure Ralph didn't escape and mess with my car while I was out gallivanting around in his.

I had a key to his car. Well, for that matter, I had keys to everybody's cars. Anyway, in no time flat, I was in his Patrol Car and gone. Knowing that on my return trip, his radio and everything else would be covered in paper, I took along my walkie-talkie...Just in case I got a call. I laid it on the seat beside me and hammered down!

When I arrived at the printing company, they were waiting. I actually drove that car through a rollup door and into the building. We opened all the car doors and even the trunk. Not many words were spoken...We all knew what had to be done. The shredded paper went in! I sat back down in the driver's seat and rolled down all the windows. Now, they really packed the paper in. We even stuffed his glove box! I made them stop so I could see out of the passenger window, the windshield and the rearview mirror, but in places, the inside of his car was packed to the top.

As I made my way back to the Charlotte Office, for the motorists I passed, it had to be an interesting sight indeed. Lucky for me, no one called in to complain. I tried to keep a nonchalant look on my face as I passed them by, in his shredded paper-packed, marked Patrol Car.

I parked his car in the same place I'd gotten it and then locked it up tight. A getaway car with a Trooper driver was waiting and we immediately left town.

After getting back to my car, I drove back to the Office, parked it, secured it, quickly brushed myself off and then casually strolled through the Office side door. Mission accomplished!…Well almost. I had left a trail of shredded paper into the Office and even worse…Oops! I just remembered…My walkie-talkie was still in his car!

If he found it before I could retrieve it, there was no doubt about it…There'd be hell to pay! There's no telling what he might do with it…He might even throw it away! That thing was issued to me and if I lost it or it got away, I'd be in deep trouble. There'd be tons of paperwork to do and lord knows, I'd already done enough paperwork today. My illustrious career was beginning to flash before my eyes. I began to visualize myself being fired and him standing there laughing nearby. Damn, how was I going to get out of this one? Well, my options were limited…There was only one way. This would be tough! I had to get back in that car before he did.

Well, so much for that option…It was almost too late! As soon as he saw me, for him it must have sparked a thought…"*I haven't looked at my car lately and where's that damn Bryan been anyway?*" Out of the Office he went! He walked quickly towards his Patrol Car. He was a few steps ahead of me, but I began to close in. Even from a distance, that car just didn't look right. The inside of it just looked a lot darker than normal. He picked up his pace. I started running and passed him, then stood by the driver's door.

Other Troopers had gathered in the parking lot now. Word had gotten out and they prepared for the show.

> "Would you look at that," I exclaimed, "somebody has paper-packed your car!"
>
> "*You SOB!*" he said. (Can you believe that? He called me a name!) "*You did it,*" he said. "*I know you!*"
>
> "What would make you think that?" I said, as I whipped out my key to his car and opened the door. Like a flash, I reached in and down through the paper, grabbed my walkie-talkie and then as I quickly left, I continued…"*Anybody who'd do something like this is a lowdown scoundrel, don't you think, Ralph?*"

I can't remember his exact words, mainly because I was increasing the distance between us and I couldn't hear them well, but whatever they were…He had nothing kind to say. I would love to have continued our conversation and I know it was rude, but for the sake of my health, I remained a good distance away.

Ralph retired not long after this and never really got me back. Now that I'm up in Pennsylvania, I feel safer. At least for the time being, I can sleep better at night.

This is not a documentary and I know it sounds like quite a tale, but that's the way I remember it…The Charlotte Race, Ralph's Birthday…And the paper trail.

Proper Authority

I enjoyed setting up driver's license checkpoints. Capps Hill Mine Road was in my area and we always had pretty good luck there. Bullethead and I loved to set up these checking stations together, and this was a fairly nice day…So we decided we'd do it.

Since the leaves were out and it was a bit cool, my thinking is that it was early Fall. At the edge of a residential area, we pulled our Patrol Cars over where the blacktop was wide. Vehicles approaching from either direction didn't have much of a chance to escape or hide. Traffic that was westbound did have one option though. Looking from where we stood, there was a small Church to our left, with a gravel parking lot that was on our side of it. It was down a small hill from us and was several hundred yards away. During the week, this Church was normally vacant…But today, it looked like the Minister was down there doing some minor repairs on the outside of it.

Traffic was fairly light. That's the way we liked it. As we got out of our cars, I fired up a cigarette. I only got a few puffs out of it before I had to put it out. Traffic started coming and we began to write tickets. I had just finished with one when I heard Bullethead call out.

> "Look down there at the Church, Bryan!" "It looks like we've got one trying to get away!"

Sure enough, an old car was just now, veering off into that Church parking lot.

Since I was closer to my vehicle than he was to his, I jumped into my Patrol Car first and took off. Bullethead followed closely in his. As we slid into the lot, the driver had jumped out of his car, left the door of it wide open, and was now hastily entering the Church. I got out of mine and headed for the same door. As I approached, the Preacher was standing there waiting for me.

> "*Officer*," with a stern voice he said. "*You're not authorized to enter a Church like this! This is a sanctuary! You don't have the authority to chase someone in here.*"

I may have missed one step, but I came right back to him.

> "I believe Romans 13:1–5 gives us that authority," I said, "now move aside Sir…I'm going in!"

As we entered the sanctuary, there was no sign of the fellow we were chasing. But he had to be in there somewhere…There were no other doors. So I got down on the floor and looked around. Sure enough, there he was…Lying down also, but about six or seven rows back, on the floor and underneath the pews. He was reaching into his pocket for something, so I continued to watch.

When I stuck my arm up and pointed in that direction, Bullethead went back there and grabbed him. As I continued to watch, I saw that right before Bullethead had reached him…He had come out of his pocket with a small object and slung it across the floor and away from him. While Bullethead was very capably dealing with him, I went back and retrieved the object he had flung. It was a test-tube filled with small cocaine rocks. In short order, that fellow found himself in deep trouble and in Jail.

What I remember most about this story is that Preacher. As we left his Church with the defendant in handcuffs…He never uttered a word. From his lack of response or complaint, I took it that he accepted…The proper Authority that we had.

The Rookies & the Flat Tire

It sure was nice being an older Trooper. I was content with my position and didn't want to move. I'd been on long enough that I knew how to make-do. My immediate Supervisors were pretty good and they left me alone. Retirement was approaching and I looked forward to that. And the Rookies?...Well, I enjoyed them a lot too.

They looked up to me. They enjoyed hearing the tales I'd tell them. They wanted to pick my brain. The younger Troopers were always seeking advice, would do what I told them, and gave me the respect I deserved. I didn't have to go looking for them either...They'd come looking for me, to set up checking stations and to take coffee breaks. Yes, older Troopers sure had it made.

One morning I met several young upstarts at The Village Restaurant. We took a long break and decided on an area to work. I was the King and played the role nicely. Surely, they were impressed by my wisdom and maturity.

As we slowly walked out of the restaurant, we came up to my Patrol Car first. *(Since I was older and wiser, I got the best spot)* Low and behold, there it was...My car had a flat tire. I was shocked! The Rookies just stood there laughing, waiting to see what this old Trooper would do. They wanted to see me in action or maybe, I'd just come unglued. *(I couldn't expect them perform a task that I wouldn't and besides...What if they refused?)* To clarify matters, I spoke out.

> "What the hell are ya'll doing just standing there?"

> "We've got a thirst for knowledge!" one of them laughed when he said, "we just want to see how an experienced Trooper changes a tire."

I had no intention whatsoever, of degrading myself in front of them. So I reached into my pocket and pulled out a wad of bills and then presented it to the Rookie closest to me.

> "If you think you're gonna stand there and watch me change this tire, you're crazy as hell! Now here! Get down to that Auto Parts Store, two blocks from here, and get me a can of Fix-a-Flat!...And bring back the change!"

That Rookie snatched the whole wad *($15)* out of my hand and took off. Fifteen dollars was a big wad of cash, for a Trooper to carry around.

(Hold on just a minute. I've got to go to the bathroom! I'll be right back)

Before long, he returned with the can of Fix-a-Flat and only $1.49 in change, and a cash register receipt that verified the same.

"What!" I loudly demanded, *"where's the rest of my change? Fix-a-Flat is no more than two dollars a can! Now where's the rest of my change?"*

Here's where the weakness and inexperience of a Rookie became clear. He was pathetic…He told me the truth. He confessed that he had talked the Clerk into making a false receipt. This receipt indicated a price of $13.51 for that damn can of Fix-a-Flat. Then to top it all off, the Rookie was so weak that he gave me back correct change…$13.21. I thought to myself… *"What's gone wrong with this younger generation? They can't even pull a prank right."*

As they stood by, I inflated my tire with the can of Fix-a-Flat. Then, I wiped the top off so it wouldn't look used. I was so disappointed. These Rookies had so much to learn.

"Give me that damn receipt!" I exclaimed, as I gathered up the empty can and stuck it back into the bag from whence it came. *"I'll show you jerks how to properly handle situations such as this,"* I told them, as I got into my car. *"Now watch, listen, and learn!"*

We all drove to the Auto Parts Store and parked. I made the Rookie who had pulled this on me wait outside. Then, I made a loud entrance into the Auto Parts Store. Like sheep, the rest of them followed me inside. No customers were in there, just the two Clerks. With a furious look on my face, I approached the first.

"$13.51 is a ridiculous price to pay for a can of Fix-a-Flat," I stated, as I waved the empty can and receipt in his face. *"I'm returning your product. Now give me my money back!"*

With and anxious look on his face, that Clerk looked at the other one and said…

"I told you we shouldn't have done this! I just knew this was gonna come back and bite us on the ass!" Then he directed his attention towards me

as he meekly said, *"Officer, this was meant as a joke. We didn't mean any harm by it. We were just having fun."*

"I don't know what you mean about fun," I slammed the receipt on the counter as I said, *"but a high price like this is no laughing matter! Now give me my damn money back…Right now!"*

That poor fellow fumbled around in his cash drawer. Finally he came up with the correct change and with a trembling hand, he gave it to me. I put it in my pocket and turned to leave the store. Only then did I break it off. I gave the Clerk his money back and we all had a big laugh.

We'd had our fun. Now it was time for work. After this, we Troopers set up a checking station on an Interstate exit ramp and really kicked butt.

The Deacon's Submarine

Trooper Steve loved to fish and looked forward to the Spring Crappie Tournament for Law Enforcement Officers. It was that time again, and he was all baited up and ready to go. Bright and early, he hooked up his boat trailer to his old white Ford work van and headed for Lake Norman. This time, he would not come back empty-handed. This time, he just knew he was going to catch The Big One. He would not be embarrassed as he had been so many times before.

He was running a little late and after arriving, he noticed that the crowds had already beat him there. This was not a good sign…And had he known what was going to happen today, he would've turned around and gone back home. In an organized fashion, those boats ahead of him began entering the water. Maybe he was a little peeved, but he waited patiently for his turn to use the ramp. Finally his turn came and he was so proud of himself…Unlike he might've done before, he had not blown up this time and got mad. He'd handled himself quite well. There was a reason for that.

This Steve was not the old Steve. This new Steve had recently become a Deacon in his Church. The coarser Steve no longer existed. Almost overnight, the polished version of Steve sprang into the light.

When his turn finally came, he tried to back his boat trailer down the steep ramp and into the lake…But his backing skills were never very good. Oh, my goodness, how embarrassing! In front of all these other Police Officers, he had managed to get that trailer hung up on the side of the ramp!

With the weight of the boat still on it, he just couldn't push it back more or pull it out. So my friend, Steve, unhitched the trailer and pulled his van up the steep ramp a little, then threw her in park and then walked back down to wrestle with the boat and trailer. A crowd was gathering now and they were snickering and laughing. But this time, although he really felt like it, he wasn't cursing…This was Deacon Steve!

By now, one of his sons had already freed the boat and was drifting out into the lake in it…So now, dealing with the empty trailer would be much easier for him. Thank goodness for that…This could've been quite awkward. Steve had almost slipped up and lost some of his "Deacon."

"*Look out!*" somebody hollered.

Steve turned around to see what was happening. Here came his van!

He'd forgotten to engage his emergency brake! That van came down the ramp and right out into the lake it went. It floated around out there for awhile...Long enough for several good photos to be made by the crowds of cackling shutterbugs on the shore...Before sinking in twenty feet of water. A skin-diver had to come out and hook a cable to it...Before they could pull his van out with a wrecker.

A few weeks passed and we were all getting a lot of laughs...Steve would even crack a smile every now and then. One day I was over at Jerry Oliver's Junkyard, scrounging around for parts for my old truck. Jerry walked up.

> "Hey Bryan," he said. "You didn't even notice. I've got Steve's old van. Its sitting right over there and it's for sale."

I looked and sure enough, there sat that same old white van of Steve's.

> "That's not a van, Jerry," I said. "That's a submarine!"

> "What the hell are you talking about?" Jerry snapped back.

I then went through the whole story of the Crappie Tournament while Jerry stood there with his mouth wide open.

> "That cotton picker never even mentioned anything about that van being under water," he ranted and raved, "and here I am...Trying to help him out and sell it for him."

We walked over to it and Jerry ran his hand up underneath the dash, and came out with a fistful of mud. He was really hot now!

> "*I'm gonna call that SOB right now,*" he said.

That's when I left.

Some time later, Jerry sold the van anyway...For a rock-bottom price. He honestly told the fellow who bought it about it being underwater, but the customer bought it anyway. He never even made it home...The motor locked up.

A few days passed and at the beginning of my shift, I walked into the Charlotte Office. A bunch of Troopers were also there and in their midst was my friend, Steve. As soon as our eyes met, he came prancing up to me.

> *"Bryan Gregory,"* with a loud voice he said, *"I can't believe that you'd tell Jerry Oliver that my van was a submarine. Why couldn't you just keep your mouth shut,"* he demanded.

> *"Steve,"* I responded, *"Jerry is a friend of mine and I wasn't about to let you screw over him. Especially since you're a Deacon of your Church...You need to check your Book and see what it says about lying."*

Steve had been trying so hard to uphold his new image and mostly, it was working. But on this occasion, some of his "Deacon" had slipped through the cracks.

The Heels of Death

Many times, I've found myself there. We try to ignore it and put it off, but we all know its coming. We'd like to think we're prepared, but promises, speculation and comfort can only be shared, once Death has appeared.

Except for the heat, 2 July 1994 started out as a beautiful day. Then the unexpected storm came. For a good twenty minutes, the torrential rains fell. Along with the thunder and lightning, the howling winds blew. Even the Weathermen were caught off guard! No one knew it was coming and it didn't hit everywhere. It was the Airport area that was hit the worse. And just as quickly as it had come, it disappeared. Except for picking up the pieces, there was not much else we could do.

Near the Charlotte/Douglas International Airport, a USAir DC-9 jetliner crashed while trying to land…Killing 37 frightened folks and injuring many others, not to mention the destruction of land. Death had come knocking. Whether we were ready or not…Here it was! All was calm now, but it was not over yet.

Most of the area's emergency resources responded to the crash area, and along with most other Troopers, I headed that way too. Then, my Dispatcher distracted me…She had something else for me to do.

Numerous traffic accidents were reported as having occurred on I85 South, just south of Little Rock Road. This area was near the Airport, was under construction and was where the storm had hit worse. With great vigor, I proceeded that way. Around Little Rock Road, I85 was undergoing great changes. The wide median was being transformed into more traffic lanes, and was protected by temporary concrete walls. Although all the normal lanes were open, two in each direction, caution and slower driving was required. *"Caution!"*, *"Reduce Speed!"* and *"Construction Area!"* the signs read.

Just after passing Little Rock Road on I85 South, there was a dip in the curve to the right…And although the sun was shining brightly now with not a cloud in the sky, a thirty foot wide river of water poured across the highway. Anyone traveling faster than 55mph, at that location, was in for an unpleasant surprise. By the time they rounded the curve and saw it…It would be too late to act. Just beyond this water and on the emergency lane to the right, was plenty of evidence to that. At different times, about half a dozen vehicles had spun out in the water, hit the concrete wall or each other and had come to rest there.

Since I had already passed this patch of flowing water and had to deal with the numerous one-car accidents that had occurred there, I called for another Trooper to approach me from the rear, then stop in the emergency lane before the curve, with his blue light and flashers on, to encourage motorists to slow down more. Within minutes, he was right there…He did just that.

Because of the curve, I could only catch a glimpse of his stationary Patrol Car. But as I gathered the drivers together, found them not to be hurt badly and began collecting information, I could see him in the distance…Walking, setting up flares and waving for the traffic to slow down. Mostly, they did…Except for one small compact car.

That little car came flying around the curve and hit the patch of water. It lost control and then began swerving sideways towards the concrete median wall. As fast as it was going, I felt surely, it would end up close to where we stood. After all, that's where everyone else who had hit the water too fast had ended up.

For the casual observer, it may not have appeared that way, but for me, my perception of time changed…All was slow motion. My senses were completely tuned towards survival. For those around me and for myself, I was scared to death!

After bouncing off the median concrete wall, that small car slid around and headed directly for…"Oh No," I thought, "*it's going to hit my Patrol Car!*" It did, but thank goodness, no one was in there. After demolishing the rear half of my car, it spun around again and headed, once again, for the median wall. "*Bam!*" After making contact this time, it began to roll over, then over again.

"*What's that flying up into the air?*" I asked myself. As my eyes focused better, I could tell…It was a young man who had been in the back seat. *(I found out later that he had not been wearing a seat belt)* I have visions of him still, as his contorted body was thrown fifteen to twenty feet off the ground. When he came down and hit the pavement, he was barely breathing…He was almost dead! Later I checked him. He never regained consciousness. Once again, Death had come knocking…And collecting. And now, as we stood on the shoulder in shock, Death approached us…In slow motion.

As the others scrambled across the guardrail, a lady near me froze up...She just couldn't move! I shoved her across it and then I also scrambled to safety. That was one close call! Death was right there...Breathing down our necks and staring at us from that torn up compact car. It had come to rest right where we were! Once again Death had knocked, but this time...There was nobody there.

During all the commotion that followed, the Trooper who had been trying to slow traffic down approached me. By now, more Troopers and Supervisors had arrived and taken over. Although it had been no more than a few minutes, he acted as though he hadn't seen me in years.

> "Bryan," with great joy in his voice, he said, "*I thought you were in your Patrol Car, and when I saw that compact car hit it...I just knew you were dead! Thank God! You're OK.*"

I had forgotten about my car. Now that we had plenty of help and things had calmed down some, we walked back to it. It was several hundred feet back from where we were and was behind all the other wrecked cars. Although it was practically new, it was really messed up...The back half was completely wiped out. Death had knocked on my door at least twice today...But I wasn't there.

Many times I had seen it, and sometimes, like today...It was face to face. My chosen profession was to slow it down some and to prevent it if I could. I could never stop it, but quite often, I felt I had put it off for awhile. Sometimes I felt as a small dog must feel...I was just chasing it, trying to run it off.

I was just nipping...Nipping at the heels of Death.

Breaking a Bad Habit

I really need to make a qualifying statement before this one. So here it goes.

I don't hate gays. Matter of fact, I've had and still have, numerous friends and even extended family members, who either are gay or claim that they are. It's just not my thing. Now, we can continue.

I thought the world of ole Darryl, but he had the habit of walking up behind me and goosing me in the rear with his thumb. Damn, that made me mad! I think that's why he did it...To get me back for all the crap that I'd pulled on him. I'd never seen him do it to anybody else. Regardless of where we were or what we were doing, that's the way he'd greet me. Although it really got under my skin and I let him know it, I more or less tolerated it because I figured I had it coming.

Although Darryl was stationed in Charlotte, he didn't spend much time there. His services as a Radar Instructor at our Patrol Training Center were frequently required and that's were he'd remain...For weeks at a time.

Once again, my turn came to return to the Training Center to become updated with law changes and Patrol Policies. In the past, every time I'd attend these classes, I'd either know or recognize at least half of the Troopers there. This time was different. It was now rather late in my career and a lot of the ones I'd known had already retired. In this batch of classmates, in this particular class, I was the only one with gray hair...I didn't know a soul. They were all younger than I was. They were the new generation and I didn't know any of them.

This morning was the first of several that we would attend classes together and casual clothing was worn by all except the Instructor. The first class ran a little long. Finally, we got a break, but it would have to be just ten minutes because the next class would be starting soon. We quickly made our way to the exit and those of us who smoked, fired up. The rest just hung around, soaking up the sunshine.

We were just standing around shooting the breeze, when off in the distance I could see Darryl approaching. In uniform, he was heading our way. I have no idea what the topic of conversation was at the time, but he was still out of range when suddenly, I burst in...

"You fella's may not realize it, but there's a lot of gays in this organization," I started out. "See that fella coming this way?...He's as queer as a three dollar bill." The group stood there in astonishment as I continued, "Yep, and he's an Instructor too. Just watch him. He'll do something and you'll just know he's gay."

I was just finishing my little speech when he came within earshot. When he came up, I shook his hand and slapped him on the back.

"How's it going Darryl?" I said.

As I expected, that's when he gave me the goose.

Silently, but ever so quickly, that group split up like a covey of quail...And he and I continued our conversation alone. I never told my classmates the truth...That he was married and had children, and thought he was a ladies man. I just let his reputation take off on its own.

It was months before I told him how it came down, that he had become a gay Trooper...With that one little move of his thumb.

The Hidden Word

This is one of the first ones I started and the last ones I finished, and I ended up changing the title many times. I'm telling you that so you'll know…Not only the great difficulty that I had with expressing it, but also to the amount of weight that it carries.

In this section, I'm not asking you to agree or disagree with me, and let me set you straight right off…Sour grapes, is not what this is about. I like to think I'm way beyond all of that. This is a problem that exists in many organizations, not just with us…And our State Highway Patrol did the best that they could to deal with it, probably better than most. For the moment, I just want you to see through my eyes and feel what I felt. Although it's going to take some explaining and it's just the tip of the iceberg, this whole section revolves around one little word.

Maybe I'm wrong, I sure hope I am, but it seems to me that especially with government and big business, sometimes, when something starts to look negative, it'll disappear briefly until the clamor has died down and then before you know it…It's right back again! But it sure does look a lot better now. *"Would you look at that!…It's had a bath and it's wearing new clothes!"* All right then, let's move on.

Years before I came on, quotas in ticket writing had been specifically outlawed, by State Law.

I never was a big ticket writer and as hard as I tried, I could never make producing numbers my goal. If I saw em, I wrote em…And it didn't make a damn to me who they were! Although my main objective was to promote highway safety and I had no tolerance at all for drunk drivers…For what I considered to be the small stuff, many times, I'd just warn a motorist and let him go. I just felt that everything wasn't always black and white…Sometimes, there was some gray in there. When I could, I tried to let people know that I cared about them while changing their perspective about compliance with the Law.

Seldom were my numbers high enough to please my Supervisors and First Sergeant Mostella was the first one to let me know. From the beginning, I felt the constant pressure to always write more. I knew I wasn't lazy! I guess I just set my standard of *"clear-cut and substantial"* a little higher than most.

Therefore, comparatively speaking, my quantity of charges made was generally low. It's not always about quality of work or public relations...It's almost impossible to put those on paper and when looking at figures, they just don't show up! As with many jobs, it's all about the amount of paperwork we can produce and how much we can make the numbers grow...As you probably already know.

I dreaded the end of each week because we always turned our weekly reports in on Sundays. As the week progressed, I could see other Troopers *"gittin fat"* and I had absolutely no problem at all with that...That was their job as they saw it. It's just that when *"fishing out of a barrel,"* many times, I preferred to throw the smaller ones back. I had no problem with making multiple charges, but if I charged a man with *"Driving Impaired"* or *"Theft of a Motor Vehicle,"* his chances were pretty good that I'd overlook his slightly *"Expired Inspection Sticker."*

I still recall the shame and humiliation I felt, when I received those regular counseling sessions. Now the first time I had one of these counseling sessions, it hurt my feelings really bad...So I went home and checked all the documents I could find relating to writing tickets. I dug into the State Laws that our State Legislature had enacted and I poured over our Policies and Procedures Manual. I looked and I searched. Nowhere could I find anything, anywhere, telling me how many tickets I was supposed to write...Even in Basic Highway Patrol School, they didn't tell us anything like that! From all I could determine, the Officer was under no obligation whatsoever, to write a ticket for every offense. He could actually use his discretion in these matters...It was up to him! Well, my hurt changed colors now and I became very upset!

I sat there steaming for a pretty good while and then I remembered what I'd heard my Daddy say.

> *"Son,"* he'd say. *"Before you get mad and do something you'll regret later, just try to put yourself in the other fella's shoes first and then see what happens."*

That part was the hardest, and it didn't happen right away. It took me years before I could even come close to putting myself in my Supervisors' place and to realize, *"Hey, it was hard for them too!"* To be honest, I still don't have that part nailed down too good. But he was right! The effort of just trying, really took off the rough edge. I wasn't quite as angry as before and it still hurt a lot, but just not as much. But the years passed and it dragged on.

"*You're not performing up to the District Average,*" they would say.

Then they'd give me a form to sign, officially acknowledging that I'd been raked over the coals. And only when I demanded a copy, would they give me one back! They said they didn't know why I would want a copy and when I kept insisting, they nervously shuffled around trying to come up with one. "*Damn,*" I thought, "*what kind of a show are they running here?*"

"*Don't worry too much,*" they'd sometimes add, "*it's not going to be a part of your Permanent Record.*"

Maybe not, but I still remember how it made me feel then, and even to this very day…It sure seemed permanent to me!

Well, it may not have been the same for everyone else, but for me, "*District Average*" meant "*quota.*" Now I could see through it better. It was the same old thing as before, except now…It was wearing new clothes.

Surely, it had to be hard for them too. Many of them had been in my shoes before and they understood. Still, at their Monday morning meetings at Troop Headquarters they wanted their numbers to look good, and I'm sure they were severely scolded because of my reports. To get me to write more, they tried every means at their disposal, but I remained stubborn…They would not get blood from a turnip!

I never really felt threatened with termination, but once during my career, I was encouraged to move to another District or to seek other employment…And I understood! I knew I wasn't helping them to make their numbers look good. "*But this wasn't a retail business, or was it?*" I thought, and "*hasn't that the old quota system already been outlawed?*"

"*We just can't justify a raise for you,*" they'd continue, "*based on your level of performance.*"

While most everyone else was getting theirs, for seven years running I missed Merit Raises…And it seemed like forever before I reached top pay. "*Merit Raises?*" I thought, "*Now why in the hell would they call them that?*" Well, since I wasn't getting any, the organization that I loved so much and for whom I put my life on the line every day, must not think I deserved much. "*Oh well,*" my thoughts continued, *"if I were killed in the line of duty, I'd be a hero! Maybe, I'll just go out and take more chances today…Nope! Can't do that! I've got a wife and family at home to support."*

Finally, I went through the formal grievance process and eventually, I went right to the top. Since it was a formal and written process, they were forced to respond in kind. Slowly and carefully, I made my way up the Chain of Command. It was tedious and I must admit, my butt remained tight…But I had never seen or heard such double-talk in my life! To this day, I've never been quite able to figure out their response. From supposedly smart and educated people, I expected much better than that. Even in the face to face meetings, the topic was never really addressed. At times, the weather was even discussed and the written responses were not any better. After reaching the top, I can't say that I was satisfied, but rather than file a class action lawsuit, I stopped.

Although they never officially addressed the issue, I never suffered any repercussions. As a matter of fact, the very next time that I came up for a Merit Raise, I received one…And they came much more frequently after that. Before I could blink my eyes, I was at top pay.

I was not the only one. There were and still remain, many like me. You might even fit in there somewhere.

So let me give you fair warning! Unless you intend to rapidly find a Police Officer's boiling point, there's one word you'd better not mention…Quota! Why? I think it's because deep down we all know that it's the same old system.

The hog is just dressed up better now. He's wearing lots of makeup…And he's regularly attending Church.

Nightmare on Wheels

Life deals each one of us a different hand and we don't have much control over that. About all we can do is deal with what we get the best that we can. Some can handle the hand we've been dealt better than others, and some of us can't handle what they've been dealt at all. These are the people who are the most unhappy. These are also the ones who can make life more miserable for the rest of us. After we've found that we can't do much to help them, these are the folks we don't want to be around…So unless they're a member of the family, we tend to stay away from them. This is the story of one such person. This is the way I remember it.

Our Dispatcher called me and gave me the assignment. On 74 East, just inside the county line, there was a male in a wheelchair, sitting on the shoulder of the road and harassing passing motorists. I thought to myself…*"How?"*

"*He's Drunk and Disorderly,*" the Dispatcher then professionally stated.

On our Highway Patrol Radio, that didn't explain much, but that was about as far as he could go.

When I arrived, two cars had pulled over onto the shoulder of the road. Two men were standing there waiting. They were about a block beyond the fellow in the wheelchair, but they were waving insistently that I come to them first. So I parked my car about halfway between him and them. Then, they came to me.

"Get him out of here, Officer," the first man said, "He's causing a disturbance!"

"He's drunk! He's cursing! He's drinking out of a liquor bottle! He's giving everybody the finger! His pants are unzipped and he's waving his tally whacker around for all to see," the smaller man added.

We could hear him well, even from where we stood. I think I've heard all of the vulgar words, but not the way he was using them. He had the most profane way of expressing himself that I've ever seen or heard. Just being near him, would make almost anyone mad.

I found out later that another Police Officer, from the adjoining county, had the same problem with him. He didn't want to deal with it, so he had simply deposited him there, just across the county line and in my county. Now, his former problem was mine. *"What in the world will I do with him?"* I wondered. I walked back to him. He was a big man.

He was obscene! He was an absolute pain! He was a stinking, sweating, cursing and obnoxious nightmare on wheels! Right in front of me, he pulled a pint of bourbon out of his pocket and took a drink. Then, before I could even touch him, he fell sideways and out of his chair. Although he had no legs, I found myself unable to even feel sorry for him. His swearing continued. For a few moments, I just let him lay there, squirming around on the ground. That did it! Now he began to throw up!

Reluctantly, I wrestled him up and into my car. What a mess! He may have been disabled, but all of his bodily functions were properly working…There was plenty of evidence of that, everywhere! I folded up his chair and threw it in my back seat.

He wouldn't tell me where he lived and his ID card just had a PO Box for his address. Besides, he didn't want to go home, he wanted me to take him to the Liquor Store! There was nothing else on his person to give me a clue…Where I should take him or what I should do. During the whole time I was with him…He was loud! He was nasty! He was crude!

Well, he was certainly drunk and disorderly, so I took him to Jail. Oops! My mistake. They didn't want him there…They didn't have accommodations for disabled persons in there.

Off to the Rehab Center we went. If anybody needed rehabilitating, I figured, he certainly did. Same old story…

> *"We aren't set up for disabled persons here,"* the Shift Supervisor said.

"Damn, where will I take him?" I thought. *"Nobody else wants him and I can't take him home with me. Nope! Not a chance! Even if he were a relative, I'd throw him out."*

I could think of only one more option…Charlotte Memorial Hospital. Since it was a weekend and they were busy, and they dealt with drunks all the time anyway…*"Yep, that's were we'll go!"* Throughout all my driving around, his demeanor and odor never changed for the better…Off we went!

When we arrived, I got him out and put him in his chair and then wheeled him up. I'd had my turn, and now…Someone else could have theirs.

"He needs your help," I told the Nurse at the desk.

A Security Guard was standing nearby. They were very busy and without further ado, I then left. I felt that a great weight had been lifted, and I laughed to myself as I quickly drove off.

A few hours passed and I had investigated a wreck. One of the occupants involved had been injured and was transported to the same Hospital. So I had to go back. When I returned, that same Security Guard was still there.

"You SOB!" as soon as he saw me, he said. *"We checked him out and other than being drunk…We found nothing wrong at all. We realized we'd been had, so we released him."*

Wait just a minute! The tale doesn't end here…It goes on!

"As he was wheeling down the ramp, he fell off of it and broke his arm," the Security Guard continued. *"He's now a patient here! You SOB!"*

Maybe I shouldn't have, but once again, I laughed. For me, the nightmare had ended and I had survived…And that's the end of this tale.

Soft & Tough

During my career as a State Trooper, I came across a wide range of characters. And not all of them were defendants...Some of them were Judges. I've had all kinds of Judges, some soft and some tough. I've had Judges who seemed to let everyone go and then others who would've nailed them to a cross. I've had them at both extremes and I've had them in the middle. I got along with all of them, because for even the ones who didn't convict my defendants much, in their own Courtrooms, I knew that they were the Boss. Now, I'm going to give an example of both ends of the spectrum. For the first one, let's go soft.

He started out as a Defense Attorney years before and had been voted in as a District Court Judge, and he stayed in that position for a good twenty years. Of course he wouldn't tolerate it in his Courtroom, but he'd do it...He drank from a coffee cup and he smoked on the bench. Rumors had it, that he even had a bottle of liquor stuck under there!

He'd arrive about thirty minutes early for Court each day and would leave his Chambers' door wide open. Before Court began, District Attorneys, Law Enforcement Officers and Defense Attorneys would wander out and in. Occasionally his door would close for a private meeting, but in general, he tried to be everyone's friend.

I'd watch as he found people *"Not Guilty!"* of some open and shut looking stuff. And many were the times that I felt I had a mighty strong case, but he'd let them go. Some Police Officers didn't take it well...They'd take it personally and get mad. But I learned not to. I learned to just grin and bear it, and sure enough, it paid off.

After we'd known each other for a pretty good while, when I had a person charged with something and they had given me a hard time, sometimes, before Court...I'd walk straight into his Chambers and get his ear. Sure enough, regardless of who they were or which Lawyers they had, he'd burn em...And for a change, I'd feel good. In later years I remember once walking through the back of his Courtroom while a trial was in full swing. When he looked up and saw me, he stopped the proceedings.

> *"How's it going, Bryan,"* he hollered out at me, *"I haven't seen you in awhile. Where have you been?"* I quietly returned the greeting and could hear him tell the filled Courtroom as I made my exit...*"That's one good State Trooper, right there."*

Boy, that made me feel good! He may not have been the strongest Judge, but he was still my good friend. Enough of the soft one, now let's go tough.

He was a retired FBI Agent who instead of playing golf in his retirement, he became a District Court Judge. To call him a *"law and order"* Judge, would not be going too far. He carried a large case load, was intimidating to look at and concealed a 45 automatic under his robe. He ran his Court like clockwork. At the beginning of Court, those pleading *"Guilty"* were told to line up at the back of the Courtroom. When their name was called out, they would walk to the front, he'd give them a stiff sentence and a Bailiff would escort them out. Most of these hearings lasted no more than a minute.

On one particular Court day, among several other Officers, I had numerous cases before him. Those pleading *"Guilty"* lined up at the back. Towards the back of the line stood an old fellow who I'd charged with *"Driving While License Revoked."* Like clockwork the process began. As the line grew shorter my attention was drawn towards him. He was obviously aware of the hefty sentences being handed out, and even from where I sat, I could see him tremble and shake. After ten minutes or so, his name was called out and the Judge socked it to him. To the floor, he fell flat! As I jumped up to go check on his health, with a strong voice, the Judge spoke out.

> *"Mister Bailiff. Get him out of here!"* without compassion he continued, *"I said get that man out of my Courtroom...Right Now!"*

Two Bailiffs had a hold of him now and literally dragged his limp body out of the hushed Courtroom. Because of the stress he'd been under, I just knew he'd had a heart attack. I followed them out into the hallway. After we placed some ammonia under his nostrils, he still had a greenish tint, but he came around.

> *"Fellow, how do you feel now,"* I asked, and *"are you OK?"*

> *"Yes, I'm feeling much better now,"* he replied, *"but I'd been holding a large chew of tobacco in my mouth and couldn't spit it out."* He went on with, *"when the Judge told me five hundred dollars and costs...Well, that's when I swallowed it and passed out."*

So now you have it. The opposite ends of the field...

      Soft   &   Tough

How to Correct a Supervisor
...or anyone else, for that matter.

This subject is rather touchy, so be careful with its application. Even a third grader can tell you…Those who fight Power do so at great risk to themselves. If you decide to try it, be prepared to find other employment, because you may find yourself out on the street again, looking for work.

I've never had much luck at judging the motives of others…And I'm just as bad as the next person is for talking about people behind their backs. I know I shouldn't do it and although I try not to, sometimes I still do. I'm not lazy and regardless of which occupation I've had, I think I've always been a pretty good employee. But I can complain and spread rumors with the very best and especially for those who have positions of authority over me, when I'm of a mind to, I can make life pretty tough.

Now that I've aged some, I look at life a little differently. And when it comes to getting a Supervisor to change his ways…Well, for myself, I've found a procedure that has worked. For one reason or another, I don't use this method as much as I could. This technique requires a lot of concentration and empathy. It certainly isn't easy, it's hard! And the first step is the most difficult of all.

First, you've got to temporarily put your anger aside. Deep breathing and long periods of silence may be needed before you can get worked up into the right frame of mind. As usual, I've already got a story lined up…So here it goes.

I worked with him when we were both Troopers, and we got along just fine. He received a promotion to Line Sergeant and moved to another area, and within a couple of years, he'd received yet another promotion to First Sergeant. He'd placed his eggs in the right basket. He'd chosen the right political horse and I didn't blame him…I'd seen how our organization worked. I didn't like the system, but I had no problem with him doing that. With all his new stripes he came back to our District. Now he was our Big Boss. Now he ran the show.

Soon, complaints within the ranks began to surface. He was not showing concern for our needs. I heard the complaints but didn't pay much attention, until his actions affected me. Sure enough, a few months later, it happened.

I asked him directly and he denied me the time off to go help my sick and aging Father…Because of lack of coverage, blah, blah, blah. A Line Sergeant beneath him overheard us. He didn't hesitate. He pulled me aside.

> "*Don't worry Bryan,*" he told me. "*You go ahead and take off. I understand your situation. I'll take the heat.*"

I went to my Father…Even if I had been fired, I would've taken off. When I came back I was boiling mad!…But I withheld my anger for a short while. I thought of our First Sergeant when he was a Trooper…He was such a different person then. How could he possibly have turned into such an asshole? As I thought about it more, I began to realize how scared and unsure of himself he must be.

He was in a new position of authority. He was not accustomed to his new power and he wanted everything to go right. He wanted to impress his Superiors. He wanted his figures to look better than the one he'd replaced. Surely, he wanted to keep moving on up and maybe he was focusing so hard on himself and his career that he'd forgotten about his best asset…His Troopers. Although he was religious, it was obvious…He was now wound up with himself, his family, his career and his problems. For the most part, he had forgotten about us. With all this in mind, I was still mad, but instead of making a big scene I decided on a different approach.

I waited until he was at the Office alone, and that wasn't long. He'd stepped on so many toes that when he was there, all who could do so, made it a point to be gone.

He was busy with his paperwork when I tapped on his Office door. It was open.

> "*Come on in, Bryan,*" he said and then asked, "*what's on your mind?*"

Without saying a word, I pulled a chair up beside his and sat down.

> "*Sarge,*" I quietly began, "*somebody has got to tell you. Your actions are affecting a lot of us.*" Then I emphatically said, "*you're not supervising worth a Damn!*"

That got his attention! From the way I had approached him, he knew I was being straight. The tears began to well up in his eyes.

"Bryan, what am I doing wrong?" he asked me. I began to choke up too, but somehow, managed to go on.

"*This is what you've done to me,*" I said and then I related the incident of my request for time off to him. "*...and it's not just me who's upset with you,*" I continued, "*you've got many other Troopers pissed off too. You've pulled similar crap on them.*"

He listened intently and then with humility, he apologized to me.

"*I didn't know,*" he tearfully said. "*Why hasn't someone told me before?*"

We began passing that box of Kleenex back and forth.

"*I'm about the only one who could do it,*" when I could talk again, that's what I said. "*I've only got a few years left. I'm not playing the promotion game. I knew you before any of them and besides that, I'm your friend. These other Troopers have worked too hard to get where they are. They're young and they don't want to jeopardize their careers, so they haven't said much to you.*" Then I topped it off with, "*but I don't give a damn...I have nothing to lose.*"

"*What have I done to them,*" he honestly asked.

"*That's not for me to answer,*" I responded. "*That's a question they'll have to answer themselves. If you want their input, just ask em. They'll have to speak for themselves.*"

"*But they won't talk to me as you have,*" he said.

"*They will if they're convinced your intentions are good. If they feel you're honestly seeking answers, and they don't think their careers will be endangered. If you talk with them one on one, like we are now, I think they will.*"

We dried our eyes. He wanted to get started right away. At his request, I left the Office first and started paving the way. I met those who were working and let them know he was coming. I could hear him on the radio as he called them, one by one. Wherever they were and whatever they were doing, he didn't call them to the Office...He went to them! They talked. He listened. He apologized.

After all this was said and done, working conditions became better. I can't say that he turned out to be perfect, but he did straighten out some. He's passed away now. Because of his health, his life was cut short. I'm so glad that I took the time to tell him how I felt. I miss him! He was my friend.

From this story, maybe you can understand why Supervisors seldom get honest feedback. One of our biggest mistakes in life may be in assuming others know how badly they're hurting us, without letting them know.

Instead, we just talk about them behind their backs...But we still work.

Decent Tomatoes

For a few years running, we'd lost a number of Troopers to violent altercations in the mountains, especially in the southwest corner of the State…That's where several State lines converge and the roads were lightly traveled. It wasn't the Mountain Folk who were killing our Troopers. It just seemed to be that criminal elements were using this area to quickly move from State to State. In many cases, the Mountain Folk seemed to love the Highway Patrol even more so than in other parts of the State. In a lot of areas up there, we were their only Law Enforcement. We loved them too.

We are a tight bunch! When someone harms a fellow Trooper, there's going to be hell to pay! On this occasion, a Trooper had stopped a vehicle and was shot and killed by two escaped convicts. These murderers were on foot and still in the area. Immediately we responded! From hundreds of miles away, even those of us who were off-duty were called. We converged on that area like greased lightning! Without delay, the roads were barricaded and Troopers with shotguns and assault rifles monitored every movement. All of the local residents were notified and kept track of. No, we weren't going to relinquish this responsibility to other departments…We'd handle it! We gladly accepted their help but this was our battle. We would avenge the death of our comrade!

More than half a dozen of us from the Charlotte area arrived. We set up a Checkpoint on I40 West and began thoroughly checking all those seeking passage, under the watchful eye of my friend and Supervisor, Line Sergeant Klink. Although this was a remote location, it was about the only way for vehicles to leave our State from that area.

Other Troopers and Law Enforcement Officers beat the bushes. With dogs and helicopters, they scoured the terrain. Every man, woman and child was informed of the dangerous felons on the loose. Some left their homes for safer havens but many remained. Time passed. Minutes turned into hours. Hours turned into days.

We began working in shifts. Some would rest up at a local Motel while the others worked. Although we were all on edge, traffic was very thin at our Checkpoint. The local folks began bringing us food and drink, to show their appreciation and support.

From time to time, the locals reported suspicious sightings and movements of the two fugitives. They were feeling the heat! They were still on foot. Time passed.

Stress turned to drudgery. As we waited in vain for action, it became more boring and monotonous. Occasionally suspicions were aroused, but in general, time became rather hum-drum. The residents were now bringing us prepared meals, even cakes and pies. We already had coolers on hand loaded with soft drinks and water. It was hot and dusty. There was a drought that year and we were sucking up the liquids.

Because of our isolated location, we had no ready access to restrooms. We just relieved ourselves the best we could on the side of the mountain. Damn, it was getting boring. Time was really dragging along now. We needed something to keep us going, something to keep us sharp. Surely, I could find some way to help.

We began by washing Sgt Klink's car. It was getting dark now, but the moon was full and we could see pretty well. Instead of urinating on the side of the mountain, we'd take turns hosing down the side of his car, while the rest of us kept his interest directed towards other locations.

We became very brazen. One of us popped the hood of his Patrol Car. Others took turns standing on his front bumper and steam cleaning his engine. *(His engine was still hot)* He never even noticed that the ground around his car was wet, while everywhere else, it was so dusty and dry. It got even worse.

I'd already thought it out beforehand and was just waiting for the right place and time. This plan involved one lonely sardine, wrapped in a napkin to contain the leaking juice, and concealed behind the horn button on the steering wheel. I knew it would work!...I'd already tested it and timed it. This installation could be preformed in 30 seconds. The only problem was, I didn't have any sardines. Steve took it upon himself to go get a can from a local store.

He never was very trusting, but of this whole group, Sgt Klink trusted me least of all. He must've thought something was up because he was getting antsy...He always had his eye on me. So I stayed with him and kept him occupied while Steve carried out the dirty work. Sgt Klink had his car locked, but that was no problem...I had a key. Steve took the key and the sardine and in no time flat, accomplished the mission. That sardine sat undisturbed for weeks, behind Sgt Klink's horn button. I'll come back to that later.

The hunt for the fugitives continued. Their actions were becoming more obvious now. They were becoming more desperate. They were taking more chances. Our Radio was becoming more active now. We were getting more calls.

> "*A Taxi has reportedly been hijacked by one of the fugitives,*" our Dispatcher said. "*Be on the lookout,*" he continued, "*he's headed west on I40.*"

The traffic was heavier and we weren't searching all cars as closely now. If they looked OK, we'd let them through. Until…

> "*That was the same Taxi that just came by!*" I shouted to my fellow Troopers, as I jumped into my Patrol Car. "*I'm going to go check him out!*" I said as I took off.

I hammered down and caught up to him about a mile up the road. As I ordered the male out of the Taxi, I heard a shotgun rack behind me but to my side. There stood Steve, locked and loaded. I was not alone here, and that made me feel mighty good! This incident turned out to be a false alarm, but I knew who'd back me up when I needed it. The search continued.

One escapee we had been hunting for came to the door of a Mountain Man, seeking food and hiding. The old man answered the door with his shotgun. In a monotone voice, this was how he related the incident…

> "*He begged me not to shoot him but I shot him anyway.*"
>
> …End of fugitive #1.

The pressure continued on the other one, but there was no place to hide…No place to flee. The Mountain Folks had no sympathy for the killers of North Carolina's Finest…There would be no support for them up here, no reprieve. Not long after the demise of the first one, the second was found by Law Enforcement Officers…Hiding under a trash pile. He survived and was jailed. Lucky for him, he had not been caught by the local folks…Or it would have been…

…End of fugitive #2.

Changing the tone some, we now go back to the sardine. The manhunt was over now. We returned to our duty stations. Except for Sgt Klink, we told everybody about that sardine. Now all we had to do was wait for it to do its work, and start stinking. Time passed, but no stink. It was summertime and with the heat, we expected quicker results...It didn't happen. He spent a lot of time at the Office and he'd leave the glasses on his car rolled down. We frequently checked, but no odor. After about five weeks I became concerned, so I checked to make sure it was still there. Yes, it was still resting comfortably there, but no odor...It just needed more time.

Finally, it ripened. The stench was remarkable!...I was so proud! Sgt Klink tried to find the source, but couldn't. He had that car washed inside and out but there was no relief. He became so frantic for liberation that he even sought advice from me, as to the cause of this smell.

> *"Damn, Sarge,"* when I stuck my head inside his car, that's what I said. *"It smells to me like you've got a bad heater core."*

He immediately drove his car to the Salisbury Patrol Garage to check it out. That wasn't it! They couldn't find anything wrong with the heater core. Again, he sought advice from his trusted Troopers. This time he approached Ralph Smeth. Ralph surveyed the situation and offered this line of bull...

> *"Sarge,"* he said, *"it's got to be in your air conditioning system. That's where it is! I'm sure of it!"*

Once again, the trip was made to the Salisbury Garage. No luck! The disgusting aroma persisted.

The Sarge was at his limit...He just couldn't stand riding in that car. He'd drive that thing back and forth from home, but that was about it...He'd leave it parked at the Charlotte Office. Soon, we all began to pay dearly. Since he wouldn't ride in his own, he started riding with us. We didn't like it...We didn't want him riding with us! He was infringing upon our freedom of movement. Something had to be done! Someone had to help him find that sardine, without giving us away.

Finally, the solution arrived at the Charlotte Office in the form of Lieutenant Gennings. He had previously been a First Sergeant there, but had received promotion and moved on to another area about a year before…He was just stopping by for a visit. As soon as I saw him, I knew he could be our salvation. I laid it all out for him…I asked him to please ride with Sgt Klink and help him find that sardine, otherwise, our torment could continue indefinitely. He did it…The sardine was located. He saved us and he kept his mouth shut about us too.

From that time on, Sgt Klink was all ears. If there were Troopers anywhere around, he was right around the corner, listening for that magic word…"Sardine." Oh, he'd hear us snickering behind his back, but he was waiting for more evidence. Months went by. That word was never mentioned…But he didn't forget! He was always on the lookout for someone to give themselves away. He never brought the subject up…Neither did we. He was patient. He just waited. So did we.

One night, he and I took a meal hour together at The Waffle House. As we ate we casually talked, and he was fascinated by the large tomatoes I'd been bringing to the Office for others to enjoy. Sgt Klink was completely lacking of any horticultural skills at all, but wanted to know how I managed to grow such nice tomatoes. So I told him how I did it.

> *"Sarge, I take a 55-gallon steel drum and cut the lid out of it, then poke large holes around the bottom edge. I then dig a hole and bury the bottom of the barrel about a foot into the ground…or up to the first ring. After this, I dig up the ground around the barrel. I then plant four tomato plants about a foot out and evenly spaced, on the perimeter of the barrel…more'n four plants are just too many. After this, I fill the barrel with cow manure and then every day…I fill the barrel with water from my garden hose and the concoction goes down to the roots of the tomatoes and they just grow like crazy."*

For a moment, Sgt Klink looked at me with wide-eyed astonishment. Not knowing his ass from a hole-in-the-ground about farming, he then said…

> *"Bryan Gregory, you don't put cow manure in that barrel! I know what you're doing! You're trying to get me to grow tomatoes that taste like shit!…That's what you're doing! Now tell me the truth…What do you use to make your tomatoes grow like that?"*

"OK, Sarge, you caught me," without ever cracking a smile, I replied. "I don't really use cow manure in there…I use sardines."

That magic word had come out! Then came those words that I had come to live for…

"Bryan Gregory! You SOB!" he said, "I knew it! I knew it all along! You're the one who did it!"

Of course, he ranted and raved and made all kinds of accusations, and I denied it. The only evidence that he really had was me telling him how to grow, decent tomatoes.

Although I'd pulled a multitude of pranks on him by now, I must admit…Sergeant Klink was right up there at the top.

He was one of the best Supervisors that I've ever had.

One of the Best

From time to time, someone will approach me.

> "I'll bet you've heard all kinds of stories to get out of speeding tickets," they'll say and then they'll ask, "what's the best one you've ever heard?"

Well, most any Officer has heard all kinds of excuses and all kinds of crap, but for me…This is one of those that take the cake.

I don't remember exactly how fast he was going, but he was flying low. I guess this fellow was running 90mph or so. He didn't know it, but I'd been way back behind him for better than a mile, clocking him with my computer and just giving him rope. Finally, I'd had enough. I stopped him. His line was pretty convincing, but he must've mistaken me for a dope.

As I walked up to his car, he jumped out!

> "Officer! This is an emergency!" he said. "I just got a call from my girlfriend and at this very moment, she's on the way to the Hospital. I've got to get to her!"

> "Well, I can understand why you're in a hurry," I replied, as I escorted him back to my car. Then we sat down in there.

Since I didn't know whether to believe him or not, I tried to question him more…But he just wasn't forthcoming with many details. He did make it plain that he had to get to the Charlotte Memorial Hospital, about fifteen miles away. There's one thing you could put your money on though…He'd rather be most anywhere, than sitting inside of my car.

> "Officer, I've really got to go! I'm not sure how bad off she is." He went on, "I don't have time for all this! I've really got to go!"

He couldn't tell me what had happened to her or where. He couldn't tell me if she'd fallen off a roof or had a stroke. He didn't even know if she was being choppered in or was driving herself there. All he could tell me is that this was an emergency and he had to get there!

Now I don't claim to know much about females, and a lot of times, I can't even recall what they've just said. But I do know this…I've never had any woman describe anything to me and then come away with no more information than that. By now, I'd pretty well heard his line…So I threw him mine.

> *"If that happened to me, I'd feel the same way,"* I compassionately said. *"Here's the deal. If you're telling me the truth, I'll let you go."* I became more stern now. *"But if this is a bunch of crap that you're feeding me, this is the time to set it straight! If you want to change your story now, I'll just give you a ticket and let you go. But if you don't, and I find out that you're lying…I'm gonna take your ass to jail! Now what's it gonna be?"*

He never even missed a beat. It was a good one and he was sticking with his story, so he kept right on with it. Maybe he thought I'd just brush him off and let him go. Maybe he thought I wouldn't waste my time with him, but he didn't know me…He didn't know how far I'd go! He kept on insisting that I let him go because he had to get to the Hospital.

> *"All right then,"* I said. *"Lock your car up! Let's go! Since this is an emergency, you're riding with me! I've got the blue light and I'm taking you there!"*

This was not what he had in mind. Reluctantly, he locked his car up and came back to mine. Surely, he would've preferred to go his way and I go mine. He wasn't under arrest and I didn't handcuff him, but he'd backed himself into a corner. There wasn't much else he could do…He was now in a bind. We left.

On the trip there, I gave him several more chances to change his story, but he declined…He wouldn't. Maybe he thought he was slick. Maybe he'd successfully used this line before. We didn't break any speed records, but before too long, we were there.

We pulled up at the Emergency Room entrance. Like a flash, he was inside…So was I. Maybe he thought he'd lose me in the crowd, but he was dead wrong…I was quick and I knew my way around! I figured he might have some rabbit blood in him and at any moment, he might take off…So every time he turned around I was on his tail. I was right there!

We checked at the main desk but nobody had heard of her…Her name wasn't there. I walked him all around the area and we looked in all the small rooms. He was getting mighty nervous…We couldn't find her anywhere!

> "Maybe the ambulance hasn't taken her away yet," I said. "Maybe you should give her a call. Even if she's already left, maybe someone is there who will know…That's the only thing I can think of. Somehow, we've got to find out how she's doing! You might as well give her a call."

How could he refuse an offer like that? We found a phone. He dialed it. She answered.

> "I'm here at the Hospital with a State Trooper," I could hear him say. "He stopped me for speeding and I told him it was an emergency. He might even take me to Jail! I told him I was on the way to the Hospital to be with you…"

I couldn't hear her end of it, but from where I stood, it sounded like he was telling her all about him and asking nothing about her. Up until now, he sure wasn't showing much concern for her health. I'd had enough! I grabbed the phone from his hand.

> "I'm Trooper Gregory with The North Carolina State Highway Patrol," I professionally stated and then politely I asked, "How are you doing today?"

> "Just fine," she sweetly replied.

> "That's all I need to know," I then said, and hung up the phone.

Without further ado, I spread-eagled him there and then cuffed him and took him straight to Jail.

As the title indicates, this is one of the best lines that I've ever heard. But the very best are the ones that were used, that I believed, and the defendant actually got away.

I'm sure I've been had many times…Maybe you've done it! But since they worked…I don't know what they were.

Bullet on the Wall

This bullet was presented to me by a stranger. It wasn't a gift, but for all intents and purposes, it was sure meant that I have it. Now it belongs to another, for whom it was never intended.

Maybe it was the Mecklenburg County Police Department or maybe it was the Charlotte Police Department, I'm not for sure. All I've got to do is check in my records. But that's not important now…It's just me and you.

> I could hear it when I came out from supper.
> The radio was like a beehive.
> Our Dispatchers were going crazy,
> Trying to keep us informed and alive.
> Police from all areas were responding,
> Near the State line, at the trailer park.
> A redneck had kidnapped his ex-girlfriend.
> By now, it was well after dark.

His girlfriend had dumped him and moved in with another fellow…In the same trailer park! With her new boyfriend in tow, she went back to Redneck's to get the rest of her belongings…This was just too much for Redneck to take! An altercation ensued and he ended up popping off a few rounds with his 45 automatic…He shot her new boyfriend in the foot. Then, he grabbed her by the hair, took her hostage and then took off in his little blue Ford Ranger pickup truck. 911 had been called by a neighbor, and the responding Police spotted him and pursued. It was on!

On the radio, I could hear them coming. I was about five miles from where I needed to be, but if I hustled, maybe, just maybe…I could get into position. I opened up my four-barrel and stretched her out good.

Where Brookshire Freeway dumps into I77 North I entered the picture. As I sped down the ramp I could see them as they passed below. The little truck came by first, followed by four or five yelping Police cars. They weren't going too fast, about 85mph or so, but that was about as fast as that little Ranger pickup would go. The pursuing Police were giving him lots of respect…It looked like maybe ten car-lengths worth. With me, it would be different.

With my Christmas tree lit and siren going, I blew their doors off and got right up on Redneck's rear end. Every light I had was on bright and I had my siren screaming...I wanted him to know I was there!

That got his attention. Boy, that made Redneck mad! He slammed on his brakes and tried to wreck me, but I didn't care...I had brakes too. I got right back up on his bumper again and this time, gave him a gentle nudge...Just to let him know I still cared. I didn't want to wreck him because she was in there.

Now the stress was getting to him, and he'd stood about all he could stand. Now, Redneck decided that he'd show me...He was the man!

I watched as he slid open his back window. So it didn't surprise me when showed me his nice chrome-plated gun. He was trying to drive with his left hand and shoot through the back window with his right. I didn't think he had rubber arms, so I just swerved to the left as he presented the first shot. *(You've seen all those gun-battles and special effects on TV. Well, it wasn't like that at all. I'd see the mussel-flash and then hear a slight pop...Nothing dramatic at all)* But he did have my attention now...So I backed off. I looked around for damage and didn't see any holes in myself or my car...So I kept moving on. I did give him a little more room though.

To be honest, it wasn't really much of a chase at all. Although I stayed behind him for a good twenty miles, I've had a lot better chases than that...He just wasn't going to stop! From time to time, we'd come up on other traffic and then we'd take to the right shoulder or the left. And whenever he pulled his right arm back in, that's when I'd slip back up on his bumper again. A few more times, he presented me one of his bullets...Each time I declined. Finally, he stopped shooting and we just drove for the next several miles.

On the radio, it sounded like there were several other Troopers behind me, but I had not seen another blue light behind me for quite awhile. Since Redneck had first started shooting, everyone else had just dropped out of sight! *"Where are they,"* I wondered, and *"are they just skittish, or what?"* In my rearview, I could see it behind me now. There was one lonely blue light, waaay back there, about a mile back.

Now, my Patrol Car didn't seem to be running right. I seemed to be running out of gas...But my gas gauge showed ¾ tank! Try as I might, my car didn't have enough juice to get up there again and nudge that little truck. Ahead of us and from the next entrance ramp, Troopers from the next county were lining up and preparing to bounce.

As we approached, my Patrol Car began to really lose power…I'd never had a Patrol Car run bad like that! Then, all my dash-lights lit up. *"Hey! What's going on here,"* I questioned myself. *"Redneck is only running 90mph and I still can't catch him!"* and *"what the hell is wrong with my car?"*

The engine died. I cranked it again. It died. I cranked. It died. I cranked. And this cycle continued several more times. I began to feel like that cartoon character, Fred Flintstone, trying to get that damn Patrol Car to go…And Redneck began walking away. As I drifted off onto the exit ramp, a Trooper from behind finally pulled up beside me.

> *"Boy, what the hell is wrong with you!"* without taking a breath, I hollered to him, *"where the hell have you been? Now get your ass up there and get him…He's getting away!"*
>
> *"Bryan,"* he was much calmer than I when he said, *"I've been behind you the whole time, but your car was throwing out so much oil that I couldn't see out of my windshield. I had to stick my head out the window to see where I was going!"* *"Don't worry,"* he continued, *"there's a crowd on the other side of the ramp. They'll take up where you've left off."*

I jumped out and checked my Patrol Car. Redneck had in fact, delivered a souvenir…And it had probably been one of the first shots that he'd taken at me. He had not hit me, but one of his slugs had penetrated my oil cooler…That cooler was located in front of, and in the lower area of, my radiator. My engine had lost all of its oil and had locked up. The chase was over for me, but it went on for another 90 miles or so. The action continued on both the outside and the inside of Redneck's truck.

From her statement, it appears that Redneck tried to force his ex-girlfriend to give him sexual satisfaction as they were speeding along, but she would have none of that…She was not in a romantic mood.

He then shot up another Patrol Car but no one was hurt. At Fancy Gap, he made his way up into Virginia. North Carolina Troopers dropped off at the state line and Virginia took over. At some point, that brave girl got Redneck's gun away from him and threw it out of the window...And then she also jumped out!

Redneck was left with nothing but an empty gas tank and his thoughts. The pressure was still on him and his options were now limited. He just drove his truck off the highway and it rolled over a few times.

Now I'm going to give you just one reason that I love Virginia...They cut the red tape! Instead of all those normal extradition hearings, involving lawyers and time and money...They just choppered his ass back to North Carolina, for medical reasons. Well, he did hurt his foot.

As far as I know, he's still in prison somewhere in North Carolina...Trying to find a new girlfriend in there. OK then, let's get back to the Bullet.

After this had all blown over, I went to the Patrol Garage to check on my Patrol Car...and the Bullet that Redneck had presented me. The Mechanics told me that they had never seen a motor locked up that tight and that a new engine had to be installed. When I asked about the Bullet, they told me that the Captain had it. *(This Captain has not appeared anywhere else in this book)* I approached him.

When I asked him for it, he lightly chucked as he turned me down. He said he had it mounted and it was at his home, hanging on his wall. Since retirement was rapidly approaching for me, that Bullet became more important. I asked him for it a couple of times more...And I let him know that it did have meaning to me.

Although he had no involvement in that incident at all...Still, he refused. And each time he did, it seemed to give him more glee.

But I ended up with so much more than he did.

Now this may sound silly to you, but it doesn't bother me at all. I've got the memory and this story. And all he's got is a symbol of his former power over me, just hanging there...

On his wall.

Long Lost Rookie

Before I get started on this one, I want to you to meet a friend of mine…Super Dave. I call him that because since I first met him, he's always been like that, super…In every way I can think of. He's the kind of friend that we all want…The kind that always laughs at your jokes, always has a smile on his face and whenever you decide you want to do something, you can always depend on him be there with you. I guess what makes him especially super to me is that he has always remained the same. Although he has attained some rank now, power hasn't gone to his head much. He can always be depended upon. He's the same ole Dave.

Whenever we had the chance, Dave and I would get together and have laughing contests. We didn't call them that, but that was our objective…To see who could make the other laugh the most. Overall, I'd have to say he was the winner, because he constantly kept me in stitches. This story coming up is one in which I was the winner though, because he can't even relate it now in a coherent manner…He still laughs until he cries when he tries to tell it. So hold on to your britches. Here it goes.

Dave and I met up on the North 29 Connector. Basically, this was a very long, two directional ramp that connected US29 and I85. Both of us were running Radar, so we positioned our Patrol Cars in opposing directions at a wide median crossover. We set up in a manner that I was clocking vehicles coming from one direction and he was shooting the ones from the other. Our driver's windows were about a foot apart and we were accomplishing two goals…We were goofing off and we were both working.

The contest began and in no time at all, we were both laughing. This went on for awhile, when suddenly, my Radar began to hum. Now, I could make it out in the distance. Another Patrol Car was approaching us and he had the hammer down.

He slid his car up close to ours. Then, the young buck Trooper who was driving it got out and came up to us. He made no bones about it…He was fresh out of Basic Patrol School. He was assigned to the next county over, and he had become lost and he couldn't find his way back to where he was. He'd been riding around for more than an hour now, trying to make heads or tails from his map. He tried not to show it, but indeed, he was scared…What in the world would he do if he got a call? He didn't know it, but he was only about five miles south of where he needed to be…So, I made it a point to comfort him with a few words.

> "Don't worry too much," I said, "we've all become lost at one time or another. But you are about 35 miles north of where you need to be."

I lied.

> "Just take this road out to I85 and head south on it. In about half an hour, you'll find yourself where you should be."

He thanked me and then got back into his Patrol Car and took off. Dave and I managed to keep straight faces until he got out of our sight. But it doesn't end here.

Since the Rookie worked in a different county than ours, he used a different radio channel than ours…So I switched my radio over to the channel he was on. Then, while disguising my voice and using one of his Sergeants call numbers, I called him specifically and asked him where he was. He hesitated to answer, but when he did, he nervously lied about his location. In the background we could hear the wind whistling and his four-barrel moaning. Neither Dave nor I were worth a damn for the rest of our shift…We couldn't stop laughing!

I'm not really sure whatever happened to the lost Rookie, but if he continued south on I85 as I instructed…He had a problem. As far as I know he may be down in South Carolina somewhere…Working as a Trooper down there, with a North Carolina uniform and Patrol Car.

It's just a matter of...

Time.

You're wondering..."*Why would he start out a story like that?*" and you're saying, "*Not only does it sound silly, but you didn't even bother to capitalize.*" It may seem ridiculous to you now, but by the time that I'm finished...They'll be words that you'll never forget.

Although I've always tried to be tender and remain a gentleman, from time to time, my rough edges come to the surface...And I'm just as good as any man is for bringing out the wrath in a woman. I remember one incident when a female threw a drink in my face. She was a little thing, but after she threw that second drink right into my eyes and then tried to block my escape...I slapped the hell out of her, shoved her out of my path and made my getaway. I'm not proud if it, but most males know that many females are quite capable of doing whatever it takes, to get their way. This narrative goes way beyond all of that. Here's how it all started...

As I earlier wrote about my children and remembered their childhood, this story began developing and took on a life of its own...But it didn't seem to fit in well anywhere except here. This is a tough story for me to tell because it involves something I've never had much exposure to. This is a story of domestic violence and spousal abuse...And time.

Until a very special Babysitter came into my life, I never really thought about it much. I just figured that if a female really wanted to get out of a bad relationship, all she had to do was just get up and leave. And there's something else I never quite understood..."*If they don't thrive on it so much,*" I thought, "*why in the world do they keep going back?*" In casual conversation, I've even heard others say..."*It's a two-way street. It's not always the fellow's fault and sometimes, maybe these women deserve what they get.*" For a while I tolerated that line, but over the years my perspective has changed a lot. I came to realize that this is not just a female issue. Any way you cut it, males are the cause of this cruelty. So sit back, get comfortable...And pay attention! I'm going to tell you about this former Babysitter of mine.

She was not the normal Babysitter. No, she was far, far, from that. She was young when I first met her and compared to me she still is. I'd say she was fifteen or so back then, when she began helping out the neighbors some with them and their kids. In addition to that, she took care of our boys when my wife was having surgery and while I was working, she took up the slack. What makes her so special is not only how much she helped us, but also how well she has dealt with the later trials in her life. She came to our aid then, she's helped many other people since then, and she's far from finished yet. It's really rather foggy to me, as to where she was and from whence she came, but just when I needed her the most…That's when the Babysitter came.

Now, I'm going to tell you something…This girl loved kids! She watched over our boys as if they were her own. She loved them, and just because she was that way, she even took them with her on trips to see her friends…Hundreds of miles away. We could really trust her with them. Yes, in many ways, she was just like a little mother hen. She must've really liked it, because lord knows we didn't pay her much. Time passed and my wife got a little better. She could get up on her own now, so the Babysitter moved on. Right before she left, I told her if she ever needed anything or I could help her out in any way, to please let me know. Shortly thereafter, the Babysitter left.

A few years passed and I still hadn't heard from her. I didn't even know exactly where she was. I did know that she was now married and had kids of her own. She lived in the next county over, which was not too far away. I was working the third shift and I was busy. It was in the wee hours of the morning when my Dispatcher called.

> "H-551!" (that was my Highway Patrol call number) "*A female subject who identified herself as Heather just called. She said that it is an emergency! She gave me her number and here it is…She abruptly hung up, but she wants you to call her right back.*"

Well, here I was in the middle of nowhere. I was busy and I didn't have a cell phone. I guess it was a good twenty minutes or so before I could call her back.

When I called, her husband answered and said she wasn't there. He sounded like he was high on something. In the background, I could hear a commotion going on, but not one peep did I hear from her. "*But something must be wrong,*" I thought, and "*with all this time that has passed, she's never called me once!*"…"*Damn, where is Heather and what's going on?*" I kept him on the phone as long as I could because in the background, I kept hearing thumps and unusual noises. But since I didn't know exactly where he was and since there's no law against getting drunk at home…Finally, as confused as I still felt, I got off the phone. The next day, I tried again to call her at the same number. Again he answered and said she wasn't there, and he didn't know where she was. I didn't want to meddle but still I wondered…"*What's going on with Heather?*" I guess the best way to continue with this story is to just lay out the sequence of events and then let you know where I fit in.

Her husband was brought up and exposed to violence towards, and suppression of, women. Although he was older than she was, he had insecurities of his own to deal with. He always had to know where she was and what she was doing. I guess the best way to say it, is that he was overly protective and jealous by nature. He had known her since she was twelve years old and by the time that they married, had come to think of her as his possession.

She was raised up right…With strong male role models who were secure in their manhood. She matured early, had a mind of her own and before most of us would even dream of doing it…She struck out on her own.

She didn't think about it much when he showed concern for her whereabouts, because she did like the attention. Yes, the signs of abuse were already showing, but she didn't know what those signs were.

It was about a month before they got married that the abuse began. She was pregnant when he shoved her to the ground and she wondered…"*Am I making a mistake going into this relationship?*" She hoped it might just be drug related and things would get better. And she also felt this was her best option, so she went ahead and got married anyway. They were married and before long his insecurities surfaced more with his continuous drug use. Soon, the accusations started and the beatings began. After abusing her, he'd sober up some and apologize…She'd give him another chance and they'd reconcile.

She began to walk on eggshells and tried to be more tender with him, because as most any therapist will tell you…It was partially her fault. But her efforts to make it right didn't help any…The beatings intensified. Slowly but surely, the abuse became more frequent and violent. He learned pretty quickly that if he gave her a black eye or busted her lip, people would start asking questions. So, he began beating her in areas that wouldn't show. He was learning how to do it. He was becoming a professional wife-beater…He was running the show! Then the big day came.

One day, while their children were at his mother's house and the two of them were home alone…A major beating occurred. He'd had just about all he could stand of her mouth and he was strung out on drugs. He was a lot larger than she was and he was certainly not afraid of his little wife. If he couldn't get her attention with his fists, he certainly would with his pistol and assault rifle. He figured he was a real man and this time he would make it plain to her. Yes, this was the proper time. He would show her now…He was the boss!

He accused her of an infidelity that she was not guilty of, but he thought he knew better…So he just went ahead and began to beat the living hell out of her right then and there. *(Somewhere during her torture is when she called my Dispatcher and tried to locate me. But just as the rest of the system has done, when she needed me the most…I was nowhere around)* He beat her some more. She fought back, but he was stronger…And he loved to see the terror in her

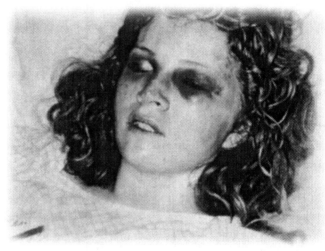

eyes. He tortured her with pliers. He squeezed them onto her small fingers and toes, and even onto her delicate earlobes, before he blackened her sensitive eyes. He made her look up at the picture of their two children and say goodbye, and then he told her…This would be the last time she saw them! At gunpoint, he made her write notes to them and then her parents…Saying goodbye. Even then he wasn't satisfied! With a broomstick, he beat her some more…And there was a lot more damage done than we'll ever see. He wrapped a belt around her neck and began choking the life out of her. But it must not have been her time to die…The belt broke. His accusations continued and he

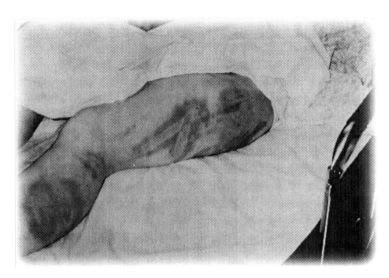

demanded to know who her lover was. After three hours of beatings, telling the truth, that she wasn't having an affair, wasn't working. Her sense of survival finally kicked in and she tried the only other option she had…She began lying. She made up a story and gave him a name…And it was only then that the dreadful beatings came to an end. Although she had asked him numerous times to go ahead and pull the trigger of the assault rifle he threatened her with, he backed off. He was content at last…Because by now he had beaten her almost to death.

Maybe he began to feel a little guilty now, because he allowed her to call a friend to come and take her to the Hospital. But the friend had only one hour to get there, or he would kill her or whoever else came down their driveway. There he sat. This was the height of his manhood. He watched every move she made and he knew how to use the firearms he carried. He was in charge now! Never again would he take any crap from his half-dead, one hundred pound wife.

The friend came in the nick of time and took her to the Hospital, and even as they escaped down the driveway…He stood there with his assault rifle aimed at their backs. The Police Department came to the Hospital and listened to her story. They then took pictures of her now not-so-pretty face. Although she gave them all the details and pressed charges against him, the police never even went to his door. He stayed right where he was…He didn't go anywhere. Warrants were drawn out for him, but never served…And not one police officer ever confronted him! Except for her statement and photo, not one piece of evidence was ever collected…And there's more.

Only after his Father finally talked him into taking a ride, did he turn himself in. He was locked up until the court date, but because of no real police work…The District Attorney didn't have much of a case. Although the charges were very serious…"Assault with a Deadly Weapon," "First Degree Kidnapping" and "Assault with a Deadly Weapon Inflicting Serious Injury with Intent to Kill," and he was facing fifty-two years in prison…The DA offered him a plea bargain of three measly years. But he was confident. Not only did his family have friends in high places, but he really didn't think he'd done much of anything wrong. He declined the plea bargain and decided to gamble on a trial. Big mistake for him and a lucky break for her…The Jury found him guilty of all charges and sentenced him to 24 years in the NC Dept. of Corrections. But we all know how that goes…He ended up serving much less than half of that. And still, we wonder why these women keep going back…We've been so blind! It's because that by allowing slaps on the wrists, we condone it! It's because we let them right back out again and abusers don't pay for their crimes, and they have no reason to expect to…That's why!

The day that he was put into prison is the day that she blossomed into the flower that she has become. In her case, she didn't need counseling, she didn't need therapy, and she didn't need to pray more…All she needed was for the threat in her life to be gone. Now is as good a time as any for me to tell you how she's handled her life and what she's become.

She did not sit still as many others have done…She didn't hide it. She went out into public without makeup on and she even allowed her battered picture to be displayed on a large billboard. Besides being instrumental in sending her spouse/abuser to prison, she became very vocal and has even influenced some of our laws. As soon as she could…She divorced him. In addition to raising four kids, she donates much of her time to any who will hear her voice…She wants to be heard! So far, she has sacrificed much to help others and has been compensated very little for any of her work. She has one of the most hectic schedules of anyone that I've ever known.

At every turn, our Legal and Social Services systems have let her down. And had she stood still for one minute and tolerated any of it, her ex-husband would've been out of prison long before now and would've made good on his promise to her…That she and her children would be dead! She had to fight her own way through this whole process. Oh, she got some help from her friends, but she didn't get the help we'd expect her to get from the taxes we pay…She had to scramble around the best that she could on her own. Anyway, he went to prison and you'd think that would be the end of the story...No Sir, far from it.

> Dear Slut,
> You better enjoy life while you still can. God forgives I don't. Pay backs are hell and you have hell to pay! There will come a day when I dance on your grave. If unable to dance, I will crawl across it! Unable to dance I will crawl. I'll be the one who puts you there and throws dirt on your body. I dream about it every night! One day you will turn around and there I'll be, and I can't wait to see the fear in your eyes... Before I kill you!!! ALL three of you will die by my hands!

She received a written "Death Threat" from prison! Even after she produced it to local authorities, still, no advice was given and no action was taken...Can you believe it? She had to really raise hell and pound on the counter before the Fed's were called in, and it was only because of her persistence that he's now serving time for the federal offense of "Communicating Threats through the Mail."

For obvious reasons, she gets no support at all from her abusive ex-husband...Because he is still in prison. But for him, if he gets an ache or pain, or needs a root canal...Our tax dollars pay for that, while he works out, gets three square meals a day, lies on his bed in jail and plots his time away. For her, it's a different ballgame altogether.

For her...The system is set up to fail. If she doesn't work and can jump through all the hoops, the government support she would get for herself and her children is not quite enough. But if she tries to supplement her income with a small job, then she won't qualify for much of any government support at all. And you know what's even harder for me to understand...She's even been advised by administrators to get married, so she would qualify for better benefits. Any way she turns, she's damned if she does and damned if she doesn't. If she were a large Corporation, we all know how she'd survive...Our government would jump right in there and spend billions to subsidize. I don't know about you, but this whole ball of wax that she's had to deal with just pisses me off!

And we aren't even touching on one of the saddest parts of this story. There are no government programs, whatsoever...For the assistance of children with a parent in prison. What the hell are we thinking about! And even worse...Why have we allowed ourselves to forget them? What about them...And on their own, how are these children supposed to make it? That brings to surface yet another subject...The message on the birthday card.

It came in the mail for his daughter's eighth birthday. Heather thought it rather odd that before now, he had not shown much interest in their children. She opened it and looked at it. I was a simple little card and obviously meant for a child's birthday. *"That's such a nice gesture,"* she thought. *"At last he's showing some concern for his kids' feelings."* But as she inspected at it further, in her throat, a lump began growing.

The card had a picture of a piece of furniture with a clock sitting on top of it. Right above the clock was his handwritten note...

"It's just a matter of..."

"How could he! Oh lord, how could he do that," she screamed internally. "Here I am, ready to give him another chance. But it's the same old thing as before...Every time I open myself up to him just a little, he beats me back down again."

The child was only eight then and would not have understood...But her Mother did! Considering his previous Death Threat that *"All three of you will die by my hands"* and that she'd known him well for ten years...She could see that he was finally learning from his blunders. Prison was helping Tommy Price, Jr. He had learned that if he wanted to relay a meaning, this time he'd better make it subtle. Yes, Heather understood...She knew him! The court system might not, but she got the message loud and clear! But as before in all of her other struggles, she would not give in to his cruelty. She and her children would be much greater than just casualties...They would endure all of this! How does she do it? How does she live, and how does she provide for herself and her dear children? Listen to me and I'll tell you.

She has very little money and for them all to survive, she must make every minute and every penny count. She must keep a beehive schedule for her kids and herself to keep a roof over their heads and food on the table. Around her children's timetable, she works at several jobs. She rides around on slick tires, can hardly pay her utilities and rent, and has never had her own home.

Most of us are raised and programmed to *"make it on our own,"* but for some of us, it's tougher than others. Although society would frown on her for doing so, it amazes me that she hasn't resorted to prostitution…What would we do if we had no more options?

Throughout all of this, she endures constant spinal pain. Yet, at the drop of a hat, whenever someone needs her help or comfort, she'll drop whatever she's doing and before you know it, she's right there…Finding refuge for a victim, mourning at a funeral, raising hell at a meeting, pounding on the desks of Politicians, District Attorneys, Lawyers or Judges. Surely, many folks who question their own status in these matters…Hate to see her coming!

She has spoken before Legislative Committees and influenced the making of better laws. She has appeared on television shows. She speaks frequently to students in High Schools and from the pulpits of Churches that allow women to speak…Her voice can also be heard. She will not sit still. She boldly fights the never-ending battle against bureaucracy. She is one of the bravest people I've ever known. Her health is less precious to her than achieving her goal and speaking out. How many of us feel so strongly about what we do with our lives? How many of us would expose ourselves, knowing that at any moment, a self-described killer might be released from prison and we could receive a shotgun blast to the back of our heads? The life that she leads is filled with potholes, but she carries on with optimism… *"Yes, I will make a difference. Yes, I will be heard!"* I'm sure Heather isn't perfect, but surely, she deserves much better than that…As do all the other women like her. *"How in the world,"* I wonder, *"does she keep her chin up and that smile on her face?"*

She has contempt for the government supported system that is so filled with flaws that it's rotten…And it's not just one person's fault, we're all guilty. Although our hearts may be in the right place, we think to ourselves… *"Hey, it's not my fault, it's that person down the hall."* Nobody takes responsibility and the situations get worse. Too many times, there's no one there to even empathize.

We don't even think about what it's like for women like her…To go through the unending maze of locked doors, only to be turned away because one single criterion was not met or one form was not signed right. We can't even imagine the horror of coming to a Shelter in the middle of the night with a murderer hot on our trail…Only to find a locked door. And if we are lucky enough to get in, to then be forced to use our own food stamps, because the benefits that were meant for us have already been taken by somebody else, probably staff. A feeling of tremendous despair must be felt, for those forced out of a Shelter early, while their abuser anxiously awaits their return. And these women must certainly wonder, *"Is my life important at all, and if so...Who cares?"*

When we serve on Juries, we constantly hear statements from the abuser like *"The devil made me do it,"* or *"I was out of my mind and didn't know what I was doing."* Where is our outrage? Will we continue to empathize with him and forget about her? Will we keep right on giving him a light sentence or sending him to a mental institution? Will we ever learn to see past the cool composure of the sorry bastard who has so obviously beaten up or killed his prey? Will we ever learn to listen to her soft voice or the silence of her grave? Are males really all that much better than females?

I can't even imagine what it must feel like for an abused woman...To be victimized by a maniac and then again by the system set up to support her, over, and over, and over again...And to be beaten almost to death and then have no one to turn to, and on top of that, to be treated as a whore.

Many of these women are not just trailer park trash, as we might think. Many are wives of Doctors, Lawyers, Ministers, Police Officers and all other professionals...And if you saw them in the Mall, you'd never know! They go through their lives with fake smiles on their faces. They hide it. They disguise the terror. Their bruises are hidden by makeup...Their pain doesn't show. In many cases, even their best friends don't know! They're embarrassed. They protect the ones who abuse them because they keep hoping and praying..."*Maybe he'll change if I just give him another chance and after all...He just apologized and sent me flowers today.*" Surely, there are hundreds of thousands, if not millions...Of women out there like that. These women who manage to live through this horror are so much more that just victims...They're Survivors.

It's not Rocket Science! Pouring more money into a system like this won't help much, unless the Battered Women themselves are leading the way. Any Politician worth his salt should be able to figure it out...Take up the cause of abused women and their children, and you'll get a helluva lot more votes. I guess it's time to focus on her abuser now. We'd better, he's still there! He still has an existence and he's just waiting. He knows his time will come.

I wonder about him and his life, and has he made good use of his time in prison? When that day comes and he gets out, will his attitude be better or will he have wasted his time and become sicker in the head? And once that choice is given to him, what will he do? Will he try to do something productive with his life or will he be consumed with taking his frustrations out on her, and make her just another statistic...Dead? And if he decides to come back and pay her back for a wrong he feels done, who's going to have a camera on him wherever he goes? Will the next time I see her be at her funeral, as I view her in her casket...Right before she's lowered into the ground? I pray to God that's not so. Maybe I'm dreaming, but can't help it...I hope for the best. I see a much better option for him than retaliation.

Although it will take a lot of determination on his part, he will now have the chance to show us his best. He will now have the opportunity to do something very constructive with his life. What will he do with this chance of a lifetime? Will he amount to something or will he just blow it again and kill her, then another...Then another? Heather shouldn't have to hide...She's done nothing wrong! Will he try to control her life again or has he matured enough to take control of his own? Your guess is as good as mine as to where it all could end.

As I'm sure you can tell by now, I've felt somewhat guilty over the years. I was a part of the system that was supposed to protect her. Heather was right there when I needed her and the only time that she called for me...I was nowhere around. Yes, I've got a conscience! Does he? Do you? Does our system?

This story was mostly written before I ever laid eyes on her again, and it was only a month or so beforehand that I had even spoken to her on the phone. I guess things like this have a purpose, because here I am at last, writing this story about her.

I'd like to leave a message for Heather's abusive ex-husband, Thomas Price, Jr...As he sits in prison until April 24, 2009 at the Bennettsville, South Carolina Federal Correctional Institution...

> *"It wasn't Heather! It's the bad choices you've made that prompted me to write this chronicle. Had it not been for your abusive actions, this wouldn't be much of a story. But don't expect royalties here for mistakes that you've made.*
>
> *Soon, you'll be out again and we're all wondering...What will you do? Surely, you're more educated now, but at the moment, even you may not have a clue. But this is my promise to you...*

> *Someday, I may offer my hand to you in friendship once you've proved honorable intentions. But if you decide to try manipulating Heather or your children, or harming her, them or anyone else in any way…Now, everyone who reads this story will know about you. At the least, I'm going to do my damnedest to make sure that's quite a few.*
>
> *There are many like me who love women out here. Also, there are many in there with you. Will you join us, or will we chase you…It's your choice. It's all up to you."*

And for the government systems that were set up to help and protect her, I also have a few words…

> "You're just as I was, years ago with my children. You need help now! You need a Babysitter…A good one! I did it before and I can do it again. I'm going to keep searching until I find one I can trust to look after you and the ones that I love…Like that little mother hen who watched over our sons!"

It's just a matter of time.

Having been in law enforcement for so long, I tend to be skeptical. I tend not to go with all of the bullshit that I read, hear or even see…But more from my own personal experiences, and even more importantly than that…From what my gut tells me! Based upon that, these are the conclusions I've drawn. Both Tommy and the system have become smarter and better…At covering up.

Education, we need more of it…From the top down and not from the bottom up. Those who represent us in government first, then Judges, then Lawyers, then Law Enforcement, and right on down the line. It's like a rope. It's got to come down…We damn sure can't push it up! Our best training will not come from Politicians, College Professors or Administrators. Our greatest learning will come from those in the trenches, the experts who've been there…The Survivors. But we'd better start now, because we can't expect that these few Survivors who do speak out will live but so long.

There are many questions left unanswered…
What will we do about the protection and care of all of our children? Will Heather and the multitude of others like her, ever be able to live normal lives without having to fight every step of the way?
Are we willing to take the necessary steps to help them get beyond just surviving…to thriving?
As a result of our ignoring their basic needs for survival, will women eventually lose their nature of compassion and nurturing?
Isn't the core of our society worth a little more effort and a few more dollars?
Is her abuser better now and if so, how will he prove it?
What will he do to restore our trust?
How can we help him to help us?
What if he's worse?
Will we ignore all the others like him?
How many like him are actually in prison?
Which is closer to the root of the problem…sex offenders or abusers?
Will there ever be a way to track them? *(Efforts are showing with sex-offenders…But what about abusers?)*
And what's all this crap about "Family Values" and other sound-bites like that? *(Because so little actions are taken, these well-placed words for the media have now lost their meaning)*
And if we're really so concerned about "Human Rights," why has a female's right to leave, live and continue to exist been so largely ignored.

Hey! It's an Emergency! Help me out here! I can't handle all of this by myself. I'm just an ole man on the porch.

For those of us males who love women and making love with them, we'd better turn the sound back on and get off of our asses. We've got to help and protect them…If we do, in fact, love them.

What's your relationship like? Is it about love and caring or is about power and control? Pay attention to your gut! If you're a female and you just feel, that it's the latter and you want to be a Survivor, don't think twice…You'd better get the hell out of there! If you're a male and it's the latter, the same may also be true…Because if you're an abuser, we'll soon be coming after you!

That message on the card that Tommy sent to his child was revealing. But who was his note meant for? Was it for his child or his ex-wife again, or was it for all of us? I'm going for the largest picture. When I visualize that little clock with the message that he scrawled…I take it as a wake-up call. We'd better hit the floor and start running!

It's just a matter of…

Transitions

Changes were coming...For myself and the North Carolina State Highway Patrol. I've adjusted to my changes pretty good, but the Patrol has much more bending to do.

I knew it was coming, so I'd been preparing myself for retirement for years. The loss of power and the drop of prestige were not dramatic for me. I was expecting it. I even welcomed it. I had come to view my employment as a hobby...That I enjoyed and loved very, very much. By the time I retired, I had found other hobbies that I took pleasure in also, so unlike many others, my departure came more easily. The Highway Patrol did not have the luxury of advance notice, so they were ill-prepared for what awaited them.

Since I left, the Patrol has begun absorbing another branch of enforcement into its ranks...Commercial Motor Vehicle Enforcement (*Weight Stations, etc*). This has been a difficult time for all involved. The members of the old Highway Patrol especially, are having a hard time adjusting.

Many feel betrayed by our Governor, our Legislature and our Command. They feel hurt. They feel that our standards have been lowered now...Because many have been allowed into the ranks that may not have been qualified to enter before. Our training was much more stringent and longer than theirs. We had twenty-two weeks of hell to go through and during this transition period, they've been allowed to get by with less than half of that. Surely, many Troopers feel as the Green Berets might feel if the Regular Army was suddenly allowed in their ranks. Initially they would balk too, if they felt unqualified persons wore their uniforms. But it's not just tough for the old Highway Patrol...It's tough for the Newcomers too.

The shuffling around of departments was not their fault. Even the shorter training they received was not their idea. These were decisions that were made by those in higher places and even for them, these choices had to be hard to make. Besides, there's not much that can be done now about that...It's a done deal! These new folks are also in an awkward dilemma. They want so desperately to be accepted and to fit in. They wear the same uniforms and have the same equipment that we have, but surely they wonder..."*How can we earn respect?*" and "*We're trying the best that we can, but we don't know what else we can do.*" Yes, it's going to be hard for everyone, and it may take years for it all to level out…But when it's all said and done, it may benefit everyone.

At least now, there will be other options for the Road Trooper. With these new positions, there are more alternatives available. As a Trooper gains seniority, he can now switch over to the Size & Weight status and get away from working those damn nights and weekends…And he won't automatically be put out to pasture now if he gets hurt. It will take time, but these new options will be positions that can be worked up to…And not to be looked down at.

This is a changeover period and soon it will pass. Transitions come for all of us. I deal with mine the best that I can and I'm sure…The new North Carolina State Highway Patrol will deal with theirs.

Epilogue

My life is real, but
My views are one-sided.
But that's OK, I'm just one person.
It's OK if I'm on my side, someone needs to be.

Originally, I really wanted to write my experiences down,
So you'd know it wasn't all work for me, it was also a lot of fun.
But it's turned out to be so much more than that.
I've tried to make you think about what we've allowed,
And to help you see what we've become.
The world and the NCSHP will go on without me,
But I sure took them both for a turn.

You say things aren't like they used to be
And we don't have fun anymore.
Only you can remedy that!
Don't do as I say.
Do like I did.
And then
Some
OK
?

Although most are gone now, I'm grateful to those who have preceded me…For making me and allowing me, to become the person that I now am and hope to be.

"*To whichever task I set my hand, I will always do the best I can.*"

www.olemanontheporch.com

978-0-595-39276-6
0-595-39276-8

Printed in the United States
70929LV00003B/253-270